D1368018

Empirical Studies of
Strategic Trade Policy

A National Bureau
of Economic Research
Project Report

Empirical Studies of Strategic Trade Policy

Edited by **Paul Krugman and Alasdair Smith**

The University of Chicago Press

Chicago and London

WILLIAM WOODS UNIVERSITY LIBRARY

PAUL KRUGMAN is a professor of economics at the Massachusetts Institute of Technology and a research associate of the National Bureau of Economic Research. ALASDAIR SMITH is professor of economics and dean of the School of European Studies at the University of Sussex and a research fellow in the international trade research program at the Centre for Economic Policy Research.

The University of Chicago Press, Chicago 60637
The University of Chicago Press, Ltd., London
© 1994 by the National Bureau of Economic Research
All rights reserved. Published 1994
Printed in the United States of America
03 02 01 00 99 98 97 96 95 94   1 2 3 4 5
ISBN: 0-226-45460-6 (cloth)

Library of Congress Cataloging-in-Publication Data

Empirical studies of strategic trade policy / edited by Paul Krugman and Alasdair Smith.
     p.   cm.—(A National Bureau of Economic Research project report)
  Includes bibliographical references and indexes.
  1. Commercial policy—Case studies. 2. Industry and state—Case studies. 3. International trade—Case studies. I. Krugman, Paul R. II. Smith, Alasdair. III. Series.
HF1411.E47 1994
382′.3—dc20   93-38665
                                                   CIP

⊚ The paper used in this publication meets the minimum requirements of the American National Standard for Information Sciences—Permanence of Paper for Printed Library Materials, ANSI Z39.48-1984.

HF
1411
E47
1994

National Bureau of Economic Research

Officers

George T. Conklin, Jr., *chairman*
Paul W. McCracken, *vice-chairman*
Martin Feldstein, *president and chief executive officer*

Geoffrey Carliner, *executive director*
Charles A. Walworth, *treasurer*
Sam Parker, *director of finance and administration*

Directors at Large

John H. Biggs
Andrew Brimmer
Carl F. Christ
George T. Conklin, Jr.
Don R. Conlan
Kathleen B. Cooper
Jean A. Crockett
George C. Eads

Martin Feldstein
George Hatsopoulos
Lawrence R. Klein
Franklin A. Lindsay
Paul W. McCracken
Leo Melamed
Robert T. Parry

Peter G. Peterson
Douglas D. Purvis
Robert V. Roosa
Richard N. Rosett
Bert Seidman
Eli Shapiro
Donald S. Wasserman

Directors by University Appointment

Jagdish Bhagwati, *Columbia*
William C. Brainard, *Yale*
Glen G. Cain, *Wisconsin*
Franklin Fisher, *Massachusetts Institute of Technology*
Saul H. Hymans, *Michigan*
Marjorie B. McElroy, *Duke*

James L. Pierce, *California, Berkeley*
Andrew Postlewaite, *Pennsylvania*
Nathan Rosenberg, *Stanford*
Harold T. Shapiro, *Princeton*
Craig Swan, *Minnesota*
Michael Yoshino, *Harvard*
Arnold Zellner, *Chicago*

Directors by Appointment of Other Organizations

Marcel Boyer, *Canadian Economics Association*
Rueben C. Buse, *American Agricultural Economics Association*
Richard A. Easterlin, *Economic History Association*
Gail Fosler, *The Conference Board*
A. Ronald Gallant, *American Statistical Association*
Robert S. Hamada, *American Finance Association*

Charles Lave, *American Economic Association*
Rudolph A. Oswald, *American Federation of Labor and Congress of Industrial Organizations*
Dean P. Phypers, *Committee for Economic Development*
James F. Smith, *National Association of Business Economists*
Charles A. Walworth, *American Institute of Certified Public Accountants*

Directors Emeriti

Moses Abramovitz
Emilio G. Collado
Thomas D. Flynn

Gottfried Haberler
Geoffrey H. Moore
James J. O'Leary

George B. Roberts
William S. Vickrey

Relation of the Directors to the
Work and Publications of the
National Bureau of Economic Research

1. The object of the National Bureau of Economic Research is to ascertain and to present to the public important economic facts and their interpretation in a scientific and impartial manner. The Board of Directors is charged with the responsibility of ensuring that the work of the National Bureau is carried on in strict conformity with this object.

2. The President of the National Bureau shall submit to the Board of Directors, or to its Executive Committee, for their formal adoption all specific proposals for research to be instituted.

3. No research report shall be published by the National Bureau until the President has sent each member of the Board a notice that a manuscript is recommended for publication and that in the President's opinion it is suitable for publication in accordance with the principles of the National Bureau. Such notification will include an abstract or summary of the manuscript's content and a response form for use by those Directors who desire a copy of the manuscript for review. Each manuscript shall contain a summary drawing attention to the nature and treatment of the problem studied, the character of the data and their utilization in the report, and the main conclusions reached.

4. For each manuscript so submitted, a special committee of the Directors (including Directors Emeriti) shall be appointed by majority agreement of the President and Vice Presidents (or by the Executive Committee in case of inability to decide on the part of the President and Vice Presidents), consisting of three Directors selected as nearly as may be one from each general division of the Board. The names of the special manuscript committee shall be stated to each Director when notice of the proposed publication is submitted to him. It shall be the duty of each member of the special manuscript committee to read the manuscript. If each member of the manuscript committee signifies his approval within thirty days of the transmittal of the manuscript, the report may be published. If at the end of that period any member of the manuscript committee withholds his approval, the President shall then notify each member of the Board, requesting approval or disapproval of publication, and thirty days additional shall be granted for this purpose. The manuscript shall then not be published unless at least a majority of the entire Board who shall have voted on the proposal within the time fixed for the receipt of votes shall have approved.

5. No manuscript may be published, though approved by each member of the special manuscript committee, until forty-five days have elapsed from the transmittal of the report in manuscript form. The interval is allowed for the receipt of any memorandum of dissent or reservation, together with a brief statement of his reasons, that any member may wish to express; and such memorandum of dissent or reservation shall be published with the manuscript if he so desires. Publication does not, however, imply that each member of the Board has read the manuscript, or that either members of the Board in general or the special committee have passed on its validity in every detail.

6. Publications of the National Bureau issued for informational purposes concerning the work of the Bureau and its staff, or issued to inform the public of activities of Bureau staff, and volumes issued as a result of various conferences involving the National Bureau shall contain a specific disclaimer noting that such publication has not passed through the normal review procedures required in this resolution. The Executive Committee of the Board is charged with review of all such publications from time to time to ensure that they do not take on the character of formal research reports of the National Bureau, requiring formal Board approval.

7. Unless otherwise determined by the Board or exempted by the terms of paragraph 6, a copy of this resolution shall be printed in each National Bureau publication.

(Resolution adopted October 25, 1926, as revised through September 30, 1974)

Centre for Economic Policy Research

The Centre for Economic Policy Research is a network of over 170 research fellows, based primarily in European universities. The centre coordinates its fellows' research activities and communicates their results to the public and private sectors. CEPR is an entrepreneur, developing research initiatives with the producers, consumers, and sponsors of research. Established in 1983, CEPR is now a European-wide economics research organization with uniquely wide-ranging scope and activities. CEPR is a registered educational charity. Grants from the Leverhulme Trust, the Esmée Fairbairn Charitable Trust, the Baring Foundation, the Bank of England, and Citibank provide institutional finance. The ESRC supports the centre's dissemination program and, with the Nuffield Foundation, its program of research workshops. None of these organizations gives prior review to the centre's publications nor necessarily endorses the views expressed therein. The centre is pluralist and nonpartisan, bringing economic research to bear on the analysis of medium- and long-run policy questions. CEPR research may include views on policy, but the executive committee of the centre does not give prior review to its publications and the centre takes no institutional policy positions. The opinions expressed in this book are those of the authors and not those of the Centre for Economic Policy Research.

Executive Committee

Chairman	Anthony Loehnis
Vice-Chairmen	Guillermo de la Dehesa
	Adam Ridley

Giorgio Basevi	Otmar Issing
Honor Chapman	Mervyn King
Sheila Drew Smith	Peter Middleton
Jacob A Frenkel	Mario Sarcinelli
Sarah Hogg	Alasdair Smith

Officers

Director	Richard Portes
Deputy Director	Stephen Yeo
Director of Finance and Research Administration	Wendy Thompson

Contents

Preface

This volume includes nine papers that were prepared as part of a research program on Empirical Studies of Strategic Trade Policy by the Centre for Economic Policy Research and the National Bureau of Economic Research. The papers were prepared for a conference held at the National Bureau of Economic Research in Cambridge, Massachusetts, in the fall of 1989 (with the exception of one paper, which was presented at a Centre for Economic Policy Research workshop in the summer of 1988).

We wish to thank the Ford Foundation for financial support of both the NBER and CEPR sides of the program.

This volume contributes to continuing research on the practical significance of new approaches to the analysis of international trade.

Paul Krugman and Alasdair Smith

Introduction

Paul Krugman

The papers in this volume represent the latest stage in an ongoing research project that has occupied international economists around the world for more than a decade. The project is the reconstruction of international trade theory to take account of increasing returns and imperfect competition; it is a project that has increasingly focused on the problem of quantification, of making the models operational.

In this introduction I will try to put the research reported in this volume in context. I begin with a brief review of the origins of the concept of strategic trade policy, then turn to a summary of the results of earlier quantitative work, and finally summarize some of the key points raised in this volume.

The Concept of Strategic Trade Policy

The revolution that swept through the theory of international trade in the first half of the 1980s—the rise of the so-called new trade theory[1]—left many of the insights of traditional trade theory intact. In particular, introducing imperfect competition and increasing returns into the picture does not alter the fundamental point that trade is a positive-sum game, generally carried on to countries' mutual benefit. Indeed, the new trade theory adds to the positive sum: by enlarging markets, international trade increases competition and allows greater exploitation of economies of scale, both of which represent gains over and above those due to comparative advantage.

Paul Krugman is professor of economics at the Massachusetts Institute of Technology and a research associate of the National Bureau of Economic Research.
1. The "new trade theory" began with models that used the device of monopolistic competition to show how economies of scale could be a source of trade and gains from trade, alongside conventional comparative advantage. Early papers include Lancaster (1980), Krugman (1979, 1981), Dixit and Norman (1980), Helpman (1981), and Ethier (1982); much of the positive theory is summarized in a common framework by Helpman and Krugman (1985).

1

Yet the new trade theory also suggests some new reasons why government intervention in international trade might prove beneficial. Traditional theory, of course, has long offered potential justifications for deviating from free trade. Large countries, able to affect their terms of trade, can benefit if they impose optimal tariffs (and other countries do not retaliate). Even small countries have a second-best justification for tariffs on particular industries if domestic distortions lead to a divergence between private and social costs. In traditional theory, however, domestic distortions are in effect imposed on a basic model of undistorted competition; the second-best justifications for activist trade policy, however plausible, always have the feel of footnotes to an approach in which free trade is optimal in the absence of specific reasons to the contrary.

In the new trade theory, by contrast, the "distortions" are woven into the basic fabric of the trade models themselves. A theory of trade that is based at least in part on increasing returns must allow for oligopoly, external economies, or both. Either necessarily implies a failure of the usual conditions for optimality of laissez-faire: if economies of scale are internal to firms, there must be an oligopoly in which price exceeds marginal cost; if the economies of scale are somehow purely external to firms, and perfect competition is thus preserved, social marginal cost is less than private. The new trade theory suggests that in practice many traded goods are produced by industries that are both oligopolistic *and* subject to external economies (e.g., because of economies of scale in the production of nontraded intermediates). Thus instead of a picture of an international economy that is at a Pareto optimum, the new trade theory offers a picture of one in which markets normally lead to suboptimal results.

But simply saying that free trade is unlikely to be strictly optimal is not the same thing as saying that any particular deviation from laissez-faire is likely to improve matters. Can anything be said about the likely direction of the bias and the likely type of national policy that can improve on free trade?

In the early 1980s James Brander and Barbara Spencer (1983, 1985) created a considerable stir with an analysis of trade policy under imperfect competition. The Brander-Spencer analysis did three things. First, it offered a particularly clever way of setting up the case for activist trade policy, one which simplified the issue enormously and thereby revealed its core. Second, it seemed to suggest that the new trade theory provided at least limited support for a kind of neo-mercantilism, for the assertion that governments could in fact raise national income at other countries' expense by supporting national firms in international competition. Third, and not without importance, the Brander-Spencer approach could be succinctly described with a term that, while accurate, seemed to promise a larger prize than Brander and Spencer themselves ever suggested: "strategic trade policy."

What the Brander-Spencer approach actually consisted of was the following: we imagine two firms, from each of two countries, competing for some export market. Domestic consumers in this sector are ignored or assumed away, so that the approach is inherently biased toward a view of trade as competition rather than mutual gain. The firms compete by choosing the level of some strategic variable: perhaps output, perhaps capacity, perhaps R&D.

In this kind of competitive situation, firms would like to convince each other of their aggressiveness. That is, each would like the other to believe that it will invest or produce massively, thereby inducing the other to produce or invest less, perhaps even to avoid entering the market at all. The problem is to find a way to make the threat of aggressive competition credible. The answer suggested by industrial organization theorists is that firms will make "strategic" moves—that is, take actions that do not directly raise profits, but that are intended to make aggressive behavior more credible and therefore have a deterrent effect on potential rivals. The quintessential strategic move is construction of excess capacity, which a firm does not expect to use, but which it builds in order to deter entry of potential competitors.

What Brander and Spencer pointed out was that trade policies could serve the same strategic purpose. Suppose that one of the two firms is backed by a government, which commits itself to subsidize the firm's sales. Then the other firm will know that an aggressive policy by the subsidized firm is rational and will curtail its own plans. The result can be to raise the firm's profits by much more than the actual subsidy outlay. And as a result, such a "strategic" trade policy can raise the aggressive nation's income at the other country's expense.

The Brander-Spencer analysis nicely cuts through the complexities. But it is also subject to abuse: it has enabled advocates of aggressive trade policies to give their views a new intellectual gloss. Thus the theory of strategic trade policy has been subject to an unusually detailed academic critique, the upshot of which has been to show that what Brander and Spencer offered was an example, not a general result. Eaton and Grossman (1986) showed that the case for strategic aggressiveness was sensitive to the assumed form of competition; Horstmann and Markusen (1986) showed that the benefits of strategic trade policy might be dissipated by entry of new firms and the resulting excess capacity; Dixit and Grossman (1986) showed that competition for scarce resources among industries complicates greatly the task of devising a welfare-improving policy; and Dixit and Kyle (1985) argued that strategic trade policies should be seen as part of a larger game in which it would often be better for governments to rule out their possibility.

What this academic critique showed was not that the strategic trade policy concept was wrong, but that it was not necessarily right. Or to put it more accurately, the case for strategic trade policies was not like the traditional case for free trade, which (in the old trade theory) could be made a priori without consideration of the specific details of industries. Strategic trade policies could be recommended, if at all, only on the basis of detailed quantitative knowledge of the relevant industries. So what the new trade theory gave rise to was not a prescription for policy, but a program of research.

Efforts at Quantification

It is not an easy task to arrive at quantitatively operational conclusions from models of imperfect competition. Indeed, to a considerable extent, the field of industrial organization seems to have given up on the task, in that the remarkable and fascinating body of industrial organization theory that has been developed since 1970 has an equally remarkable lack of operational content or empirical confirmation.

In international economics, however, such a state of affairs has been viewed as unacceptable by all concerned. Perhaps because free trade is such a powerful symbol, perhaps because international economists are more likely than industrial organization theorists to commute to Washington or Brussels, there was almost immediately a demand to put up or shut up: to determine when, if ever, the new arguments against free trade were relevant.

But how was this to be done? Ideally one would estimate models of imperfectly competitive industries econometrically. In practice this is extremely hard to do, because of the difficulty of identifying firm behavior. In fact, it is actually very hard to estimate models even of perfectly competitive industries; adding the potential complexities of oligopoly is beyond what anyone has managed to do.

In a seminal paper, however, Dixit (1988) offered a way to make some progress. (Harris and Cox [1984] independently developed a similar approach.) He suggested using a "calibration" technique similar to that used in computable general equilibrium (CGE) models. In this technique, parameter estimates are drawn from econometric and engineering estimates wherever possible; the number of remaining parameters of the model is then narrowed down by a priori assumptions until the model can be fully identified by requiring that it match data for some base period. Dixit used this technique to quantify a simple model of the U.S. auto industry. Once the model has been quantified, it then becomes possible to carry out policy experiments. It is also possible to carry out sensitivity analysis, to see whether the conclusions of these experiments are crucially dependent on the particular a priori assumptions made.

In general, this technique is no worse when applied to the new trade theory than in conventional constant-returns models (e.g., Whalley 1985). In imperfect competition, however, there is a special problem: the need to represent the behavior of firms. In the theoretical literature in trade (and for that matter in industrial organization) it is generally simply assumed that firms act noncooperatively, either as Bertrand price-setters or as Cournot quantity-setters. When one tries to calibrate a model, however, the data generally seem to be inconsistent with either assumption. Dixit's answer to this problem was to represent firms' behavior by the device of conjectural variations, leaving the conjectural variation parameter to be decided by the data. The problems with this method are, first, that the use of conjectural variations cannot be properly justified analytically and, second, that there is no reason to expect the conjectural variations parameter to remain stable in the face of alternative policies.

This has not stopped other authors from using the conjectural variations technique—Baldwin and Krugman (1988b), for example, is an early post-Dixit paper that complains about the approach but uses it nonetheless. In another key early paper, however, Venables and Smith (1986) proposed an alternative. They suggested that the modeler assume either Bertrand or Cournot behavior and reconcile this with the data by positing an unobserved elasticity of substitution between the products of different firms. This approach has the virtue of theoretical tightness; it has the defect that the data are not given the chance to tell us anything about the behavior of firms.

By 1985, then, an approach had been developed that allowed quantification of imperfect-competition models of trade and industrial policy. It was by no means an ideal method—most papers in this area contain some kind of disclaimer, an acknowledgment that the results should not be taken too seriously—but it at least allowed research to go beyond purely theoretical speculation. There is now a reasonably large selection of calibrated new trade models, including Dixit (1988), Baldwin and Krugman (1988a, 1988b), Smith and Venables (1988), Venables and Smith (1986), Baldwin and Flam (1989), and others.

What do these models tell us? Three main points seem to have emerged. First, the models generally suggest that the *positive* economics of trade policy—its consequences for output and trade flows—are quite different from the predictions of conventional trade theory. In particular, protection, by encouraging entry of domestic firms, often promotes exports. In some cases, as in Baldwin and Krugman (1988b), this result alone is of some importance for policy disputes.

Second, the models have for the most part supported the view that modest tariffs and/or subsidies, if imposed unilaterally, do improve on free trade. Dixit's initial model suggested that tariff rates in the low double-digit range were optimal; similar results have recurred in a number of other papers.

Third, however, the calibrated models generally suggest quite large costs to trade war and, conversely, large gains from mutual removal of trade barriers. These pro-free-trade results have actually played a significant role in two key policy debates in recent years: Harris and Cox (1984) provided some valuable ammunition to Canadian advocates of free trade with the United States, and Venables and Smith provided much of the technical background to the Cecchini Report (Emerson et al. 1989) that stated the economic case for the completion of the European internal market in 1992. But these results are all very preliminary. It is clearly necessary to refine and extend empirical work in strategic trade.

An Overview of the Volume

The papers in this volume fall into three main groups: refinement of the basic calibration technique, efforts to extend that technique to encompass industry dynamics, and renewed efforts to replace some of the ad hockery of calibration with actual testing of the implications of new trade models.

Refining the Technique

Krishna, Hogan, and Swagel offer a paper very much in the Dixit mode but suggest that an alternative formulation of demand is more satisfactory. In implementing this formulation, they discover something disheartening— namely, that even the sign of optimal policies is sensitive to the prior assumptions. They confirm, however, Dixit's basic results that the gains from intervention are in any case small, and that the gains from trade policy are negligible if appropriate domestic policies are implemented.

Venables and Smith, in their separate contributions to this volume, follow their own slightly different approach—in Venables's case by calibrating a basic model to a battery of industries, in Smith's by a more in-depth look at European autos. The results here are more heartening than in the Krishna et al. paper. Venables, in particular, notes that when the a priori assumptions about the form of competition are changed, the parameters fitted in calibration change as well; fortunately, they do so in a way that usually makes the predicted results of policies similar. So he finds that the typical result that modest tariffs or export subsidies can produce small gains is quite robust. Smith, too, finds some results that are robust to changes in the specification of the model, but other aspects of his results are quite sensitive to ad hoc assumptions.

Finally, the paper by Norman and Strandenes is on a very different subject, that of competition and entry in a regulated service industry. It shows, however, that the basic issues of modeling remain much the same as they are in ordinary trade policy.

Dynamics

Klepper addresses the effects of trade policy in an industry that is often cited as a classic case for strategic trade policy, aircraft. As he points out, however, it is a far more complex industry than is often realized, due to the combined dynamic effects of heavy initial R&D and a steep learning curve. Perhaps as interesting as his results is the evidence his paper offers on the difficulty of adequately modeling even a seemingly straightforward duopoly.

The paper by Harris represents a cleverly innovative attack on a difficult problem: in this case, the role of trade policy in an industry in transition. He models the U.S. steel industry, with its declining large-scale producers and rising minimills, and shows that the U.S. protection of that industry looks very different in the dynamic context than it would in a static model. He also shows, interestingly, that while free trade would be better than the existing protection, a tightening of the current quotas would actually raise welfare.

It has been argued by some analysts—myself included—that the case for strategic policies is substantially stronger if these policies are implemented "upstream," e.g., by subsidizing the supply of specialized inputs like skilled manpower. Ulph and Winters use a calibrated approach to study such strategic manpower policies; they suggest that such policies may indeed be powerful, but also that issues of international mobility of high-skill workers are surprisingly critical.

Evidence

In the final section of the book, Rodrik and Winters use unusual sources of evidence to test the importance of new trade factors. Rodrik exploits one of the world economy's natural experiments. Taiwan and South Korea are very similar economies by many measures. Their industrial organization, however, is spectacularly divergent. Rodrik argues that Korea's highly concentrated industry ought to be better at assuring customers of quality and finds evidence that this is in fact the case; in so doing, he indirectly confirms the importance of industrial organization in the process of international trade.

Winters uses an even more exotic test. He argues that import surveillance—which puts foreign sellers on notice that they are being watched, but does not impose any current restriction on imports—should not matter for a competitive industry. The fact that it does in fact appear to lead to a reduction in imports is indirect evidence that the typical industry is in fact composed of imperfectly competitive firms that engage in strategic behavior.

Directions for Future Research

What can we learn from the research represented in this volume? The empirical implementation of the new trade theory has not been an easy matter. In spite of the growing body of experience with such empirical work, each new application is a painful process: after hard work learning details of a particular industry, the researcher typically constructs a model that, while capturing some crucial aspects of reality, is less than fully satisfactory. There have been no stunning empirical successes.

It is also true that the research generally provides little support for a drastic rethinking of trade policy. Nobody has yet provided empirical evidence that would suggest large gains from protection or export subsidy. This is itself a useful result, but it does not excite as much attention as would a striking pro-interventionist result.

Yet research in this area will clearly go on. For one thing, it remains important to understand as well as we can the positive effects of trade policy—and while the style of modeling represented here may not represent the final word on the effects of trade policy in imperfectly competitive industries, it is surely a much better guide than treating the market for aircraft as if it were similar to the market for wheat. The experience with the debates over regional free trade agreements in North America and Europe has already shown that even crude models of this kind can enter where conventional trade models are unable to tread. As experience is gained with dynamic models, in particular, we can expect to see them play an increasingly large role in actual policy debate.

It is also true that modeling efforts thus far have focused exclusively on one source of potential gains from activist policy: the divergence between price and marginal cost. At the time of writing, the cutting edge of theoretical speculation has now shifted to divergences between private and social cost, with new models of the externalities that may lead to long-term growth, to divergences among national growth rates, and to industry localization. Such external economies, arising from interactions in the markets for specialized labor and intermediate inputs, cry out for quantification. Thus there will surely be future waves of empirical work on international trade in the presence of imperfect markets, and this future work will draw heavily on the style of modeling represented in this volume.

References

Baldwin, R., and H. Flam. 1989. Strategic trade policy in the market for 30–40 seat aircraft, *Weltwirtschaftliches Archiv* 125 (3): 484–500.
Baldwin, R., and P. Krugman. 1988a. Industrial policy and international competition in wide-bodied jet aircraft. In *Trade policy issues and empirical analysis,* ed. R. Baldwin. Chicago: University of Chicago Press.
————. 1988b. Market access and international competition: A simulation study of 16K random access memories. In *Empirical methods for international trade,* ed. R. Feenstra. Cambridge: MIT Press.
Brander, J., and B. Spencer. 1983. International R&D rivalry and industrial strategy, *Review of Economic Studies* 50:707–22.
————. 1985. Export subsidies and market share rivalry. *Journal of International Economics* 18:83–100.
Dixit, A. 1988. Optimal trade and industrial policies for the US automobile industry. In *Empirical research in international trade,* ed. R. Feenstra. Cambridge: MIT Press.
Dixit, A., and G. Grossman. 1986. Targeted export promotion with several oligopolistic industries. *Journal of International Economics* 21:233–50.
Dixit, A., and A. Kyle. 1985. The use of protection and subsidies for entry promotion and deterrence. *American Economic Review* 75:139–52.
Dixit, A., and V. Norman. 1980. *Theory of international trade,* Cambridge: Cambridge University Press.
Eaton, J., and G. Grossman. 1986. Optimal trade and industrial policy under oligopoly. *Quarterly Journal of Economics* 101:383–406.
Emerson, M. et al. 1989. *The economics of 1992: An assessment of the potential economic effects of completing the internal market of the European economy.* Oxford: Oxford University Press.
Ethier, W. 1982. National and international returns to scale in the modern theory of international trade. *American Economic Review* 72:389–406.
Harris, R., and D. Cox. 1984. *Trade, industrial policy, and Canadian manufacturing.* Toronto: University of Toronto Press.
Helpman, E. 1981. International trade in the presence of product differentiation, economies of scale, and monopolistic competition: A Chamberlinian-Heckscher-Ohlin approach. *Journal of International Economics* 11:305–40.
Helpman, E., and P. Krugman. 1985. *Market structure and foreign trade.* Cambridge: MIT Press.

Horstmann, I., and J. Markusen. 1986. Up your average cost curve: Inefficient entry and the new protectionism. *Journal of International Economics* 20:225–49.

Krugman, P. 1979. Increasing returns, monopolistic competition, and international trade. *Journal of International Economics* 9:469–79.

———. 1981. Intraindustry specialization and the gains from trade. *Journal of Political Economy* 89:959–73.

Lancaster, K. 1980. Intraindustry trade under perfect monopolistic competition. *Journal of International Economics* 10:151–75.

Smith, A., and A. Venables. 1988. Completing the internal market in the European Community: Some industry simulations. *European Economic Review* 32:1501–25.

Venables, A., and A. Smith. 1986. Trade and industrial policy under imperfect competition. *Economic Policy* 1:622–72.

Whalley, J. 1985. *Trade liberalization among major world trading areas.* Cambridge: MIT Press.

1

The Nonoptimality of Optimal Trade Policies: The U.S. Automobile Industry Revisited, 1979–1985

Kala Krishna, Kathleen Hogan, and Phillip Swagel

1.1 Introduction

A central theme of recent work on trade policy for imperfectly competitive markets has been that by precommitting to tariffs or subsidies, governments can affect firms' strategic positions, thereby shifting profits toward domestic firms.[1] Eaton and Grossman (1986) show, however, that the form of optimal trade policies depends critically on the nature of the competition between firms.[2] Hence, if such models are to be used to justify activist trade policy, it is necessary to have information not only on demand and cost conditions, but also on the nature of the competition between rival firms.

There has recently been some success in implementing these theories using calibration models. Dixit (1988) applies a calibrated model to U.S.-Japan competition in the automobile industry. He uses a conjectural variations (CV) approach to capture firm interactions, where the conjectures result from use of profit maximization equations calibrated to market data. The CVs then combine with calibrated estimates of demand to determine the optimal trade and industrial policies.

This work has generated excitement both in policy circles and among econo-

Kala Krishna is professor of economics at Pennsylvania State University and a research associate of the National Bureau of Economic Research. Kathleen Hogan is the senior technical marketing manager at Oracle Corporation. Phillip Swagel is an economist at the Board of Governors of the Federal Reserve System.

The authors thank Ling Hui Tan for extremely helpful assistance. Avinash Dixit, Garth Saloner, and seminar participants at the IIES Stockholm and NBER provided valuable comments. Kala Krishna gratefully acknowledges funding from the World Bank, the Project on Empirical Studies of Strategic Trade Policy at the NBER, and NSF grant SES-8822204.

1. See Dixit (1988) for a survey of this literature.

2. Optimal policy, of course, depends on what other distortions exist. See Krishna and Thursby (1989), who look at overall optimal policies using a targeting approach.

mists, as policy recommendations can be made even when only minimal data is available.[3] Richardson (1989), Srinivasan (1989), and Helpman and Krugman (1989) survey work in this area. Applied econometricians, however, look upon these models with considerable suspicion, because they appear to elicit policy recommendations out of tiny data sets and often poorly known elasticity parameters. Sensitivity analysis is typically limited to simply examining the effects of changing the parameters used in calibration.

In this paper, we explore the robustness of such models to changes in model specification itself. Since Dixit's model (1988) is probably the most influential of these models to date, we examine how an alternative specification of this model alters the policy recommendations and welfare results of the calibration exercise. As does Dixit, we apply the model to U.S.-Japan competition in the automobile industry, expanding the years examined to the full range from 1979 to 1985. The specification we employ is richer than Dixit's in that we allow product differentiation not only between U.S. and Japanese goods, but also between goods made within each of the countries.[4]

The advantages of doing so are twofold. First, the richer specification allows us to get estimates for the extent of product differentiation, as well as time-varying behavioral parameters for firms and consumers. Second, it allows us to ask which results from Dixit's simpler model are robust and which are artifacts of the model specification.

The effect of the richer specification is to completely reverse the sign of the resulting optimal trade policy: we find the optimal policy to be a subsidy to rather than a tax on imports. In fact, following the policies recommended by Dixit's model can result in a welfare loss if the "true" model is as we specify. The more detailed specification also greatly affects the implicit estimates of collusion/competition between firms. Our results suggest that auto industry firms behave more competitively than Bertrand oligopolists, as opposed to Dixit's finding of competition somewhere between that of Bertrand and Cournot oligopolists. Dixit's result is in part a byproduct of his assumption that firms within a nation produce a homogeneous good. With this assumption, the existence of any markup of price above marginal cost implies that behavior is more collusive than Bertrand.

On the other hand, some results are robust. For example, the effects on firms' behavior of trade policies, particularly the voluntary export restraints (VERs) imposed at the end of 1981, correspond to the effects noted by Dixit. Our implicit estimates of demand cross-elasticities are also consistent with

3. Other examples of work in this area include that of Baldwin and Krugman (1988) and Venables and Smith (1986).

4. Dixit (1988), in contrast, assumes that goods produced within a country are perfect substitutes for one another—that a Chevrolet is the same as a Lincoln or a Pontiac. Although our specification allows for imperfect substitution between all products, the separability we impose groups together all U.S. cars and all Japanese cars. That is, our model puts a Chevy in the same group as a Cadillac, and a Civic in the same group as an Acura.

other sources. In addition, the targeting of instruments to distortions evident in Dixit's results seems to carry through. Finally, as is common with most calibrated trade models, the extent of welfare gains from optimal policies, particularly optimal trade policies alone, remains quite limited.

In section 1.2, we develop the model, present the data and sources, and explain the calibration procedure. Section 1.3 contains our results. We examine the years from 1979 to 1985, which includes years when VERs were in force. Krishna (1989) shows that in the presence of such restraints the behavior of firms is likely to become more collusive as foreign firms become effectively capacity-constrained. The results in Dixit (1988) are consistent with this. Dixit looks at the years 1979, 1980, and 1983. The behavior he finds in 1983 appears more collusive than that in 1980. Our results in section 1.3.1 similarly indicate that VERs allowed Japanese firms to act more collusively from 1981 to 1983. After 1983, however, we find that both U.S. and Japanese firms acted less competitively than prior to the VERs.

In section 1.3.2 we derive the welfare function, which we then maximize to obtain the optimal tariff and production subsidy. As in Dixit (1988), we estimate optimal polices both with and without monopoly (union) labor rents. We then compare our results to Dixit's. Dixit finds that the optimal policy consists of a tariff on imports and a subsidy to domestic production. In contrast, our model indicates a subsidy to both imports and domestic production to be optimal. We suspect that this is related to our demand specification, which increases the importance of consumer surplus in welfare, thereby increasing the attractiveness of import subsidies which raise consumption. In addition, competition in our model appears to be quite vigorous.[5] This tends to limit the gains from using the optimal production subsidy, as these gains are largest in the face of less competitive behavior. As does Dixit, we find that the existence of labor rents raises the optimal subsidy to production and reduces, and in some cases reverses, the optimal import subsidy.

The final section offers some concluding comments and directions for future research. Our work indicates that there is good reason to be suspicious of the results of such simple calibration exercises. Indeed, policymakers should be extremely cautious in the application of "optimal" trade policies suggested by calibrated models, as the nature of the recommended policies may simply be an artifact of the model specification and calibration procedure. Since the optimal policy resulting from one model can differ dramatically from that of another model, and since use of the "wrong" policies can actually reduce welfare, it is important to specify a flexible form which does not dictate the direction of the results. Even if the optimal policies are found and implemented, the gains from

---

5. The direction of optimal trade policy is known to be related to the extent of competition, as parametrized by the choice of the strategic variable and thus in our model by the CVs. For example, in Eaton and Grossman's (1986) simple model of duopolistic competition in third party markets, a tax on exports turns out to be optimal with price competition, while a subsidy is optimal with quantity competition.

doing so are relatively limited, even without foreign retaliation. This result, that only fairly small welfare gains are to be had from optimal tariffs and subsidies, seems common to many such models.

Calibration models should thus probably not be used to determine trade and industrial policy without detailed empirical work to guide the model selection. Sufficiently well specified, however, they prove to be a valuable tool in the analysis of imperfectly competitive industries, since many important results are not sensitive to model specification. Guidance from careful empirical work as to the correct demand and cost parametrizations to use in such calibration models is vital for them to serve as useful guides to determine trade policy.

1.2   A Model with Product Differentiation

We extend Dixit (1988) by allowing for product differentiation among home and foreign firms, as opposed to Dixit's assumption that all firms in a country produce the same good. This is important, since Dixit's results, which suggest that behavior lies between Cournot and Bertrand, could be a result of this assumption. With homogeneous goods and many firms, any markup over cost implies behavior more collusive than that of Bertrand oligopolists. The richer specification allows changes in the parametrization to affect not only the magnitude of the optimal tariff, but also the sign. In contrast, Dixit's parametrization restricts tariffs and subsidies to be positive.[6]

1.2.1   The Model

Demand raises from an aggregate consumer who receives all profits and tariff revenues and maximizes a utility function of the form:

$$u = n_0 + U(S),$$

where n_0 is a numeraire good, and $U(S)$ is the subutility function,

$$U(S) = \beta S^\alpha,$$

with

$$S = \left(\left[\sum_{i=1}^{n} (x^i)^{\rho_x} \right]^{\rho/\rho_x} + \left[\sum_{i=1}^{m} (y^i)^{\rho_y} \right]^{\rho/\rho_y} \right)^{1/\rho}.$$

This form allows ρ to parametrize the extent of product differentiation between U.S. goods x and Japanese goods y, while ρ_x and ρ_y parametrize substitution within home goods and within foreign goods, respectively.[7]

---

6. In Dixit's model, welfare increases with a subsidy or a tariff from an initial position of zero tariffs and subsidies. With a well-behaved welfare function this implies that the optimal tariff and subsidy is positive.

7. Anderson, De Palma, and Thisse (1989) show that these CES demands can arise from the aggregation of consumers with Lancasterian preferences over characteristics. The key restriction needed is that the number of characteristics exceeds the number of varieties (models) minus one.

To best understand the form of the demand functions, think of this subutility function as a particular separable form, and think of β as a scale parameter. To derive the demand functions for the goods, think of S as the level of services produced by all new cars purchased, both domestic and foreign.

Consumers purchase U.S. cars x^i from each of the n domestic firms and Japanese cars y^i from the m foreign firms. The goods of the individual firms are then used to make the aggregate goods X and Y. These X and Y in turn make the services S from which consumers derive utility. Since consumers produce the services using a household production function, the price of a service equals its marginal cost. Firms' market power, of course, creates a wedge between the price and marginal cost of the products from which the services are produced.

The actual forms of these functions can be obtained from the CES parametrization. Equating the marginal utility of S with its marginal cost C and inverting gives the demand for services:

$$D(C(\cdot)) = S = \left(\frac{C}{\alpha\beta}\right)^{1/(\alpha-1)}$$

The production functions for X and Y give rise to the associated cost functions:

$$p(v^1, \ldots, v^n) = \left[\sum_{i=1}^{n} (v^i)^{r_x}\right]^{1/r_x}$$

and

$$q(w^1, \ldots, w^m) = \left[\sum_{i=1}^{m} (w^i)^{r_y}\right]^{1/r_y},$$

where v denotes U.S. price, w Japanese price, and $r_x = \rho_x/(\rho_x-1)$ and $r_y = \rho_y/(\rho_y-1)$.

These cost functions can then be differentiated to obtain the unit input requirements for the output of individual firms in the aggregate goods X and Y, while the cost function for services, $C(p(\cdot),q(\cdot))$, can be differentiated to obtain the input requirements of X and Y in services S, which we denote as a and a^*.

To calibrate the model, assume that firms within each country are symmetric, and then use the CES structure to obtain the demands for individual U.S. and Japanese firms' goods, $x^i(\cdot)$ and $y^i(\cdot)$:

$$x^i = \frac{n^{(1-r_x)/r_x}}{(\alpha\beta)^{1/(\alpha-1)}} (vn^{1/r_x})^{r-1} (v^r n^{r/r_x} + w^r m^{r/r_y})^{((\alpha-1)(1-r)+1)/(\alpha-1)r},$$

and

$$y^i = \frac{m^{(1-r_y)/r_y}}{(\alpha\beta)^{1/(\alpha-1)}} (wm^{1/r_y})^{r-1} (v^r n^{r/r_x} + w^r m^{r/r_y})^{((\alpha-1)(1-r)+1)/(\alpha-1)r},$$

Note that $x^i(\cdot)$ and $y^i(\cdot)$ thus depend on the variables n, m, v, w, r, r_x, r_y, α, and β, where n and m, the number of domestic and foreign firms, and v and w, domestic and foreign prices, are taken from the data. From the cost function for services, C, $r = \rho/(\rho - 1)$.

Summing these demands over the n domestic firms and m foreign firms gives the demands for U.S. and Japanese autos. Since we assume that both markets clear, these demands are observable as actual sales, which we denote as Q_1 for U.S. cars and Q_2 for Japanese cars:

(1) $$Q_1 = \frac{n^{1/r_x}}{(\alpha\beta)^{1/(\alpha-1)}} \, (vn^{1/r_x})^{r-1} \, (v^r n^{r/r_x} + w^r m^{r/r_y})^{((\alpha-1)(1-r)+1)/(\alpha-1)r},$$

(2) $$Q_2 = \frac{m^{1/r_y}}{(\alpha\beta)^{1/(\alpha-1)}} \, (wm^{1/r_y})^{r-1} \, (v^r n^{r/r_x} + w^r m^{r/r_y})^{((\alpha-1)(1-r)+1)/(\alpha-1)r}.$$

Before we derive the remaining equations for the calibration, recall that the elasticity of substitution between domestic and foreign goods equals

$$\sigma = \frac{1}{1 - \rho} = 1 - r,$$

which is defined so as to be positive. The analogous σ_x and σ_y parametrize the degree of substitutability between goods produced by two firms of the same nationality, with

$$\sigma_x = 1 - r_x,$$

and

$$\sigma_y = 1 - r_y.$$

The demand elasticity for the aggregate good, ε, defined so as to be positive, equals

$$\varepsilon = -\frac{\partial D(C(\cdot))}{\partial C(\cdot)} \frac{C(\cdot)}{D(\cdot)} = \frac{1}{1 - \alpha}.$$

We next use a number of relationships implied by the CES structures to derive price elasticities of demand. We then use these elasticities, along with the demand functions for each good, to derive expressions for firms' profit maximizing conditions.[8]

Differentiating $x^i(\cdot)$ gives domestic elasticities of demand:

$$\varepsilon^{ii}(x,x) = -\frac{\partial x^i}{\partial v^i}\frac{v^i}{x^i} = \frac{1}{n}\left[(1 - r_x)(n - 1) + \frac{1 - r + \varepsilon\phi}{1 + \phi}\right],$$

and

---

8. Krishna, Hogan, and Swagel (1989) contains a fuller derivation of these elasticities.

$$\varepsilon^{ij}(x,x) = \frac{\partial x^i}{\partial v^j}\frac{v^j}{x^i} = \frac{1}{n}\left[(1 - r_x) - \frac{1 - r + \varepsilon\phi}{1 + \phi}\right],$$

where

$$\phi = \left(\frac{p}{q}\right)^r.$$

Similarly, differentiating $y^i(\cdot)$ gives foreign elasticities of demand:

$$\varepsilon^{ii}(y,y) = -\frac{\partial y^i}{\partial w^i}\frac{w^i}{y^i} = \frac{1}{m}\left[(1 - r_y)(m - 1) + \frac{(1 - r)\phi + \varepsilon}{1 + \phi}\right],$$

and

$$\varepsilon^{ij}(y,y) = \frac{\partial y^i}{\partial w^j}\frac{w^j}{y^i} = \frac{1}{m}\left[(1 - r_y) - \frac{(1 - r)\phi + \varepsilon}{1 + \phi}\right].$$

Note that $\varepsilon^{ij}(a,b)$ is the elasticity of demand for the ith good in country a with respect to the price of the jth good in country b. For example, $\varepsilon^{ii}(x,x)$ denotes domestic firms' own elasticity of demand, while $\varepsilon^{ij}(y,y)$ represents foreign firms' cross-elasticity of demand when both i and j are foreign goods. Similarly, cross-elasticities of demand between the goods of different countries equal

$$\varepsilon^{ij}(x,y) = \frac{\partial x^i}{\partial w^j}\frac{w^j}{\partial x^i} = \frac{1}{m}\left[\frac{1 - r - \varepsilon}{1 + \phi}\right],$$

and

$$\varepsilon^{ij}(y,x) = \frac{\partial y^i}{\partial v^j}\frac{v^j}{\partial y^i} = \frac{1}{n}\left[\frac{(1 - r - \varepsilon)\phi}{1 + \phi}\right].$$

We are now ready to use firms' first-order conditions for profit maximization. The profits of a typical U.S. firm are

$$\pi^i = (v^i - d + s)x^i(v^1, \ldots, v^n, w^1, \ldots, w^m),$$

where s is the specific subsidy to home firms and d is the (constant) domestic marginal cost of production.

This yields the first-order condition for a U.S. firm:

(3) $$\varepsilon^{ii}(x,x) - \gamma = v^i/(v^i - d + s),$$

with the cv,

$$\gamma = (n - 1)\varepsilon^{ij}(x,x)\gamma^{11} + m\varepsilon^{ij}(x,y)\frac{v}{w}\gamma^{12},$$

where

$$\gamma^{11} = \frac{\partial v^j}{\partial v^i},$$

$$\gamma^{12} = \frac{\partial w^j}{\partial v^i}.$$

Similarly, the first-order condition for a Japanese firm is:

(4) $\qquad \varepsilon^{ii}(y,y) - \gamma^* = w^i/(w^i - d^* - t),$

where t is the specific tariff on the foreign firm and d^* is the (constant) foreign marginal cost of production. The foreign cv is thus

$$\gamma^* = n\varepsilon^{ij}(y,x)\frac{w}{v}\gamma^{21} + (m - 1)\varepsilon^{ij}(y,y)\gamma^{22},$$

where

$$\gamma^{21} = \frac{\partial v^j}{\partial w^i},$$

$$\gamma^{22} = \frac{\partial w^j}{\partial w^i}.$$

We now have four equations, but seven unknowns: γ, γ^*, α, β, r, r_x, and r_y. There are many possible ways to complete the calibration; available elasticity estimates typically determine the route chosen. Since Dixit cites several estimates for ε, the total elasticity of demand for all automobiles, and σ, the elasticity of substitution between U.S. and Japanese cars, we employ these in the calibration. Following Dixit, we take 2.0 as the base case for σ and perform sensitivity analysis using values of 1.5 and 3.0. For ε, Dixit's figure of 1.0 would imply $\alpha = 0$. We therefore use 1.1 as our central case and perform sensitivity analysis for values of 1.05, 1.30, and 1.50.[9] Table 1.9 contains the results of this sensitivity analysis, which we describe in section 1.3.4. For U.S. and Japanese cars to be substitutes, e.g., $\varepsilon^{ij}(x,y) > 0$, ε must be less than σ, so we report no results for the case where both ε and σ equal 1.50.

Given data for v, w, n, m, Q_1, and Q_2 and estimates for ε and σ, the demand equations (1) and (2) become a system of two equations with the three unknowns β, σ_x, and σ_y. We solve the system recursively. Dividing (1) by (2) eliminates β. Taking a value for σ_y as given then gives σ_x. Substituting σ_x into (1) or σ_y into (2) gives β.

Since Japanese cars are probably closer substitutes for one another than they are for U.S. cars, σ_y should be larger than σ. We take σ_y as 3.0 for our central case; this is larger than the central case estimate for σ of 2.10.[10] As described in section 1.3.4, table 1.10 shows the effects of changing σ_y on firms' implied conduct. In general, a larger σ_y implies that Japanese firms act more collusively, since they persist in charging a price above marginal cost even as their products become less distinguishable. The effect on the implied conduct of U.S. firms is small.

Given σ_x and σ_y, we can calculate ϕ as $(p/q)^r$. Another way to get ϕ would be to use the result of Krishna and Itoh (1988) that $\theta = \phi/(1 + \phi)$, where θ is domestic producers' share in expenditure, which equals ap/C. Thus, using the data described below to find θ determines the value of ϕ. The calibration procedure ensures that both methods produce the same ϕ. Once we know ϕ, r, ε, r_x, and r_y, the first-order conditions (3) and (4) provide γ and γ^*.

These aggregate CVs can in turn be decomposed into the component γ^{ij}s using the definitions of γ and γ^* given above. Since there are four γ^{ij}s and only two equations that define them, we must set either $\gamma^{11} = \gamma^{12}$ and $\gamma^{21} = \gamma^{22}$, or set $\gamma^{11} = \gamma^{22}$ and $\gamma^{12} = \gamma^{21}$. The first set of restrictions implies that firms have the same conjectures about both domestic competitors and foreign firms. As demonstrated in Krishna (1989), this is not a good idea for years with VERs. The second set of restrictions implies that domestic firms' conjectures about other domestic firms is the same as the foreign firms' conjectures about other foreign firms and, similarly, that each nation's firms hold identical conjectures about firms in the other nation. U.S. and Japanese firms are thus required to behave similarly, which again may not be true. Since neither set of restrictions is particularly appealing, we simply use the aggregate CVs γ and γ^* in our simulations.[11]

1.2.2   Data

Table 1.1 contains our data. Prices and quantities for both U.S. and Japanese cars are taken from the *Automotive News Market Data Book (ANMDB)*. Prices are calculated as a weighted average of the suggested retail prices for March or April of each year, exclusive of optional equipment and domestic transport costs, with expenditure shares as the weights. Japanese prices include import duties and freight (transport) charges. Quantities are the total sales of all models; though for U.S. cars this differs slightly from Dixit's use of production minus exports plus imports from Canada, the difference is far less than 1 percent for the three years of Dixit's data. For Japanese cars, the difference between Dixit's use of imports and our use of sales amounts to nearly 10 percent in 1983, the difference being reflected in changes in inventory stocks. To facilitate comparisons, we use Dixit's numbers for 1979, 1980, and 1983;[12] either way, our results change only slightly.

As always, cost data is more difficult to obtain. As Dixit notes, true marginal costs should take into account the shadow price of investment. Following

---

11. Simulations using the disaggregated CVs can be found in Krishna, Hogan, and Swagel (1989).

12. Japanese sales were 1,833,744 in 1979, 1,977,018 in 1980, and 1,911,318 in 1983.

Table 1.1   Data

		1979	1980	1981	1982	1983	1984	1985
Autos (million)	Q_1	8.341	6.581	6.206	5.757	7.020	7.952	8.205
	Q_2	1.546	1.819	1.892	1.801	2.112	1.906	2.218
Price ($)	v	5,951	6,407	6,740	6,880	7,494	8,950	10,484
	w	4,000	4,130	4,580	4,834	5,239	5,518	6,069
Cost ($)	d	5,400	6,100	6,362	6,636	7,000	7,301	7,615
	d^*	3,400	3,800	3,963	4,121	4,400	4,589	4,786
Firms	n	2.250	2.077	2.100	2.200	2.262	2.300	2.310
	m	4.040	4.034	4.210	4.250	4.350	4.460	4.400
Labor rent		1,000	1,200	1,272	1,327	1,400	1,460	1,523
Total elasticity of demand		$\varepsilon = 1.1$						
Elasticities of substitution		$\sigma = 2.0$						
		$\sigma_y = 3.0$						

Dixit, however, we ignore this complicated intertemporal issue and include only labor and materials costs in our data. The costs in table 1.1 should thus be seen as a lower bound on actual marginal costs. We use Dixit's cost figures for 1979, 1980, and 1983 and adjust these figures for other years, following the method described by Dixit. For domestic autos, production costs are broken into labor and component/materials costs. Labor costs are adjusted in each year by Bureau of Labor Statistics (BLS) figures for automobile industry compensation rate changes and then by an additional 2 percent for productivity changes. Component/materials costs are adjusted by the wholesale price index from the IMF *International Financial Statistics* (*IFS*). For Japanese costs, we use the *IFS* manufacturing wages index to adjust Dixit's figures for materials costs, the *IFS* wage/price index for labor costs, *IFS* statistics for exchange rate changes, and data from the World Bank *Commodity Trade and Price Trends* to adjust for changes in ocean freight costs.

We use market share data in the *ANMDB* to calculate Herfindahl numbers-equivalents on a firm basis, which we denote as n for the United States and m for Japan.[13]

1.3   Implementing the Model

We use the data in table 1.1 to calibrate the model for the years 1979 to 1985. The resulting parameter values for market (consumer) and firm behavior are summarized in tables 1.2 and 1.3, respectively.

13. Note that since we assume product differentiation within each country, the Herfindahl numbers-equivalent—the number of symmetric firms that would reproduce the existing market shares—is not really the proper measure, as the number of firms n and m are not truly exogenous. Our use of the Herfindahl index should thus be taken as an approximation. While it is a simple matter to add two equations to endogenize n and m, the computational burden becomes much greater.

1.3.1 Calibration Results

Table 1.2 summarizes the parameters which describe market (consumer) behavior. For $\sigma_y = 3.0$, the value of σ_x is remarkably constant and lies around 1.3 for all years. That the elasticity of substitution between U.S. goods is always smaller than that for Japanese goods suggests that U.S. autos are less interchangable than Japanese autos. This seems plausible as U.S. cars seem more differentiated from one another than are Japanese cars.

This is reflected in the elasticities of demand. That $\varepsilon^{ii}(x,x)$ and $\varepsilon^{ij}(x,x)$ are respectively smaller than $\varepsilon^{ii}(y,y)$ and $\varepsilon^{ij}(y,y)$ shows that demand for Japanese cars with respect to other Japanese cars is more price elastic than demand for U.S. cars with respect to other U.S. cars. Indeed, the demand for Japanese cars in general reacts more to price changes, by both national and international competitors. That $\varepsilon^{ij}(y,x)$ is an order of magnitude larger than $\varepsilon^{ij}(x,y)$ illustrates this. The two "own" elasticities $\varepsilon^{ii}(x,x)$ and $\varepsilon^{ii}(y,y)$ are orders of magnitude larger than the ε^{ij}'s because they reflect the effect on a firm which raises its own price and thus loses demand to all other firms. The four ε^{ij}'s, on the other hand, are smaller because they measure the gain of only one of the many firms which benefit when another firm changes its price.

Table 1.2   **Market Behavior**

	1979	1980	1981	1982	1983	1984	1985
β^{a}	10.574	9.813	10.150	9.838	12.681	15.532	18.838
σ_x	1.255	1.255	1.277	1.304	1.308	1.265	1.267
Elasticities of demand							
$\varepsilon^{ii}(x,x)$	1.231	1.246	1.266	1.285	1.285	1.244	1.247
$\varepsilon^{ij}(x,x)$	0.025	0.009	0.011	0.019	0.023	0.021	0.019
$\varepsilon^{ii}(y,y)$	2.728	2.718	2.726	2.727	2.734	2.750	2.745
$\varepsilon^{ij}(y,y)$	0.272	0.282	0.274	0.273	0.266	0.250	0.255
$\varepsilon^{ij}(x,y)$	0.025	0.034	0.037	0.038	0.036	0.026	0.028
$\varepsilon^{ij}(y,x)$	0.356	0.368	0.355	0.335	0.329	0.341	0.337
Cross-elasticities of demand							
$L(Q_1,v)$	1.200	1.236	1.254	1.262	1.256	1.216	1.222
$L(Q_1,w)$	0.100	0.136	0.154	0.162	0.156	0.116	0.122
$L(Q_2,w)$	1.900	1.864	1.846	1.838	1.844	1.884	1.878
$L(Q_2,v)$	0.800	0.764	0.746	0.738	0.744	0.784	0.778
Calibration using Levinsohn's cross-elasticities							
$\varepsilon^{ii}(x,x)$	1.219	1.226	1.238	1.251	1.251	1.227	1.228
$\varepsilon^{ij}(x,x)$	−0.022	−0.019	−0.009	0.003	0.004	−0.016	−0.014
$\varepsilon^{ii}(y,y)$	2.662	2.662	2.676	2.679	2.686	2.694	2.690
$\varepsilon^{ij}(y,y)$	0.338	0.338	0.324	0.321	0.314	0.306	0.310
$\varepsilon^{ij}(x,y)$	0.014	0.021	0.024	0.026	0.024	0.015	0.016
$\varepsilon^{ij}(y,x)$	0.197	0.228	0.234	0.227	0.218	0.198	0.200
$L(Q_1,w)$	0.055	0.084	0.102	0.110	0.104	0.067	0.072
$L(Q_2,v)$	0.444	0.473	0.491	0.499	0.493	0.456	0.461

[a] β is reported in 10 billions.

As a further check on these demand elasticities, we calculate the resulting aggregate cross-elasticities of demand and compare them to estimates in Levinsohn (1988).[14] The U.S.-U.S. cross-elasticity, which we denote as $L(Q_1,v)$, is the percentage quantity change in U.S. auto sales given an equiproportionate change in the price of all U.S. cars. Similarly, we denote the U.S.-Japan cross-elasticity—the response of U.S. sales to an equiproportionate change in Japanese prices—as $L(Q_1,w)$. The Japan-Japan and Japan-U.S. cross-elasticities are $L(Q_2,w)$ and $L(Q_2,v)$, respectively. As usual, we define these elasticities so that they are typically positive.

For our specification,

$$L(Q_1, v) = -\left[\frac{\partial nx(v^1, \ldots, v^n, w^1, \ldots, w^m)}{\partial v}\right]\frac{v}{nx} = \frac{1 - r + \varepsilon\phi}{1 + \phi},$$

$$L(Q_1, w) = \left[\frac{\partial nx(v^1, \ldots, v^n, w^1, \ldots, w^m)}{\partial w}\right]\frac{w}{nx} = \frac{1 - r - \varepsilon}{1 + \phi},$$

$$L(Q_2, w) = -\left[\frac{\partial my(v^1, \ldots, v^n, w^1, \ldots, w^m)}{\partial w}\right]\frac{w}{my} = \frac{(1 - r)\phi + \varepsilon}{1 + \phi}, \text{ and}$$

$$L(Q_2, v) = \left[\frac{\partial my(v^1, \ldots, v^n, w^1, \ldots, w^m)}{\partial v}\right]\frac{v}{my} = \frac{(1 - r - \varepsilon)\phi}{1 + \phi}$$

Table 1.2 contains the aggregate cross-elasticities which result from our model, along with the ε^{ij}'s—the individual firm elasticities of demand. Our results of 1.200–1.263 for $L(Q_1,v)$ correspond well with Levinsohn's estimates of 0.967–1.412. For $L(Q_1,w)$, our results of 0.100–0.162 are similarly roughly in line with Levinsohn's estimates of 0.086–0.226. Note that after 1979, U.S. firms become markedly more responsive to changes in Japanese prices; 1979 is the year in which U.S. auto manufacturers first appealed for import protection. However, our results of 1.838–1.900 for $L(Q_2,w)$ differ significantly from Levinsohn's estimates of 1.080–1.636, while our results of 0.738–0.800 for $L(Q_2,v)$ differ from Levinsohn's figures of 0.122–0.231.

An alternative approach to the calibration sheds light on the implications of these differences. Since ϕ can be calculated from market-share data, assuming values for the own-country cross-elasticities $L(Q_1,v)$ and $L(Q_2,w)$ lets us solve for ε and σ. The rest of the calibration then proceeds as before. The bottom of table 1.2 shows the behavioral parameters and jointly optimal policies and welfare which result from setting $L(Q_1,v) = 1.247$ and $L(Q_2,w) = 1.636$, which are the Levinsohn estimates with the smallest standard errors. Except in 1982 and 1983, $\varepsilon^{ij}(x,x)$ is negative, indicating that U.S. cars are complements for one

---

14. Levinsohn's estimates come from an econometric study using a panel of data for 100 different models over the years 1983–85. He presents four different estimates for each of the cross-elasticities, which he takes as constant over the years examined. See Levinsohn (1988, tables 2.4–2.7).

Table 1.3   **Firm Behavior**

	1979	1980	1981	1982	1983	1984	1985
Conjectural variations							
γ	−9.57	−19.62	−16.56	−26.91	−13.89	−4.18	−2.41
γ^*	−5.27	−15.24	−6.13	−5.16	−4.36	−3.91	−2.39
γ_C	0.0410	0.0510	0.0537	0.0520	0.0496	0.0417	0.0413
γ_C^*	0.2064	0.2287	0.2354	0.2385	0.2311	0.2002	0.2013
U.S. prices							
v	5,951	6,407	6,740	6,880	7,494	8,950	10,484
v_B	23,895	25,257	24,898	25,028	26,626	31,450	32,788
v_C	26,553	28,434	27,928	27,827	29,494	34,851	36,308
Japan prices							
w	4,000	4,130	4,580	4,834	5,239	5,518	6,069
w_B	5,567	6,220	6,471	6,723	7,152	7,416	7,733
w_C	5,857	6,591	6,867	7,139	7,574	7,780	8,117
U.S. costs							
d	5,400	6,100	6,362	6,636	7,000	7,301	7,615
d_B	1,115	1,265	1,417	1,527	1,662	1,753	2,077
d_C	1,032	1,147	1,283	1,390	1,521	1,618	1,915
Japan costs							
d^*	3,400	3,800	3,963	4,121	4,400	4,589	4,786
d_B^*	2,433	2,511	2,800	2,961	3,223	3,411	3,758
d_C^*	2,357	2,419	2,696	2,849	3,106	3,307	3,640

another, rather than substitutes. While the optimal policies and welfare do not change by much, this improbable result makes us wary of Levinsohn's estimate for $L(Q_2, w)$.

Table 1.2 also summarizes the value of β, which gives an indication of the strength of demand. While demand for autos was relatively strong in 1979, it weakened in 1980, a year in which the three major U.S. producers all suffered losses.[15] This is picked up by the fall in β between these years. The rise in β in 1983 coincides with the comeback of U.S. firms, as Ford and General Motors edged back into profitability after the dismal years (for U.S. firms) of 1980–82.

Table 1.3 summarizes the parameters which describe firm behavior. The estimates of γ and γ*, parametrize the degree of competition among U.S. and Japanese firms, respectively. A zero value for γ indicates Bertrand competition. The estimates derived are uniformly negative, suggesting that firms' behavior is more competitive than that of Bertrand oligopolists. This contrasts with Dixit's result that competition lies somewhere between Cournot and Bertrand. With Dixit's assumption of perfect substitutability between all home goods and between all foreign goods, any markup of price over cost implies conduct less competitive than Bertrand. By introducing product differentiation within

15. Halberstam (1986) provides a fascinating history of the U.S. and Japanese automobile industries.

goods made at home and within those made abroad, we do not implicitly restrict the calibrated conjectures in this way.

From 1979 to 1980, these conjectures become more negative, suggesting a greater degree of competition in 1980 than in 1979. This is not surprising, as demand was relatively slack in 1980. With VERs in place starting in 1981, Japanese firms appear to behave less competitively, while U.S. firms continue to act in a relatively competitive manner. This is consistent with Dixit's result that collusion between U.S. firms does not appear to be greatly strengthened by VERs. By 1984, however, U.S. firms appear to match Japanese firms in acting less competitively, though both continue to behave more competitively than Bertrand duopolists. The need to catch up to Japanese competitors apparently prodded U.S. firms into a period of competitive behavior, after which they reverted to relatively collusive behavior.

In order to better interpret the meaning of the values of the CVs γ and γ^* we also calculate the prices of U.S. and Japanese autos that would exist were behavior Bertrand or Cournot. The Bertrand-equivalent prices are calculated by solving for v and w in (3) and (4), with γ and γ^* fixed at zero, and substituting for $\varepsilon^{ij}(x,x)$ and $\varepsilon^{ii}(y,y)$. These are given by v_B and w_B in table 1.3.

To calculate the Cournot-equivalent prices, we solve (3) and (4) in conjunction with equations (5)–(8) given below, which restrict firms' beliefs (γ^{ij}'s) to competition in quantities. The Cournot-equivalent prices v_C and w_C and aggregate CVs γ_C and γ_C^* are presented in table 1.3.

For a U.S. firm to assume that other U.S. firms do not vary their output, it must assume that prices change so that

$$(5) \qquad \varepsilon^{ij}(x, x)(1 + (n - 2)\gamma^{11}) - \varepsilon^{ii}(x, x)\gamma^{11} + m\varepsilon^{ij}(x, y)\gamma^{12}\frac{v}{w} = 0.$$

For a U.S. firm to assume that Japanese firms do not change their output, it must assume that

$$(6) \quad \varepsilon^{ij}(y, x)(1 + (n - 1)\gamma^{11}) + \frac{v}{w}\gamma^{12}[\varepsilon^{ij}(y, y)(m - 1) - \varepsilon^{ii}(y,y)] = 0.$$

Similarly, for a Japanese firm to assume that other Japanese firms do not change their output as it varies its own price, it must assume that

$$(7) \qquad \varepsilon^{ij}(y, y)(1 + (m - 2)\gamma^{22}) - \varepsilon^{ii}(y, y)\gamma^{22} + n\varepsilon^{ij}(y, x)\gamma^{21}\frac{w}{v} = 0.$$

For a Japanese firm to assume that U.S. firms do not vary their output, it must assume that

$$(8) \quad \varepsilon^{ij}(x, y)(1 + (m - 1)\gamma^{22}) + \frac{w}{v}\gamma^{21}[\varepsilon^{ij}(x, x)(n - 1) - \varepsilon^{ii}(x, x)] = 0.$$

For firms to behave in a Cournot fashion and for this behavior to replicate the market outcome, v, w, γ^{11}, γ^{12}, γ^{21}, γ^{22} must be such that equations (3)–(8) are satisfied simultaneously.

We similarly calculate the Bertrand- and Cournot-equivalent costs for both U.S. and Japanese firms. These appear at the bottom of table 1.3 as d_B, d_C, d_B^*, and d_C^*. We discuss these results in section 1.3.4.

Because we find behavior to be less collusive than that of Bertrand oligopolists, the Bertrand-equivalent price for both domestic and foreign cars is higher than the actual price, while the Cournot-equivalent price is higher still. Note, however, that while the Bertrand- and Cournot-equivalent prices for U.S. firms are much higher than actual prices, the equivalent prices for Japanese firms are quite close to actual prices v and w, which are shown in the middle of table 1.3. This indicates that the behavior of Japanese firms is fairly close to that of Bertrand (and Cournot) oligopolists, while U.S. firms exhibit far more competitive behavior.

1.3.2   Welfare

We now calculate the optimal policies which arise from maximization of the welfare function. The first-order conditions (3) and (4) together define how domestic price, v, and foreign price, w, adjust for a given subsidy, s, and tariff, t. In turn, v and w determine U.S. and Japanese outputs. Since v and w are nonlinear simultaneous functions of s and t, (3) and (4) must be solved numerically for every s and t. The resulting v and w are then used to calculate a value for welfare. The jointly optimal subsidy and tariff are thus the s and t which maximize the welfare function. For the optimal tariff by itself, s is set to 0, while for the optimal subsidy by itself, we set t to the most-favored-nation (MFN) level of \$100.

As explained in section 1.2.1, we assume a numeraire good, n_0, and a utility-maximizing aggregate consumer. We assume that all revenues are given back to this aggregate consumer, so that welfare is given by

$$W(s, t) = U(S(s, t)) - ndx(s, t) - (w - t)my(s, t)$$

when there are no rents to labor. Following Dixit, we assume labor rents to be a constant 20 percent of domestic costs in each year. For 1979, Dixit notes that this corresponds to about half of the wage bill. Rents are then subtracted from domestic cost d in the second term of the welfare function.

1.3.3   Optimal Policies

Tables 1.4 and 1.5 summarize the policy and welfare results for 1979–85. In all following tables, welfare is shown in billions of dollars. The first thing to notice is that in all years the jointly optimal policy is to subsidize both domestic production and imports. This contrasts with Dixit's results, which call for a subsidy on domestic production but a tariff on imports.

In order to understand why the sign of the import policy differs between our model and Dixit's, consider the derivative of welfare with no labor rents at t and s equal to zero:

Table 1.4   Policy Results—No Labor Rent

	1979	1980	1981	1982	1983	1984	1985
Jointly optimal policies							
Subsidy	528	312	405	298	528	1,389	2,139
Tariff	−245	−122	−268	−318	−377	−404	−558
v	5,369	6,079	6,311	6,571	6,929	7,249	7,545
w	3,606	3,895	4,165	4,355	4,684	4,925	5,251
Q_1	9,339,751	6,966,457	6,641,703	5,996,750	7,611,905	10,135,979	12,028,153
Q_2	1,734,165	1,949,192	2,146,008	2,108,682	2,449,221	2,001,047	2,249,905
Welfare[a]	563.279	499.049	507.623	484.829	640.654	831.912	1,023.592
Optimal tariff only							
Subsidy	0	0	0	0	0	0	0
Tariff	−102	−41	−166	−245	−244	−24	27
v	5,951	6,407	6,740	6,880	7,494	8,950	10,480
w	3,769	3,891	4,280	4,439	4,839	5,372	5,978
Q_1	8,290,636	6,547,626	6,140,050	5,674,886	6,930,603	7,927,060	8,190,322
Q_2	1,730,508	1,948,058	2,142,799	2,105,861	2,444,186	2,004,723	2,281,226
Welfare[a]	562.982	498.981	507.516	484.780	640.463	830.154	1,018.548
Optimal subsidy only							
Subsidy	491	277	342	219	447	1,339	2,085
Tariff	100	100	100	100	100	100	100
v	5,410	6,116	6,378	6,653	7,016	7,311	7,624
w	4,000	4,130	4,580	4,834	5,239	5,517	6,067
Q_1	9,347,531	6,969,203	6,650,342	6,005,257	7,624,480	10,148,407	12,049,094
Q_2	1,432,016	1,755,363	1,815,162	1,757,361	2,010,503	1,623,802	1,723,339
Welfare[a]	563.225	499.027	507.561	484.754	640.546	831.814	1,023.412
Status quo							
Subsidy	0	0	0	0	0	0	0
Tariff	100	100	100	100	100	100	100
v	5,951	6,407	6,740	6,880	7,494	8,950	10,484
w	4,000	4,130	4,580	4,834	5,239	5,518	6,069
Q_1	8,341,000	6,581,000	6,206,296	5,756,660	7,020,000	7,951,517	8,204,721
Q_2	1,546,000	1,819,000	1,891,769	1,801,481	2,112,000	1,906,208	2,217,850
Welfare[a]	562.963	498.972	507.483	484.727	640.406	830.148	1,018.545

[a]Welfare reported in billion dollars.

Table 1.5   Policy Results—With Labor Rent

	1979	1980	1981	1982	1983	1984	1985
Jointly optimal policies							
Subsidy	1,426	1,448	1,590	1,557	1,814	2,567	3,231
Tariff	−242	−119	−263	−311	−370	−398	−550
v	4,379	4,886	5,056	5,266	5,552	5,806	6,046
w	3,609	3,898	4,170	4,363	4,691	4,931	5,260
Q_1	11,904,968	9,104,444	8,753,861	7,920,674	10,034,817	13,219,449	15,673,308
Q_2	1,468,333	1,643,050	1,810,673	1,782,521	2,066,796	1,670,132	1,875,887
Welfare[a]	573.809	508.592	517.308	493.962	652.872	848.785	1,044.467
Optimal tariff only							
Subsidy	0	0	0	0	0	0	0
Tariff	180	290	178	111	135	369	409
v	5,951	6,407	6,740	6,880	7,494	8,951	10,490
w	4,091	4,331	4,668	4,847	5,280	5,834	6,452
Q_1	8,359,537	6,622,834	6,224,367	5,759,085	7,028,460	8,000,855	8,261,727
Q_2	1,481,012	1,664,472	1,826,520	1,792,889	2,082,063	1,716,007	1,976,865
Welfare[a]	571.307	506.883	515.379	492.366	650.234	841.781	1,031.076
Optimal subsidy only							
Subsidy	1,401	1,425	1,547	1,504	1,760	2,534	3,195
Tariff	100	100	100	100	100	100	100
v	4,407	4,910	5,101	5,321	5,610	5,848	6,098
w	4,000	4,130	4,579	4,833	5,238	5,517	6,066
Q_1	11,913,770	9,108,249	8,761,021	7,929,342	10,048,377	13,325,997	15,692,584
Q_2	1,211,527	1,478,861	1,530,159	1,484,537	1,694,871	1,647,189	1,436,555
Welfare[a]	573.764	508.574	517.256	493.899	652.783	848.704	1,044.318
Status quo							
Subsidy	0	0	0	0	0	0	0
Tariff	100	100	100	100	100	100	100
v	5,951	6,407	6,740	6,880	7,494	8,950	10,484
w	4,000	4,130	4,580	4,834	5,239	5,518	6,069
Q_1	8,341,000	6,581,000	6,206,296	5,756,660	7,020,000	7,951,517	8,204,721
Q_2	1,546,000	1,819,000	1,891,769	1,801,481	2,112,000	1,906,208	2,217,850
Welfare[a]	571.304	506.869	515.377	492.366	650.234	841.757	1,031.041

[a]Welfare reported in billion dollars.

$$\frac{\partial W}{\partial t}\bigg|_{s=t=0} = n(U_x - d)\frac{\partial x}{\partial t} - my\left(\frac{\partial w}{\partial t} - 1\right).$$

Note that at this point there are only two terms in this expression. The first term is positive in both models, since marginal utility equals price, which exceeds costs, and since a tariff raises domestic production in both models, which implies that $\partial x/\partial t$ is positive. In Dixit's model, however, $\partial w/\partial t$ is less than unity, while it exceeds unity in ours. Hence the second term, $-my(\partial w/\partial t - 1)$, is positive in Dixit's model but negative in ours. As the welfare function is well behaved this leads to the optimal tariff being positive in his model. In ours, the second term outweighs the first at $s = t = 0$, so that a subsidy on imports improves welfare.

Intuitively, trade policy seems to play two roles here. The first is a profit-shifting role in correcting any "strategic distortion" à la Eaton and Grossman (1986). Second, since trade policy affects domestic consumption, it also affects the size of consumer surplus. Our model implies that the behavior of firms is fairly competitive. This by itself should work toward reversing the sign of the optimal trade policy, since the direction of the profit-shifting policy depends on the degree of competition. In addition, our CES demand parametrization implies that consumer surplus is quite important, since demand resembles a hyperbola. This in turn strengthens the reasons to subsidize both domestic and foreign output. Hence, we believe that the calibration results for implied conduct together with the effect of the demand parametrization itself on the importance of consumer surplus in welfare is responsible for the differences between our results and Dixit's.

Next compare the jointly optimal subsidy when there are no labor rents to the case with labor rents. The optimal policy with rents involves a higher subsidy on production than without. This is to be expected, as the presence of rents makes domestic production more desirable. Also notice that the optimal tariff changes only very slightly. This suggests a targeting interpretation. The presence of labor rents distorts production, as firms produce too little, both because they have monopoly power and because they do not take labor rents into account in their production decisions. Hence the optimal policy to correct this distortion is a domestic production subsidy, which targets the domestic distortion directly, rather than a trade policy, which targets the distortion only indirectly.

When the production subsidy is unavailable, the optimal tariff in the presence of labor rents is positive for all years, as opposed to the import subsidy typically optimal in the absence of labor rents. Again this is expected, as the tariff must partly do the job of the unavailable production subsidy, and the higher tariff encourages domestic production. The presence of labor rents thus dramatically changes the nature of the optimal policies.

Next compare the jointly optimal tariffs with and without labor rents to the optimal tariffs when a production subsidy is unavailable. The tariff is always larger (less negative) in the latter case. Again, this has a targeting interpretation. When a subsidy is unavailable, the tariff targets the monopoly distortion which is really best targeted by the subsidy. Similarly, comparing the jointly optimal subsidy and the optimal subsidy when the tariff is set to the MFN level shows that the subsidy is slightly lower when applied by itself. When the tariff is not available, reducing the subsidy on production acts to encourage imports.

In the above comparisons, we see at work the general principle of targeting instruments to the relevant distortion. We also see that in the absence of an instrument, the optimal level of the remaining instrument is set to help reduce other distortions. Dixit offers similar interpretations.

A natural question to ask next is how valuable such policy is in raising welfare. The welfare levels with both t and s set optimally, with only t set optimally, and with only s set optimally are also given in tables 1.4 and 1.5. Here our results are in line with Dixit's—the gains to be had are very limited, with most of the benefit coming from the production subsidy rather than from a tariff on imports.

In the absence of labor rents, gains range from a high of about \$5 billion in 1985 to less than \$80 million in 1980.[16] Welfare gains are larger when labor rents constitute a share of the domestic wage bill, since the increased domestic production that results from optimal policies adds to consumer surplus and to workers' rents, both of which the price-setting firm ignores. With our assumption of labor costs as 20 percent of unit cost (half of the wage bill), welfare gains from jointly optimal policies range from \$13 billion in 1985 to \$1.7 billion in 1980. The presence of labor rents thus provides greater scope for strategic trade policy (see, e.g., Katz and Summers 1989). And yet these gains remain fairly minor relative to the size of the markets involved.

Moreover, it may be worse to implement the wrong policy than to do nothing. For example, if the optimal policies that result from Dixit's model are used instead of the ones identified as optimal by our model, welfare is slightly lower in some years. Table 1.6 compares the status quo (MFN tariff, no subsidy) welfare level (W^{MFN}) with the welfare which results from application of the optimal policies suggested by our CES model (W^{CES}) and the welfare which results from Dixit's optimal policies (W^D). Implementing Dixit's policies reduces welfare in the absence of labor rents in 1981, 1982, and 1983 but raises welfare over inaction in the remaining years. With labor rents, Dixit's policies reduce welfare in 1985 but increase it in other years. Of course, the lack of responsiveness in welfare also implies that the loss from following the wrong policies is likely to be small—a conclusion borne out for 1981–83. In 1985,

---

16. Potential gains in 1985 are particularly large because firm behavior in that year is not very competitive. This increases the welfare gains available from increasing output with a production subsidy.

Table 1.6   **Comparison of Models**

	1979	1980	1981	1982	1983	1984	1985
			No Labor Rent				
CES model							
Subsidy	528	312	405	298	528	1,389	2,141
Tariff	−245	−122	−268	−318	−377	−404	−558
Dixit's linear model							
Subsidy	611	325	408	258	538	2,029	3,847
Tariff	408	211	440	521	604	621	809
Welfare[a]							
W^{CES}	563.28	499.05	507.62	484.83	640.65	831.91	1,023.59
W^D	563.09	499.00	507.42	484.57	640.26	830.81	1,023.11
W^{MFN}	562.96	498.97	507.48	484.73	640.41	830.15	1,018.55
			With Labor Rent				
CES model							
Subsidy	1,426	1,448	1,590	1,557	1,814	2,567	3,231
Tariff	−242	−119	−263	−311	−370	−398	−550
Dixit's linear model							
Subsidy	1,712	1,590	1,768	1,643	2,044	3,812	5,871
Tariff	357	181	389	461	529	553	731
Welfare[a]							
W^{CES}	573.81	508.59	517.31	493.96	652.87	848.79	1,044.47
W^D	573.46	508.52	517.09	493.74	652.46	843.37	971.07
W^{MFN}	571.30	506.87	515.38	492.37	650.23	841.67	1,031.04

[a]Welfare reported in billion dollars.

however, application of the optimal tariff and subsidy which result from Dixit's model entails a decline in welfare of nearly $60 billion in the presence of labor rents. Misguided policy decisions can indeed prove costly in certain cases.

As shown by Krishna (1989), however, quantitative restraints such as VERs differ fundamentally from tariffs in that they facilitate collusive behavior by the competing firms. The existence of VERs starting in 1981 thus affects firm behavior, as reflected in the CVs γ and γ^*. The rise in γ^* corresponding to the imposition of VERs in 1981, and in γ after 1983, supports this theory. Our simulation results for these years, however, take γ and γ^* as fixed behavioral parameters. These CVs are surely inappropriate for calculating the optimal tariff and subsidies, since these policies do not have the collusion-increasing effects of VERs.

As an attempt to correct for this problem of static CVs, we double the γ and γ^* that result from the calibration for 1983 before finding the optimal subsidy and tariff. This experiment, which makes γ and γ^* more negative, thus imposes the more competitive conjectures Krishna (1989) tells us should exist in the absence of a VER. Of course, we have no way of knowing whether our modification is sufficient (or too much); we mean this only as a first step.

Table 1.7 compares the prices, policies, and welfare which result from the

Table 1.7   **Effect of Voluntary Export Restraints**

	MFN Tariff		Tariff Rate Quota	Jointly Optimal	
	Actual CVs	Modified CVs		Actual CVs	Modified CVs
			No Labor Rent		
γ	−13.885	−27.770	−27.770	−13.885	−27.770
γ^*	−4.355	−8.710	−8.710	−4.355	−8.710
v	7,494	7,249	7,250	6,929	6,954
w	5,239	4,931	5,170	4,684	4,570
Subsidy	0	0	0	528	285
Tariff	100	100	318	−377	−229
Q_1	7,020,000	7,249,339	7,303,303	7,611,905	7,546,347
Q_2	2,112,000	2,304,043	2,111,708	2,449,221	2,568,974
Welfare[a]	640.406	641.189	641.117	640.6549	641.277
			Labor Rent = $1400		
γ	−13.885	−27.770	−27.770	−13.885	−27.770
γ^*	−4.355	−8.710	−8.710	−4.355	−8.710
v	7,494	7,249	7,250	5,552	5,570
w	5,239	4,931	5,170	4,691	4,576
Subsidy	0	0	0	1,814	1,622
Tariff	100	100	318	−370	−224
Q_1	7,020,000	7,249,339	7,303,303	10,034,817	9,962,263
Q_2	2,112,000	2,304,043	2,111,708	2,066,796	2,170,450
Welfare[a]	650.2346	651.338	651.342	652.872	653.398

[a]Welfare reported in billion dollars.

modified CVs for 1983 with those from the original CVs, both at the actual MFN tariff and at the jointly optimal policy. The first two columns compare the actual MFN tariff results with the results of the modified CFs. Without the VER, both domestic and foreign prices would be lower, and consumption of both countries' cars higher. Welfare rises by about $700 million or $1.1 billion, depending on whether labor rents exist. This experiment thus highlights the point that a tariff is (from the standpoint of efficiency) a far better instrument with which to protect domestic industries than a quantitative restraint. The third column shows the quota-equivalent tariff rate, that is, the tariff (to the nearest dollar) required to duplicate the original level of Japanese imports assuming the less collusive conjectures. Notice that for the same volume of imports, U.S. production is substantially larger with a tariff than with a VER.

The next two columns compare the jointly optimal subsidy and tariff outcomes with the results of modifying the CVs. The more competitive behavior on the part of firms lessens the size of the oligopoly distortions, so that both domestic and import subsidies decline. U.S. producers thus lose some market share to Japanese firms, but the increased consumer surplus results in a slight gain in welfare.

1.3.4   Sensitivity Analysis

We next consider how sensitive our results are to the calibration parameters we obtain from outside sources. In the interest of brevity, we present sensitivity results only for 1979; similar results obtain for the other years.

Table 1.8 shows the effect of changing U.S. and Japanese costs over the same range considered by Dixit. This affects firms' behavioral parameters γ and γ^* and the resulting optimal policies and welfare. Notice that the estimate of γ (γ^*) becomes more negative as costs in the United States (Japan) rise, since a smaller markup of price over marginal cost indicates more competitive behavior. Similarly, γ and γ^* rise to reflect more collusive behavior as costs decline, though both remain negative for the range of plausible costs.

As Japanese costs rise, the optimal subsidy falls slightly, while the optimal tariff rises markedly, though it remains negative. Similarly, as U.S. costs rise, the optimal subsidy falls, while the optimal tariff remains relatively constant. This further reinforces the targeting interpretation given before. As Japanese firms' costs rise, their implied behavior becomes more competitive, thereby reducing the desirability of subsidizing imports. Similarly, as U.S. costs rise, implied U.S. firm behavior becomes more competitive, reducing the size of the domestic distortion targeted by the subsidy.

Welfare at the optimum falls when U.S. costs rise, since the resource costs of production enter the welfare function directly. Welfare is relatively unaffected by Japanese costs, since these enter only via their impact on prices. Again, however, welfare falls, as higher costs mean higher prices.

Table 1.8   Cost Sensitivity: 1979 (labor rent = 0)

U.S. Cost		Japan Cost		
		3,000	3,400	3,600
5,000	γ	−5.027	−5.027	−5.027
	γ^*	−1.717	−5.272	−10.606
	Subsidy	842	822	812
	Tariff	−408	−244	−151
	Welfare[a]	567.280	567.189	567.162
5,400	γ	−9.570	−9.570	−9.570
	γ^*	−1.717	−5.272	−10.606
	Subsidy	553	528	516
	Tariff	−410	−245	−152
	Welfare[a]	563.376	563.279	563.250
5,600	γ	−15.724	−15.724	−15.724
	γ^*	−1.717	−5.272	−10.606
	Subsidy	389	361	348
	Tariff	−411	−246	−152
	Welfare[a]	561.552	561.451	561.422

[a]Welfare reported in billion dollars.

Table 1.9 shows the sensitivity of our results to the assumed values for the elasticity of demand for auto services, ε, and the elasticity of substitution between U.S. and Japanese autos, σ. While the choice of ε significantly alters the resulting optimal welfare level, the behavioral parameters and the optimal subsidy and tariff levels change only slightly for reasonable values of σ and ε. Furthermore, as ε rises, $\varepsilon^{ij}(x,x)$ and $\varepsilon^{ij}(y,y)$ become negative, which implies that autos are complements in demand. Our parametrization thus puts an upper bound of about 1.3 on the total elasticity of demand. As σ rises, U.S. and Japanese cars become more similar to consumers, so that firms' implied behavior becomes more collusive. The optimal subsidy rises along with the tariff, which becomes less negative.

Table 1.10 shows the sensitivity analysis of the elasticity of substitution among Japanese autos, σ_y. As σ_y increases, σ_x rises only slightly, and σ_y always remains larger. American cars are thus quite differentiated from one another,

Table 1.9   **Sensitivity to Elasticity of Demand and Elasticity of Substitution: 1979 (labor rent = 0)**

Elasticity of Demand (ε)		Elasticity of Substitution (σ)		
		1.5	2.0	3.0
1.05	β[a]	42.010	46.650	49.159
	γ	−9.670	−9.590	−9.471
	γ^*	−5.384	−5.274	−5.053
	Subsidy	519	531	541
	Tariff	−308	−247	−182
	Welfare[b]	1,121.482	1,121,480	1,121.484
	$\varepsilon^{ij}(x,x)$	0.024	0.044	0.050
	$\varepsilon^{ij}(y,y)$	0.384	0.274	0.053
1.1	β[a]	8.657	10.574	11.686
	γ	−9.651	−9.570	−9.452
	γ^*	−5.382	−5.272	−5.052
	Subsidy	517	528	538
	Tariff	−307	−245	−180
	Welfare[b]	563.281	563.279	563.282
	$\varepsilon^{ij}(x,x)$	0.004	0.025	0.031
	$\varepsilon^{ij}(y,y)$	0.382	0.272	0.052
1.3	β[a]	0.167	0.278	0.359
	γ	−9.572	−9.491	−9.372
	γ^*	−5.377	−5.267	−5.047
	Subsidy	507	518	529
	Tariff	−300	−239	−174
	Welfare[b]	191.184	191.182	191.186
	$\varepsilon^{ij}(x,x)$	−0.075	−0.054	−0.048
	$\varepsilon^{ij}(y,y)$	0.377	0.267	0.047

[a]β is reported in 10 billions.
[b]Welfare reported in billion dollars.

Table 1.10   **Sensitivity to Elasticity of Substitution among Japanese Automobiles (σ_y): 1979**

	σ_y				
	1.5	2.1	3.0	5.0	50.0
σ_x	1.154	1.216	1.255	1.287	1.323
β[a]	8.741	10.039	10.574	10.915	11.238
γ	-9.626	-9.591	-9.570	-9.552	-9.532
γ^*	-6.401	5.949	-5.272	-3.767	30.094
$\varepsilon^{ii}(x,x)$	1.174	1.209	1.231	1.248	1.268
$\varepsilon^{ij}(x,x)$	-0.020	0.007	0.025	0.039	0.055
$\varepsilon^{ii}(y,y)$	1.599	2.051	2.728	4.233	38.094
$\varepsilon^{ij}(y,y)$	-0.099	0.049	0.272	0.767	11.906
$\varepsilon^{ij}(x,y)$	0.025	0.025	0.025	0.025	0.025
$\varepsilon^{ij}(y,x)$	0.356	0.356	0.356	0.356	0.356

[a]β is reported in 10 billions.

as opposed to Japanese cars, which are far more substitutable in demand. As σ_y becomes large, Japanese cars become closer substitutes, and γ^* becomes very large, implying substantial collusion between Japanese firms. Without differentiation between Japanese cars, any markup of price above cost is evidence of monopoly power. A small σ_y, on the other hand, results in implausible negative values for $\varepsilon^{ij}(x,x)$ and $\varepsilon^{ij}(y,y)$. We thus find a lower bound on σ_y of about 2.0. Again, however, the choice of σ_y does not at all affect prices, which satisfy (3) and (4), or the resulting optimal policies and welfare. An econometrically derived estimate for σ_y would thus allow a more definitive determination of Japanese firms' behavior but would not otherwise affect our results.

These sensitivity analyses imply that the calibration results and the optimal policies are quite insensitive to changes in the parameter values, with the exception of costs. Marginal costs, however, are the least reliable of our data. To ensure that our crucial result of firm behavior more competitive than Bertrand is not merely an artifact of poor data, we calculate the costs which would be necessary for firms to act as if they were Bertrand and Cournot duopolists. These were presented at the bottom of table 1.3.

For U.S. firms, notice that even the higher Bertrand-equivalent costs are far smaller than our data for actual costs. Costs for Japanese firms, on the other hand, are much closer to the Bertrand costs. As with prices, the Bertrand and Cournot costs are fairly close together. While this further illustrates the more collusive behavior of Japanese firms, both U.S. and Japanese firms still appear to behave fairly competitively.

In general, the sensitivity analyses highlight our point that what is most important is not the parameter values, but rather the specification of the model itself.

1.4 Conclusion

Our results indicate that simple calibration models of trade in oligopolistic industries are quite sensitive to the model structure imposed. Though we have taken one step in elaborating Dixit's model, further extensions seem worthwhile.

As noted previously, further disaggregation such as between large cars and small cars would more accurately reflect industry conditions. Whether this would give strikingly different results, however, is uncertain. What is clear is that the resulting model would be extremely complex; our model is already highly nonlinear. Further differentiation would require a substantial amount of additional data, perhaps broken down even by each particular model. Much of this, such as market-share data, is publicly available; other data, particularly costs and elasticities of substitution, would no doubt prove more elusive. Feenstra and Levinsohn (1989) provide an excellent beginning.

Less difficult to implement would be the inclusion of quality effects, an extension on which we are currently at work. Indeed, many studies examine the effects of trade policy on quality upgrading; Feenstra (1988) focuses on the Japanese auto industry. In unpublished work, we show that Dixit's calibration procedure cancels out quality effects, so that quality upgrading plays no role in the determination of optimal policies in his model.[17] This clearly unsatisfactory result stems primarily from Dixit's linear demand structure and is, we hope, not a general feature of calibration models.

One result common to both our model and Dixit's is that the presence of labor rents substantially enlarges the potential benefits of optimal trade policies. This is particularly important since wages in import-competing industries such as steel and autos probably include a large rent component. Following Dixit, we include only the most rudimentary attempt at capturing the effects of these rents. Endogenizing the wage process through inclusion of a formal model of union-firm bargaining (cooperative or not) would no doubt provide great insight. Eaton (1988) provides several suggestions for fruitful research, and work on this is under way.

Our results similarly accord with Dixit's in that we find a surprising amount of "targeting" of instruments to particular distortions. Only limited theoretical work exists on targeting rules for oligopolistic industries analogous to targeting rules for distortions in competitive industries. Krishna and Thursby (1991) provide a beginning, but there remains more work to be done.

We make only a limited attempt to take into account the effects of preexisting quantitative restraints on firms' behavioral conjectures. A more satisfactory way to measure firm interactions is clearly necessary. Recent work on dynamic differential games, such as Driskill and McCafferty (1989), may prove useful here.

---

17. The proof, which will appear in future work, is available from the authors.

For the present, however, our results suggest that the policy recommendations of simple calibrated trade exercises should be interpreted with extreme caution. Moreover, as the gains from activist policy appear quite small, the case for activist policy is far from clear. However, such exercises provide valuable insights into the behavior of firms over time and the effects of policies on this behavior. They also provide good estimates of demand elasticities. But our understanding of calibrated trade models is far from perfect, and more work is clearly necessary. Until our ability to apply theory to actual industry conditions improves, it remains vital not to oversell such models to policymakers.

References

Anderson, S., A. De Palma, and J-F. Thisse. 1989. Demand for differentiated products, discrete choice models, and the characteristics approach. *Review of Economic Studies* 56:21–35.

Automotive News Market Data Book. 1977–87. Detroit: Automotive News.

Baldwin, R., and P. Krugman. 1988. Market access and international competition: A simulation study of 16K RAM's. In *Empirical methods for international trade,* ed. R. Feenstra. Cambridge: MIT Press.

De Melo, J., and D. Tarr. 1990. Welfare costs of U.S. quotas in textiles, steel, and autos. *Review of Economics and Statistics* 72(3): 489–97.

Dixit, A. 1988. Optimal trade and industrial policy for the U.S. automobile industry. In *Empirical methods for international trade,* ed. R. Feenstra. Cambridge: MIT Press.

Driskill, R., and S. McCafferty. 1989. Dynamic duopoly with output adjustment costs in international markets: Taking the conjecture out of conjectural variations. In *Trade policies for international competitiveness,* ed. R. Feenstra, 125–37. Chicago: University of Chicago Press.

Eaton, J. 1988. Comment on Dixit. In *Empirical methods for international trade,* ed. R. Feenstra. Cambridge: MIT Press.

Eaton, J., and G. Grossman. 1986. Optimal trade and industrial policy under oligopoly. *Quarterly Journal of Economics* 100:383–406.

Feenstra, R. 1988. Quality change under trade restraints in Japanese autos. *Quarterly Journal of Economics* 103:131–46.

Feenstra, R., and Levinsohn, J. 1989. Distance, demand, and oligopoly pricing. NBER Working Paper no. 3076. Cambridge, Mass.: National Bureau of Economic Research, August.

Halberstam, D. 1986. *The reckoning.* New York: Avon Books.

Helpman, E., and P. Krugman. 1989. *Market structure and trade policy.* Cambridge: MIT Press.

Katz, L., and L. Summers. 1989. Can inter-industry wage differentials justify strategic trade policy? In *Trade policies for international competitiveness,* ed. R. Feenstra, 85–116. Chicago: University of Chicago Press.

Krishna, K. 1989. Trade restrictions as facilitating practices. *Journal of International Economics* 26 (3/4): 251–70.

Krishna, K., K. Hogan, and P. Swagel. 1989. The Non-optimality of optimal trade policies: The U.S. automobile industry revisited, 1979–1985. NBER Working Paper no. 3118. Cambridge, Mass.: National Bureau of Economic Research, September.

Krishna, K., and M. Itoh. 1988. Content protection and oligopolistic interactions. *Review of Economic Studies* 55:107–25.

Krishna, K., and M. Thursby. 1991. Optimal policies with strategic distortions. *Journal of International Economics* 31 (3/4): 291–308.

Levinsohn, J. 1988. Empirics of taxes on differentiated products: The case of tariffs in the U.S. automobile industry. In *Trade policy issues and empirical analysis,* ed. R. E. Baldwin. Chicago: University of Chicago Press.

Richardson, J. David. 1989. Empirical research on trade liberalization with imperfect competition: A survey. *OECD Economic Studies* no. 12 (Spring): 7–50.

Srinivasan, T. N. 1989. Recent theories of imperfect competition and international trade: Any implications for development strategy? *Indian Economic Review* 24(1):1–23.

Venables, A., and A. Smith. 1986. Trade and industrial policy under imperfect competition. *Economic Policy* 1 (October):622–71.

Comment   Garth Saloner

Krishna, Hogan, and Swagel's (KHS) purpose is to demonstrate the sensitivity of calibration models of trade to the assumptions that are made about the nature of imperfect competition. They succeed in this goal and reach the appropriate conclusion that "until our ability to apply theory to actual industry conditions improves, it remains vital not to oversell such models to policymakers."

In order to interpret the results in this class of models, it is useful to lay out the essence of the basic approach. The basic structure of the conjectural variations models and the calibration procedure is transparent in the case of homogeneous-goods Cournot duopoly. In that case a typical firm, say firm 1, maximizes its profits given by

$$\pi_1 = P(q_1 + q_2)q_1 - C_1(q_1),$$

where q_i is the output of firm i, $P(\cdot)$ is the industry inverse demand curve, and $C_i(\cdot)$ is firm i's cost function. Maximizing π_1 with respect to q_1 yields:

(1) $$\frac{\partial \pi_1}{\pi q_1} = P + q_1\frac{\partial P}{\partial q_1} + q_1\frac{\partial P}{\partial q_2}\left(\frac{dq_2}{dq_1}\right) - C_1' = 0.$$

Calling the part of Equation (1) in braces γ (i.e., $dq_2/dq_1 \equiv \gamma$) and rearranging yields:

(2) $$\frac{P - C'}{P} = \frac{s_1(1 + \gamma)}{\varepsilon},$$

where $(P - C')/P$ is the price-cost margin (PCM), $\varepsilon \equiv -(\partial Q/\partial P)P/Q$ is the industry elasticity of demand, and s_1 is firm 1's market share.

Garth Saloner is professor of economics and management at the Massachusetts Institute of Technology and visiting associate professor of business administration at Harvard University.

The calibration models begin with equations like (2) and, by making assumptions about ε, s_i, and the PCM, calculate γ. The now discredited conjectural variations models (see Tirole [1988] for a discussion) interpret the term in parentheses in equation (1), and hence γ, as a behavioral change in firm 2's action in response to a change in firm 1's action. In a static game the notion of a behavioral response by one firm to another is meaningless and so a *fortiori* is the term dq_2/dq_1 in equation (1).

Taking equation (2) as the starting point, however, γ does have a meaningful interpretation. If the Cournot duopoly model applies, then the PCM is equal to the inverse of the elasticity, i.e., γ is equal to 0 in equation (2). (To see this, simply note that firm 1's first-order condition under Cournot is that given by equation (1) with the third, "nonsense", term omitted). If γ exceeds 0, then the appropriate interpretation is simply that the PCM is higher than would be expected from Cournot duopolists facing an elasticity of ε. Thus γ is a meaningful measure of the degree to which the firms are able to elevate the PCM above "the competitive level" defined in terms of the Cournot equilibrium.

But what is the appropriate inference to make if one finds, as indeed Dixit does, that γ is negative? Then the PCM is lower, and hence competition is fiercer, than in the Cournot model. Since models in which price is the strategic variable can yield much lower PCMs, a natural alternative is to consider a differentiated products model of that kind.

This is the approach that KHS adopt. In their formulation, the crucial equation which is the equivalent of equation (2) above is their equation (3) which can be abbreviated as

$$(3) \qquad \frac{P - C'}{P} = \frac{1}{\varepsilon^{ii} - \gamma},$$

where ε^{ii} represents firm i's own price elasticity.

The interpretation here is similar to that above. If the firms are competing as static price competition suggests they should, the PCM is again equal to the inverse of the elasticity so that $\gamma = 0$. If the firms are competing less aggressively than that, the PCM should exceed the inverse of the elasticity so that, in order for equation (3) to hold, γ must be positive.

An advantage of this formulation is that it accommodates very competitive outcomes, rather than bounding them from below by the Cournot outcome. If there is a great deal of competition the own-price elasticity will be high and the PCM's will be very low. For example, if the firms face constant marginal costs and compete in prices, the Bertrand result with price equal to marginal cost (and infinitely large own-price elasticity) obtains. Thus in this formulation it should be extremely surprising to encounter negative values of γ.

As KHS's table 1.3 shows, however, not only does γ turn out to be uniformly negative in their calibrations, but γ is less than -9 in five of the seven years, and in 1982 it is -26.91. Referring to equation (3), there are three possible explanations for such a finding: (a) the calibration is plausible and behavior "is more competitive than Bertrand," (b) ε has been mismeasured and is actually greater than the calibration suggests, or (c) the PCM has been mismeasured and is actually lower than the calibration suggests.

Taking (a) first, Might competition actually be more competitive than Bertrand? The "fundamental theorem of industrial organization" asserts that with a sufficiently rich assumption space, modern I.O. can explain any observation! A number of "solutions" readily suggest themselves: (i) the firms are involved in an implicitly collusive supergame and what is being measured is a punishment phase during which firms are using severe punishments of the kind advocated by Abreu (1986), (ii) as in Froot and Klemperer (1989) firms are "buying market share" which will earn them high profits in the future, (iii) the incumbent firms are deterring potential entrants by signaling low costs as in the Milgrom-Roberts (1982) limit-pricing model, (iv) some of the incumbents are attempting to drive out others through predatory pricing, or (v) firms are selling automobiles as a way of later selling automobile parts, and hence the "price" variable understates the value of a sale.

None of these explanations is particularly plausible. First, several of them are really explanations for short-term pricing behavior, whereas the authors find that γ is negative for seven years in a row. Second, KHS calculate the automobile price that would be predicted by their model if the firms were simply behaving as static price competition suggests they should and were not taking into account the kinds of considerations listed in the previous paragraph. The predicted price for a U.S. automobile is of the order of $25,000! If that is correct, the automobile manufacturers are paying a great deal in short-term forgone profits to deter entry, build market share, drive out or punish rivals, or sell auto parts!

This suggests that either ε or the PCM or both are mismeasured. The estimate of ε is around 1.25. Studies which examine the own-price elasticities of particular automobile models tend to find elasticities in the range 5–16 (see Adams and Brock 1982). One troubling feature of the way in which ε^{ii} is measured by KHS is the way in which it is derived from the degree of substitutability between goods of two producers of Japanese cars, σ_y, and the corresponding measure for substitutability between goods produced by U.S. producers, σ_x.

The procedure they use is as follows: Their equations (1) and (2) specify the demands for U.S. and Japanese cars, Q_1 and Q_2, respectively, as functions of inter alia σ_x and σ_y, i.e., $Q_1 = f(\sigma_x, \sigma_y, \ldots)$ and $Q_2 = f(\sigma_x, \sigma_y, \ldots)$. In the calibration σ_y is set by the authors and σ_x is then *derived* using the assumed functional form of the demand functions and the observed sales of U.S. and Japanese cars. This procedure places a large burden on the functional-form assumptions on demand to yield information on the value of underlying taste parameters. That is, the degree of substitutability between cars produced by two U.S. firms, a "marginal" concept, is inferred from the ratio of actual sales of U.S. and Japanese cars each year, an "average" measure.

Nonetheless, it is unlikely that mismeasurement in ε alone is enough to explain the observed γ's. In 1982 the PCM is about 1/33, so that for γ to be nonnegative, ε^{ii} would have to be 33, which seems implausibly large.

Thus the measured PCMs must probably share in the blame: they are too low to be consistent with "reasonable" elasticity estimates. One possible reason why the measured PCMs may be too low is the difficulty of measuring marginal costs correctly. For example, the PCMs compiled by the Census Bureau use a measure of "payroll and materials." Yet many of the payroll costs represent the fixed costs of the minimum number of workers required to operate the assembly line and the hoards of paper shufflers who contribute to a fixed overhead rather than to marginal costs.

In the end, however, for the conclusion that the authors reach, it doesn't matter whether it is ε or the PCM that is mismeasured. If, as seems likely, there is significant mismeasurement in one or the other or both, then as KHS conclude, it is premature to use models of this kind for policy analysis.

References

Abreu, D. 1986. Extremal equilibria of oligopoly supergames. *Journal of Economic Theory* 39:191–225.

Adams, W., and J. W. Brock. 1982. The automobile industry. In *The structure of American industry,* ed. W. Adams. New York: Macmillan.

Froot, K. A., and P. D. Klemperer. 1989. Exchange rate pass-through when market share matters. *American Economic Review* 79:637–54.

Milgrom, P., and D. J. Roberts. 1982. Limit pricing and entry under incomplete information: An equilibrium analysis. *Econometrica* 50:443–60.

Tirole, J. 1988. *The theory of industrial organization.* Cambridge: MIT Press.

2 Trade Policy under Imperfect Competition: A Numerical Assessment

Anthony J. Venables

2.1 Introduction

The literature on international trade under imperfect competition is now more than 10 years old. Many of the papers in this literature have been motivated by policy concerns, yet much uncertainty remains about the possible effects of employing trade policy in a particular industry. This is partly because we now know that it is possible to construct models in which policy conclusions are sensitive to aspects of market conduct about which little is known. It is partly because little work has been done that attempts to quantify the effects of policy on particular industries.

This paper takes a reasonably wide range of industries and a number of alternative theories of trade and systematically investigates the effects of trade policy on each industry under each theory. The policy instruments studied are those most widely discussed in the literature—an import tariff and an export subsidy. The equilibrium types covered include the cases of price and quantity competition, segmented and integrated markets, and oligopoly and monopolistic competition.

The effects of policy under these different possibilities are established by undertaking a rather large number of numerical simulations. Using the results of these simulations the paper addresses the following questions. First, are results sensitive to the equilibrium concept employed? Do we observe the magnitude, or even the sign, of the welfare effect of policy changing according to the theoretical model which has been chosen? Second, can we identify the

Anthony J. Venables is professor of international economics at the London School of Economics and a research fellow of the Centre for Economic Policy Research.

The author thanks Jim Markusen and other conference participants for useful comments. This research is supported by the Ford Foundation through the NBER/CEPR project on Empirical Studies in Strategic Trade Policy, and by UK ESRC grant no. R000231763.

WILLIAM WOODS UNIVERSITY LIBRARY

characteristics of industries in which policy is successful in achieving welfare gains? Third, how large are the gains from policy? Do the qualitative effects established in the theoretical literature lead to quantitative effects of a significant magnitude?

The first stage of this project involves specifying the theoretical models (sec. 2.2) and calibrating these models to each of the industries under study (sec. 2.3). For given parameters, each theory predicts different levels of output and volumes of trade. The calibration procedure turns this around; data are available on levels of output and trade and on some parameters of the industry. Different theories then imply different values of unobserved parameters in order to support observations on the industry as an equilibrium. Of course, if there were sufficient observations one might reject some theories in favor of others. Calibration does not attempt this, but merely solves for unobserved parameters. This procedure is described in section 2.3, which discusses the way in which different theories lead to different interpretations of an industry data set.

Having calibrated each industry under each of the different theories, the second part of the project is to investigate the effects of trade policy. Import tariffs and export subsidies are evaluated in sections 2.4 and 2.5, and section 2.6 presents some concluding comments.

2.2   The Models

We investigate four different equilibrium concepts, each applied within the framework of the same general model. This model has the same structure as that used in Smith and Venables (1988), and is briefly outlined here.

The model is one of partial equilibrium, operating at the level of a single industry. There are J producing and consuming countries. The ith of these countries has n_i firms, and all firms in country i are assumed to be symmetric and to produce m_i product types. These products are tradable, and x_{ij} denotes the quantity of a single product type produced by a firm in country i and sold in country j at price p_{ij}.

Demands in each country are derived from a Dixit and Stiglitz–type welfare function (1977). Consumers in country j may consume products which are produced in each country, so the number of product types available for consumption is $\sum_{i=1}^{J} n_i m_i$. Subutility derived from consumption of these products is denoted y_j and takes the form

(1)
$$y_j = \left(\sum_{i=1}^{J} n_i m_i a_{ij}^{1/\varepsilon} x_{ij}^{(\varepsilon-1)/\varepsilon} \right)^{\varepsilon/(\varepsilon-1)}, \quad \varepsilon > 1, \quad j = 1, \ldots, J,$$

where the a_{ij} are demand parameters describing the preferences of a consumer in country j for a product produced in country i. The variable y_j can be regarded as a quantity index of aggregate consumption of the industry output. Dual to the quantity index is a price index (or unit expenditure function), q_j, taking the form

$$(2) \qquad q_j = \left(\sum_{i=1}^{I} n_i m_i a_{ij} p_{ij}^{1-\varepsilon} \right)^{1/(1-\varepsilon)}, \quad j = 1, \ldots, J.$$

The p_{ij} are the prices of individual varieties, and q_j can be interpreted as the price of the aggregate, y_j. Income effects are ignored, so that demand for the aggregate product is a function only of the price index, q_j. This demand function is iso-elastic, taking the form

$$(3) \qquad y_j = b_j q_j^{-\eta}, \quad j = 1, \ldots, J,$$

where the b_j reflect the size of the respective country markets. Utility maximization implies that demand for individual product varieties depends both on the price of the individual variety and on the aggregate price index, and demand functions take the form

$$(4) \qquad x_{ij} = a_{ij}(p_{ij}/q_j)^{-\varepsilon} y_j = a_{ij} b_j p_{ij}^{-\varepsilon} q_j^{\varepsilon - \eta}, \quad i,j = 1, \ldots, J.$$

The profits of a single representative country-i firm are

$$(5) \qquad \pi_i = m_i \sum_{j=1}^{J} x_{ij} p_{ij} (1 - T_{ij}) - C_i(x_i, m_i), \quad i = 1, \ldots, J,$$

where the T_{ij} are the ad valorem costs of selling in market j (transport costs or trade taxes, for example). The function C_i is the firm's cost function, assumed to depend on the output per variety, $x_i = \sum_j x_{ij}$, and on the number of varieties, m_i. The form of this function is a weighted average of linear and loglinear functions in m_i and x_i, so it takes the form

$$(6) \qquad C_i(x_i, m_i) = c_i[z(c_0 + m_i c_m + m_i x_i) + (1 - z) m^\alpha x^\beta],$$

where z describes the linear/loglinear share, c_0, c_m, α, and β are parameters common to all countries, and c_i is a country-specific cost parameter.

We investigate four different types of competitive interaction between firms. The first is the case of segmented-market Cournot behavior and is denoted case C in the following discussion. Under this hypothesis firms choose the quantities they sell in each market, x_{ij}, given other firms' sales. The first-order condition for profit maximization takes the form

$$(7) \qquad p_{ij}(1 - T_{ij})\left(1 - \frac{1}{e_{ij}}\right) = \frac{1}{m_i}\left(\frac{\partial C_i}{\partial x_i}\right), \quad i,j = 1, \ldots, J,$$

where e_{ij} is the perceived elasticity of demand and is given by

$$(8) \qquad \frac{1}{e_{ij}} = \frac{1}{\varepsilon} + \left(\frac{1}{\eta} - \frac{1}{\varepsilon}\right) s_{ij}, \quad i,j = 1, \ldots, J,$$

where s_{ij} is the share of a single firm from country i in the country j market.

The second form of competition we investigate is Bertrand price competition, referred to as case B. Profit maximization given rivals' prices gives first-order condition (7) with e_{ij} taking the form

$$(9) \qquad e_{ij} = \varepsilon - (\varepsilon - \eta)s_{ij}, \quad i,j = 1, \ldots, J.$$

In the preceding two cases markets were segmented in the sense that firms played a separate game in each market, ignoring linkages between markets. We now turn to cases in which there is some degree of market integration, as some of firms' decisions are taken with respect to all markets. This is modeled by assuming that, instead of playing a single-stage game, firms play a two-stage game, choosing total output at the first stage and the distribution of output between markets at the second stage. Two different forms of the second-stage game will be investigated. In the first, referred to as case CB, we assume that, in the second stage, firms play a segmented-market price game. At the second stage of the game each firm therefore chooses its sales in each market, x_{ij}, to maximize profits, taking as constant its total sales $x_i = \sum_j x_{ij}$ and the prices of other firms. This gives first-order conditions:

$$(10) \qquad p_{ij}(1-T_{ij})\left(1 - \frac{1}{e_{ij}}\right) = p_{ik}(1 - T_{ik})\left(1 - \frac{1}{e_{ik}}\right), \quad i,j,k = 1, \ldots, J,$$

where $e_{ij} = \varepsilon - (\varepsilon-\eta)s_{ij}$. At the first stage each firm chooses total output x_i given the total output of other firms' and fully incorporating the reallocations of sales between markets implied by the second-stage equilibrium, equation (10), so establishing a perfect Nash equilibrium of the two-stage game. (For theoretical analysis of this case see Venables [1990]).

The case of full market integration will be referred to as case CI. If the second-stage game has fully integrated markets then, for a given total x_i, at the second stage sales x_{ij} are determined by arbitrage, so as to equate the producer price of a particular product in each market. Second-stage equilibrium therefore has $x_i = \sum_j x_{ij}$ and prices satisfying

$$(11) \qquad p_{ij}(1 - T_{ij}) = p_{ik}(1 - T_{ik}), \quad i,j,k = 1, \ldots, J.$$

At the first stage, each firm chooses total output x_i given other firms' total output and fully incorporating the reallocations of sales between markets implied by the second-stage equilibrium, equation (11). The perfect equilibrium of this game corresponds to the integrated market equilibrium analyzed by, for example, Markusen (1981).

We assume throughout this paper that the number of varieties produced per firm, m_i, is a constant. The number is set so that output per model, x_i, is the same for all i. In some of the simulations reported below the number of firms in each country will be held constant, and in others the number will be allowed to adjust in response to profit changes, so giving a monopolistically competitive equilibrium.

2.3 Calibration

The theoretical models outlined above are applied to a world of six countries—France, the Federal Republic of Germany, Italy, the United Kingdom, the rest of the European Community and the rest of the world. Our treatment of the rest of the world is somewhat crude, and in the two-stage games described above, the rest of the world is treated as being segmented from the European economies.

The industries to which the models are applied are listed in table 2.1 and use the same data as Smith and Venables (1988). Production and trade flows for each industry were derived from the Eurostat Annual Industrial Survey and from Eurostat NACE-CLIO trade tables for 1982. Numbers of firms in each industry were derived from Eurostat Structure and Activity of Production data on the size distribution of firms. These numbers were adjusted to capture the number of "subindustries" operating within the broadly defined industry, and then a Herfindahl index of concentration was computed for each country and for each industry. The cross-country average values of these indexes are reported in table 2.1 and provide a summary measure of the degree of concentration of each industry. This ranges from its highest values in motor vehicles (350) and office machinery (330) to lows in machine tools (322) and footwear (451).

The second column of table 2.1 gives the price elasticity of demand for the aggregate output of each industry, η. Sources used to obtain these estimates were Piggot and Whalley (1985), Deaton (1975), Houthakker (1965), and Houthakker and Taylor (1970). The third and fourth columns of table 2.1 give some characteristics of the technology of the industry. These are drawn from

Table 2.1   **Industry Characteristics**

NACE Number: Name	Herfindahl Index	η	Returns to Scale (%)	Loglinear Share	U.K. Exports/ production (%)
257: Pharmaceutical products	0.05	0.8	22	0	32
260: Artificial and synthetic fibers	0.05	0.5	10	0.5	20
322: Machine tools	0.004	1.1	7	0.2	55
330: Office machinery	0.12	0.9	10	0.2	52
342: Electric motors, generators, etc.	0.022	1.1	15	0.5	46
346: Domestic electrical appliances	0.11	1.7	10	0.5	15
350: Motor vehicles	0.19	1.6	16	0.5	36
438: Carpets, linoleum, etc.	0.031	0.9	6	0.5	20
451: Footwear	0.009	0.7	2	0.5	15

the study of Pratten (1987). The returns to scale column gives the estimated increase in average costs associated with reducing per firm output from minimum efficient scale to half minimum efficient scale. This is largest in pharmaceuticals (257), motor vehicles (350), and electric motors and generators (342) and least in footwear (451), carpets (438), and machine tools (322). The loglinear share column reflects the z parameter of equation (6) and gives the proportion of marginal cost at minimum efficient scale (MES) coming from the two components of the cost curve. Choice of these numbers was judgmental and informed by Pratten's work. If this weight is zero, then marginal costs are constant, but average cost is falling; this is appropriate if returns to scale are due to fixed costs, for example, research and development. A positive loglinear share means that both average and marginal costs are declining and so, for example, captures industries where learning occurs. The final column in table 2.1 gives the ratio of U.K. exports of each industry's output to U.K. production, a ratio which is an important determinant of the welfare effect of some of the policy experiments undertaken.

The calibration procedure involves solving unknown parameters of the model so that the observed values of endogenous variables constitute an equilibrium of the model. There are a number of aspects to this, two of which are of economic interest: solving for the degree of product differentiation, ε, and for the implicit barriers to trade.

We assume that the base data set represents a long-run equilibrium in which profits are zero. Technology and firm scale imply a relationship between average cost and marginal cost, and, with the assumption of long-run equilibrium, this also gives a relationship between price and marginal cost. This price–marginal cost margin is supported at equilibrium by two considerations: product differentiation and market power stemming from the degree of concentration in the industry and the form of interaction between firms. If the degree of product differentiation is known, then this relationship can be solved for the form of the competitive interaction between firms. This is the approach of Dixit (1988) and Baldwin and Krugman (1988), who use this relationship to solve for a conjectural variations parameter. However, for the industries under study here, products are certainly differentiated, but we have little information about the elasticity of substitution between different products. The approach we follow is therefore to assume a form of competition between firms and see what this implies for the degree of product differentiation consistent with observed price-cost margins. Of course, we do not know that the assumed form of competition is correct. This is therefore an essential dimension in which to conduct sensitivity analysis, so we undertake the calibration procedure for a variety of different forms of competition. Table 2.2 reports the results of doing so for the four different types of equilibria described in section 2.2 above. The ε reported in the table are to be interpreted as the elasticities of demand for individual products, holding constant the prices of all other varieties.

Table 2.2   **Calibrated Elasticities (ε)**

NACE Number	C	CB	CI	B
257	5.77	5.36	5.16	4.72
260	21.11	12.72	12.29	8.70
322	13.55	13.44	13.41	13.25
330	35.21	15.52	14.48	10.9
342	7.36	7.17	7.06	6.77
346	10.76	9.60	8.79	7.75
350	13.38	10.44	8.86	7.20
438	21.39	18.68	18.49	17.59
451	53.32	46.17	46.02	42.57

We learn a number of things from table 2.2. First, looking across equilibrium concepts we see a ranking of ε (which holds for all industries) in the order C, CB, CI, B. The relationship between cases C and B is as would be expected; as quantity competition (C) is inherently less competitive than price competition (B), so less product differentiation (higher ε) is required to support a given price-cost margin as an equilibrium. The two two-stage games (CB and CI) are intermediate. Market power is lost as firms are no longer able to fully segment markets, but, at the aggregate level, both these cases assume quantity competition, so are less competitive than the Bertrand equilibrium. The difference between cases C and CI alerts us to the importance of the degree of country disaggregation. If markets are truly segmented, then we cannot aggregate them into country blocs; to do so would be to implicitly assume intrabloc integration, and thereby overstate the level of competition.

Looking across industries in table 2.2 we see a wide range in the extent of product differentiation. Firms derive relatively little market power from product differentiation in 451 (footwear), 438 (carpets), 330 (office machinery), and 322 (machine tools). The market power derived from product differentiation is greatest in 257 (pharmaceuticals), 342 (electric motors, etc.), 346 (household appliances), and 350 (motor vehicles). The variation in ε across the equilibria is largest for 260 (artificial fibers), 330 (office machinery), and 350 (motor vehicles). These are all industries with a relatively high level of concentration as measured by the Herfindahl index; this influences ε because the difference between Cournot and Bertrand competition is an increasing function of firms' market shares.

Inspection of the data on trade and production indicates that firms have very much larger shares of their domestic markets than they do of foreign markets, which suggests the presence of barriers to trade. For given trade barriers, each of the theories described in section 2.2 implies different equilibrium volumes of intraindustry trade. The analog of this in calibration is that we solve for a matrix of trade barriers consistent with observed trade flows between countries and with the observed market shares of firms in different countries. These calibrated matrices of trade barriers will be different for each theory. Table 2.3 presents the average height of these trade barriers for intra-EC trade for each industry and each equilibrium type. The calibration reported in table 2.3 took place using the same elasticity ε for each of the cases C, CB, CI, and C (with ε set at its Cournot level, ε^C). The numbers are expressed in "tariff-equivalent" form, as a proportion of price. We see that these implicit barriers are very high in some industries, notably 257 (pharmaceuticals) and 342 (electric motors, generators, etc.). The implicit barriers are greatest in case C, followed by CB, followed by CI. This reflects the implications of each of these equilibrium concepts for trade volumes (for analysis of these volumes see Venables [1990]). Case CB gives the same trade barriers as case B because international price relativities are the same in these cases, (see eqq. [7], [9], and [10]).

The tariff-equivalent trade barriers reported in table 2.3 were derived using the same value of ε for all equilibria, in order to illustrate the way in which different equilibria support different trade volumes. Computing the trade barriers simultaneously with the elasticities reported in table 2.2 gives the numbers contained in table 2.4. Trade barriers in cases CB, CI, and B are higher in this case than in table 2.3 because, although theories CB, CI, and B predict lower trade volumes than case C (given parameter values), the lower values of ε asso-

Table 2.3   **Tariff Equivalent Trade Barriers ($\varepsilon = \varepsilon^c$)**

NACE Number	C	CB	CI	B
257	0.556	0.526	0.521	0.526
260	0.178	0.089	0.087	0.089
322	0.176	0.173	0.173	0.173
330	0.152	0.063	0.060	0.063
342	0.439	0.426	0.423	0.426
346	0.310	0.270	0.261	0.270
350	0.289	0.198	0.181	0.198
438	0.138	0.125	0.124	0.125
451	0.065	0.057	0.057	0.057

Table 2.4   **Tariff Equivalent Trade Barriers**

NACE Number	C	CB	CI	B
257	0.556	0.557	0.568	0.614
260	0.178	0.147	0.148	0.213
322	0.176	0.175	0.175	0.177
330	0.152	0.142	0.146	0.201
342	0.439	0.435	0.439	0.457
346	0.310	0.300	0.315	0.364
350	0.289	0.250	0.269	0.352
438	0.138	0.142	0.143	0.151
451	0.065	0.066	0.066	0.071

ciated with these equilibria mean that higher tariff equivalents are consistent with observed trade levels.

Tariff-equivalent trade barriers are a way of displaying the size of implicit trade barriers consistent with equilibrium. Calibration incorporates each industry's matrix of tariff-equivalent trade barriers into the model in the following way. Off-diagonal elements of T_{ij} are set at 10 percent to capture the real costs of trade, and any further implicit trade barrier is attributed to demand differences, as measured by the demand parameters, a_{ij}. This approach means that trade barriers are viewed as real costs.

2.4   Import Tariffs

In this section we study the effects of tariffs imposed by a single country on its imports from all sources. We take the United Kingdom as the country imposing the tariff. This is of course a hypothetical experiment, the United Kingdom having treaty obligations prohibiting it from following such a policy. The role of the experiment is to demonstrate the possible effects of a unilateral tariff and to compare these effects both across equilibrium concepts and across industries. We shall initially study oligopoly, holding the number of firms in each industry and country constant, and then move on to cases in which entry and exit occur.

In order to focus on cross-equilibrium differences, we first consider a single industry and, for these purposes, take NACE 346, electrical domestic appliances, an industry with moderate returns to scale and a moderate level of concentration. Figure 2.1 gives the U.K. welfare gains (i.e., the sum of the change

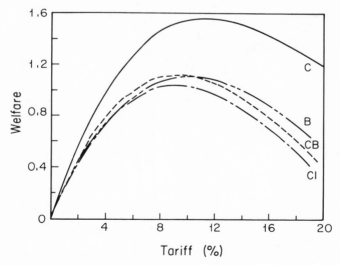

Fig. 2.1   Import tariff and welfare

in consumer surplus, profits, and government revenue expressed as a percentage of U.K. base consumption of the product) as a function of the tariff rate for each of the four different equilibria. Positive tariffs raise welfare in all cases, but the main thing to note from this figure is that case C—Cournot equilibrium in segmented markets—gives welfare gains which are very much higher than the other cases. Following case C, the gains are next highest for the other segmented-market case, B, followed by the two integrated-market cases, CB and CI. The optimal tariff rate is greatest in case C, although optimal tariff rates vary little between the four cases. The absolute size of the welfare gain, relative to the size of the industry, is rather small. For example, at a 10 percent tariff rate, case C yields welfare gains amounting to 1.54 percent of U.K. base consumption, and in case CI gains are 1.03 percent.

The change in the components of welfare are significantly larger than the change in overall welfare, and these are illustrated in figures 2.2–2.4. For example, in case C, consumer surplus at a 10 percent tariff is reduced by an amount equal to some 4 percent of U.K. base consumption, and profits increased by an amount equal to 3 percent of the value of U.K. base production. The most noteworthy feature of figures 2.2 and 2.3 is that the impact of the tariff on consumers and producers is smallest in case B, segmented-market price competition. Equations (7) and (9) illustrate that changes in market share have relatively little effect on price—marginal cost margins in this case; we therefore see that the profit gains of domestic firms following the tariff are approximately half the size they are under case C. The reduction in consumer surplus is correspondingly small, although tariff revenue is relatively large; the

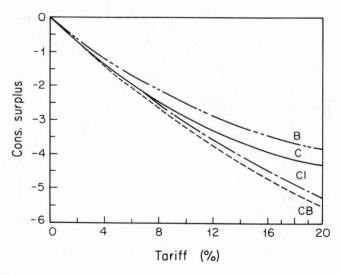

Fig. 2.2   Import tariff and consumer surplus

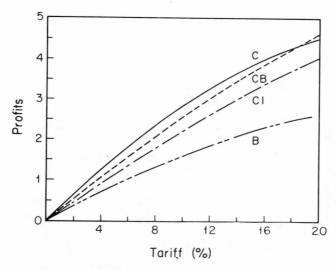

Fig. 2.3   Import tariff and profits

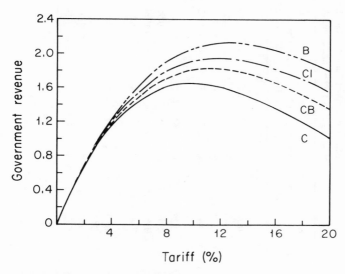

Fig. 2.4   Import tariff and government revenue

lower value of ε calibrated in case B means that imports decline relatively slowly as a function of the tariff.

The conclusions derived from NACE 346 are supported by study of the other eight industries. For 346 the welfare gain from a relatively high tariff is largest in case C, followed by B, CB, then CI. This ranking is broadly con-

Table 2.5 Welfare Effects of Import Tariffs under Oligopoly (welfare gain as a percentage of base consumption, by NACE class and equilibrium type)

Equilibrium Type	Tariff Rate			
	5%	10%	15%	20%
			257	
C	0.59	0.96	1.15	1.20
CB	0.46	0.71	0.79	0.73
CI	0.44	0.67	0.74	0.67
B	0.44	0.70	0.80	0.77
			260	
C	2.23	3.93	5.07	5.64
CB	1.58	2.27	2.31	1.98
CI	1.53	2.15	2.15	1.80
B	1.15	1.55	1.44	1.07
			322	
C	0.67	0.44	−0.20	−0.81
CB	0.65	0.40	−0.25	−0.88
CI	0.65	0.40	−0.26	−0.89
B	0.64	0.40	−0.27	−0.90

Equilibrium Type	Tariff Rate			
	5%	10%	15%	20%
			330	
C	1.52	2.09	1.97	1.81
CB	0.88	0.81	0.10	−0.70
CI	0.84	0.76	0.02	−0.85
B	0.70	0.62	−0.15	−1.22
			342	
C	0.76	1.04	0.96	0.65
CB	0.72	0.96	0.84	0.51
CI	0.71	0.94	0.83	0.49
B	0.71	0.96	0.85	0.52
			346	
C	1.15	1.54	1.46	1.18
CB	0.92	1.11	0.86	0.41
CI	0.85	1.03	0.77	0.31
B	0.86	1.11	0.94	0.55

Equilibrium Type	Tariff Rate			
	5%	10%	15%	20%
			350	
C	1.44	2.13	2.24	1.99
CB	0.99	1.19	0.78	−0.03
CI	0.92	1.11	0.75	0.03
B	0.90	1.22	1.09	0.64
			438	
C	0.74	0.64	0.48	0.39
CB	0.60	0.43	0.21	0.07
CI	0.59	0.42	0.19	0.05
B	0.55	0.37	0.12	−0.03
			451	
C	0.60	0.48	0.47	0.47
CB	0.22	0.03	0.00	0.00
CI	0.21	0.02	−0.01	−0.01
B	0.12	−0.10	−0.14	−0.15

firmed across the other eight industries. Table 2.5 reports the U.K. welfare gain (as a percentage of base U.K. consumption) for tariff rates of 5, 10, 15, and 20 percent, for each industry. For every industry, case C gives significantly larger welfare effects than the other cases, and the gains in CB exceed those in CI. The results from these industries (obtained, of course, with the functional forms of this model) therefore confirm the Markusen and Venables (1988) findings that, with Cournot behavior, tariff policy is more powerful when markets are segmented than when they are integrated. However, the relative ranking of CB and CI against B varies across industries. Segmented-market Bertrand behavior may produce even smaller welfare gains from tariff policy than arise under integrated markets.

Looking across industries we see that the four industries with the largest gains from tariffs are 260 (artificial fibers), 330 (office machinery), 346 (domestic appliances), and 350 (motor vehicles). These are the four industries with the highest levels of concentration as measured by the Herfindahl index (see table 2.1), although they are not the industries with the highest returns to scale. Even in these industries the gains from the tariff are rather modest reaching, in case C, gains of around 1.5–2.5 percent of base consumption. The exception to this is artificial and synthetic fibers (NACE 260), in which gains from the tariff exceed 5 percent of base U.K. consumption. The main reason for this industry to be exceptional seems to be its low aggregate demand elasticity, η, which is equal to 0.5. This means that the deadweight loss associated with the tariff is small.

So far we have assumed that the number of firms in the industry is held constant. How do things change when entry and exit occur to restore profits to their pretariff levels? Table 2.6 gives for this case information analogous to that in table 2.5. Several noteworthy features are apparent. First, comparing the effects of policy across equilibria C, CB, CI, B, we see that the gains from the tariff are now greatest in case B—reversing the position when the number of firms are constant. The reason for this follows from the observation made above about the effect of tariffs on profits. Under price competition (B) tariffs raise profits relatively little (see fig. 2.3); correspondingly, there is a relatively small increase in the number of firms operating in the United Kingdom, leaving firms operating at a relatively larger scale. Under price competition (B) tariffs therefore give rise to more significant achievement of economies of scale than is the case with Cournot behavior (C).

Free entry also reverses the ranking of cases CB and CI, with the welfare gain in case CI now always exceeding that in case CB. Furthermore, for most (although not all) of the experiments reported in table 2.6, case CI yields larger gains than case C, i.e., policy is more powerful when markets are integrated than when they are segmented. This reverses the relative magnitudes of the effects of tariffs under oligopoly, where we saw that with Cournot behavior policy was more powerful when markets were segmented. This also alerts us to the possible sensitivity of results with respect to functional form. We know

Table 2.6 Welfare Effects of Import Tariffs under Free Entry (welfare gain as a percentage of base consumption, by NACE class and equilibrium type)

Equilibrium Type	Tariff Rate			
	5%	10%	15%	20%
257				
C	0.60	0.40	0.99	0.96
CB	0.57	0.86	0.94	0.89
CI	0.59	0.90	1.01	0.98
B	0.65	1.03	1.22	1.26
260				
C	0.93	0.70	0.45	0.33
CB	1.02	0.84	0.36	−0.08
CI	1.04	0.89	0.43	−0.01
B	1.45	1.79	1.66	1.36
322				
C	1.27	1.17	0.77	0.43
CB	1.28	1.18	0.79	0.45
CI	1.28	1.19	0.79	0.45
B	1.29	1.21	0.82	0.47

Equilibrium Type	Tariff Rate			
	5%	10%	15%	20%
330				
C	0.73	0.33	0.21	0.19
CB	1.53	1.33	0.90	0.59
CI	1.62	1.48	1.05	0.71
B	2.01	2.21	1.85	1.40
342				
C	1.13	1.53	1.50	1.26
CB	1.14	1.55	1.53	1.30
CI	1.15	1.57	1.57	1.34
B	1.17	1.64	1.67	1.47
346				
C	1.15	1.29	1.05	0.73
CB	1.11	1.23	0.95	0.57
CI	1.18	1.40	1.19	0.84
B	1.34	1.76	1.71	1.44

Equilibrium Type	Tariff Rate			
	5%	10%	15%	20%
350				
C	1.31	1.33	0.97	0.64
CB	1.24	1.25	0.82	0.34
CI	1.38	1.60	1.31	0.86
B	1.69	2.31	2.33	2.05
438				
C	0.51	0.31	0.14	0.06
CB	0.58	0.39	0.18	0.06
CI	0.59	0.40	0.19	0.07
B	0.63	0.47	0.26	0.13
451				
C	0.12	0.02	0.01	0.01
CB	0.16	0.01	−0.01	−0.01
CI	0.16	0.01	−0.01	−0.01
B	0.21	0.05	0.02	0.02

from the work of Horstman and Markusen (1986) that if demands are linear and product differentiation is country (rather than firm) specific, then, with Cournot behavior and free entry, tariff policy raises welfare when markets are segmented, but has no effect on welfare when markets are integrated.

The absolute magnitude of the welfare effects are, in this case as under oligopoly, rather small, never exceeding 2.5 percent of base consumption. It is worth noting however that, whereas under oligopoly there were large redistributions from consumers to profits and to government, in this case profits are unchanged (by the free-entry assumption), there is in most cases a small increase in consumer surplus (for reasons analyzed in Venables [1985]), and most of the welfare gains accrue in the form of government revenue. Looking across industries, we see that, as was the case under oligopoly, the largest gains from policy come in the most highly concentrated industries, namely 260 (artifical fibers), 330 (office machinery), 346 (domestic appliances), and 350 (motor vehicles).

2.5 Export Taxes

The second policy experiment we consider is an export tax or subsidy. It is on this topic that the theoretical literature has most clearly highlighted the possible sensitivity of results to the equilibrium concept. We consider first the case of oligopoly and then turn to the effect of export subsidies under free entry.

In order to illustrate the difference between equilibrium concepts , we concentrate first on a single industry—once again taking NACE 346 (domestic electrical appliances) as our example. Figure 2.5 illustrates the effect of an export tax/subsidy on this industry. The figure plots U.K. welfare gain as a function of the export tax, and from the figure we see positive gains from an export subsidy under all four equilibrium concepts. The optimal subsidy is in the range 4–5 percent in all cases, but the optimal policy yields only small gains—somewhat less than 0.1 percent of consumption in case B and only 0.25 percent of base consumption in the most powerful case, CB.

In interpreting these results it is important to note that the gains from the export subsidy consist of an increase in profits, a loss of government revenue, the sum of these being a net loss, plus a consumer surplus gain. Export policy is transmitted back to domestic consumers through two possible routes. The first is that in this industry marginal costs are a decreasing function of output; export-subsidy-induced expansion therefore reduces the price charged to domestic consumers. It is this effect which means that there are welfare gains even when markets are segmented and there is price competition (case B). However, the gains are smallest in this case, as would be expected from the work of Eaton and Grossman (1986).

The second route by which export policy is transmitted to domestic consumers is through integration of markets. In cases CB and CI there is some market

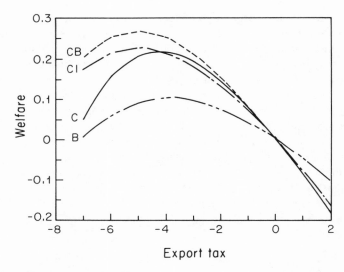

Fig. 2.5   Export tax and welfare

integration (i.e., firms do not take decisions on a segmented market basis). This means that subsidization in one market will reduce prices in others; export subsidies therefore give domestic consumer surplus gains, and it is this that accounts for the fact that welfare gains are relatively large in cases CI and CB. This is seen most clearly for NACE 257 (pharmaceutical products). This is the only industry in the sample in which, we assume, there are constant marginal costs (loglinear cost share = 0; table 2.1). At a 2 percent export subsidy, the sum of profits and government revenue is negative for all four cases. In the segmented-market equilibria, cases B and C, domestic consumer surplus is unchanged by export policy. However, in cases CB and CI export subsidies raise domestic consumer surplus, giving the net welfare gains reported in table 2.7.

Table 2.7 summarizes the position in all the industries, reporting the U.K. welfare gain from export subsidies set at 4 percent and 2 percent, and from a 2 percent export tax (with changes measured from a base position of zero export tax). The most frequent ranking of welfare gain by equilibrium type is that the gains are largest (or losses smallest) in case C, followed by cases CB, CI, and B. In all cases the gains from an export subsidy are small, only reaching as much as 1 percent of base consumption in one case (260). Although a 2 percent export tax reduces welfare in all cases, the range of values of the export tax/subsidy which produces an improvement over free trade seems extremely small—in six of the nine industries there are losses from export taxes set as high as +2 percent or as low as −4 percent, under all types of equilibria. In only three industries (260, artificial fibers, 346, domestic electrical appliances, and 350, motor vehicles) are there gains, under all types of equilibria, from

Table 2.7   Welfare Effects of Export Tariffs under Oligopoly (welfare gain as a percentage of base consumption, by NACE class and equilibrium type)

Equilibrium Type	Export Tax Rate			Equilibrium Type	Export Tax Rate			Equilibrium Type	Export Tax Rate		
	−4%	−2%	2%		−4%	−2%	2%		−4%	−2%	2%
	257				*330*				*350*		
C	−0.23	−0.06	−0.03	C	−1.09	0.23	−0.96	C	0.92	0.66	−0.77
CB	−0.01	0.04	−0.13	CB	−0.49	0.03	−0.36	CB	0.87	0.54	−0.63
CI	−0.02	0.04	−0.11	CI	−0.46	0.02	−0.33	CI	0.63	0.40	−0.50
B	−0.24	−0.08	0.00	B	−0.63	−0.10	−0.17	B	0.15	0.16	−0.27
	260				*342*				*438*		
C	1.01	0.55	−0.48	C	−0.38	−0.05	−0.17	C	−0.65	0.04	−0.21
CB	0.46	0.26	−0.29	CB	−0.34	−0.03	−0.18	CB	−0.40	0.03	−0.18
CI	0.42	0.25	−0.27	CI	−0.34	−0.03	−0.17	CI	−0.39	0.03	−0.18
B	0.06	0.07	−0.12	B	−0.36	−0.05	−0.15	B	−0.41	0.00	−0.16
	322				*346*				*451*		
C	−1.34	−0.25	−0.24	C	0.22	0.14	−0.18	C	−3.49	−0.19	−0.14
CB	−1.31	−0.25	−0.23	CB	0.25	0.15	−0.18	CB	−2.39	−0.16	−0.13
CI	−1.31	−0.25	−0.23	CI	0.21	0.13	−0.16	CI	−2.38	−0.16	−0.13
B	−1.31	−0.25	−0.23	B	0.10	0.08	−0.11	B	−2.44	−0.17	−0.21

export subsidies set at both 2 percent and 4 percent. These industries share the common characteristics of high concentration and a relatively low volume of exports (see table 2.1). The low volume of exports means that the revenue cost of export subsidies is relatively small. The effect of export subsidies at the margin is therefore obtained without the revenue cost of large subsidies being paid on existing, intramarginal export quantities.

The effects of export subsidies under free entry are summarized in table 2.8. The same three industries (250, 346, and 350) have unambiguous gains from 2 percent and 4 percent export subsidies, as was the case under oligopoly. The magnitude of the gains remains extremely modest, generally not exceeding 1 percent of base consumption. Notice that in some, although not all industries, the ordering of equilibria by welfare gain is changed; for example, in industry 350, free entry reverses the ordering of equilibria as compared to oligopoly giving the largest welfare gain in case B, followed by CI, CB, and C. The reason for this is as it was for tariffs; the policy has a relatively smaller profit effect in equilibrium B than in C, so fewer firms enter the industry, giving an equilibrium with fewer firms and lower average costs. The most striking feature of table 2.8 is the extremely large welfare losses imposed by export subsidies in some cases—322 (machine tools), 330 (office machinery), and 451 (footwear). In these industries the U.K. export subsidy is sufficient to drive the number of firms in some other countries to zero. There are then very large increases in U.K. exports, and the revenue cost of the subsidy becomes extremely large, this accounting for the size of the welfare loss.

2.6   Constant Parameters

Each experiment so far has been based on the following method. Assume a type of equilibrium, calibrate this equilibrium of the model to the data, and then simulate policy changes. As we saw in section 2.3, this implies different values for some parameters of the model (ε and a_{ij}) in each of the cases C, B, CB, and CI. Comparison of the effects of policy changes for different cases therefore incorporates different equilibrium types *and* different parameter values—these being chosen to support the same base equilibrium. An alternative procedure (and the standard one in theoretical work) would be to compare the effects of policy for different equilibrium types given the same parameter values in all cases—although this implies different values of endogenous variables in the initial equilibrium. What difference does it make if we follow this route?

We can address this question in the following way. First, calibrate an industry to a particular equilibrium type. Second, given the calibrated parameters compute the equilibrium of the model under an alternative equilibrium concept, so generating a new "base" equilibrium. Third, introduce policy changes, and simulate the way in which the equilibrium moves from this new base.

Table 2.9 reports the results of following this procedure for one industry

Table 2.8 Welfare Effects of Export Taxes under Free Entry (welfare gain as a percentage of base consumption, by NACE class and equilibrium type)

Equilibrium Type	Export Tax Rate			Equilibrium Type	Export Tax Rate			Equilibrium Type	Export Tax Rate		
	-4%	-2%	2%		-4%	-2%	2%		-4%	-2%	2%
	257				*330*				*350*		
C	-0.23	-0.03	-0.10	C	-19.10	-4.42	-1.72	C	0.44	0.80	-1.04
CB	0.20	0.18	-0.26	CB	-7.33	-0.50	-2.11	CB	0.88	0.84	-1.02
CI	0.29	0.22	-0.33	CI	-12.30	-0.19	-2.17	CI	1.07	0.82	-0.96
B	0.28	0.21	-0.31	B	-7.26	0.93	-2.23	B	1.13	0.73	-0.86
	260				*342*				*438*		
C	0.52	0.51	-0.50	C	-0.01	0.45	-0.82	C	-1.03	0.01	-0.22
CB	0.33	0.28	-0.32	CB	0.17	0.54	-0.92	CB	-0.64	0.07	-0.23
CI	0.32	0.27	-0.31	CI	0.25	0.58	-0.94	CI	-0.61	0.07	-0.24
B	0.34	0.22	-0.27	B	0.39	0.62	-0.97	B	-0.49	0.09	-0.24
	322				*346*				*451*		
C	-12.56	-0.20	-1.76	C	0.30	0.20	-0.23	C	-10.32	-0.43	-0.16
CB	-12.77	-0.19	-1.82	CB	0.42	0.24	-0.29	CB	-9.01	-0.32	-0.18
CI	-12.77	-0.18	-1.82	CI	0.46	0.25	-0.27	CI	-8.98	-0.31	-0.18
B	-12.42	-0.14	-1.83	B	0.45	0.25	-0.26	B	-7.35	-0.21	-0.19

Table 2.9   **Trade Policy Comparisons with Parameters Constant across Equilibria (welfare gain as a percentage of base consumption for NACE 346)**

Equilibrium Type	Calibration on Equilibrium Type C		Calibration on Respective Equilibrium Type[a]		Welfare Change due to Change in Equilibrium Type
	(1)	(2)	(3)	(4)	(5)
	Tariff Rate				
	5%	15%	5%	15%	
C	1.15	1.46	1.15	1.46	0
CB	0.77	0.64	0.92	0.86	0.79
CI	0.69	0.50	0.85	0.77	0.91
B	0.82	0.72	0.86	0.94	0.85
	Export Tax Rate				
	−4%	−2%	−4%	−2%	
C	0.22	0.14	0.22	0.14	
CB	0.24	0.15	0.25	0.15	
CI	0.20	0.13	0.21	0.13	
B	0.08	0.07	0.10	0.08	

[a]From tables 2.5 and 2.7.

(once again NACE 346, electrical domestic appliances) taking case C as the equilibrium type against which the model is calibrated. Column (5) of this table gives the welfare change associated with moving from the equilibrium of type C to an alternative type of equilibrium (with no policy change and unchanged parameters). There are welfare gains because, as noted previously, case C is the least competitive of the equilibrium types under study. From this new base equilibrium policy changes are introduced and reported in columns (1) and (2) of the table. Columns (3) and (4) reproduce results from sections 2.3 and 2.4 for purposes of comparison. Results are reported only for two values of each experiment, and only for cases in which the number of firms is held constant.

From table 2.9 we see that the gains from policy, both import tariffs and export subsidies, are somewhat reduced when simulations are undertaken using parameters obtained from calibration under equilibrium type C (columns [1] and [2], compared to [3] and [4]). The reason for this is that the calibrated elasticity ε is highest for case C (see table 2.2). Using this higher elasticity reduces firms' price-cost margins in the new base equilibrium. The distortion due to imperfect competition is thereby reduced, and consequently policy has a smaller welfare effect. However, the basic conclusions of previous sections still hold. For example, the export subsidy raises welfare in all cases, and by considerably more in case C than in case B.

2.7 Conclusions

The simulations reported in this paper study the welfare implications of two trade policy instruments, an import tariff and an export tax. The effects of these instruments are examined in a family of models of trade under imperfect competition, applied to nine industries in the European Community. From the large number of simulations undertaken, what conclusions can be drawn?

The first message to emerge from the simulations is the small size of the welfare gains that can be derived from use of these policy instruments. Under oligopoly there is only one industry in which tariffs yield welfare gains in excess of 2.5 percent of the base value of consumption of the industry's output. Taking simple averages across industries and equilibrium types we see that the gains from tariffs of 5, 10, 15, and 20 percent average out at 0.48, 0.81, 0.99, and 0.82 percent of base consumption, respectively. With free entry the average gains are somewhat larger, at 0.66, 0.88, 1.05, and 1.00 percent of base consumption for these tariff rates. Export subsidies give even smaller welfare gains, only reaching 1 percent of base consumption in a few of the cases studied. Under oligopoly the net welfare figure is the difference between increases in firms' profits and losses for either consumers or government. This means that if these components of welfare were weighted differently, then results could easily be changed. For example, attaching a premium to government revenue would strengthen the case for import tariffs and rapidly destroy the case for export subsidies.

The second message from the simulations is that, looking across industries, the gains from policy intervention are greater the more concentrated the industry. This is as would be expected. Tariff policy offers welfare gains for all industries studied, these gains arising both from the distortions associated with imperfect competition and from standard terms of trade effects. The effect of export subsidies is more varied across industries, with only three of the nine industries studied giving unambiguous welfare gains from a 4 percent export subsidy, these three being industries with a relatively high level of concentration. The reason for the greater ambiguity in the effects of export subsidies is, of course, that the effect of the policy on distortions and its effect on the terms of trade work in opposite directions. Another industrial characteristic that is important in determining the effects of an export subsidy is the base volume of exports. An industry with a large volume of exports will incur a heavy revenue cost of subsidizing existing exports, in order to achieve the marginal expansion in exports, and is therefore less likely to generate welfare gains from the export subsidy.

Third, although the welfare gains from these policies are relatively small, the quantity effects are quite large. Some part of a tariff is absorbed by the supplying firm, but the larger part is passed on to consumers, and with elasticities of demand for individual models at the levels reported in table 2.1, the order of magnitude of the quantity effect is apparent. Quantity effects are particularly large in the case of trade-promoting policies—export subsidies— since they permit exporters to undercut firms in their home markets and lead, in some cases, to some degree of international specialization of production. This suggests that in order to adequately capture the effects of trade policy, models of imperfect competition need to be put into a general equilibrium framework. Factor price changes would then reduce the size of quantity changes and reduce the likelihood of specialization.

Fourth, the simulations of this paper explored a number of different equilibrium concepts: from the case of price competition (B) to the less competitive behavior implied by Cournot equilibrium (C), from pure market segmentation to pure integration (CI), as well as the intermediate case of integrated-market Cournot competition followed by segmented-market price games (CB). These cases cover a wide range of possible behavior, although it cannot be claimed that actual industry behavior is necessarily within the range spanned by these cases—for example, the industry may be more collusive than is implied by Cournot behavior. The four different equilibria studied lead to significantly different interpretations of the base data sets, as calibration generated different elasticities of demand, in each case, and different levels of the implicit barriers to trade.

How do results differ across these four types of equilibria? Ranking the effectiveness of policy across cases yield some quite surprising results. As would be expected, under oligopoly, policy is more effective if the industry has Cournot competition than if it has Bertrand competition. But with free entry this is (in most cases) reversed; in the long run there are greater gains from policy under the more competitive Bertrand interpretation of the industry, similarly, with the segmented/integrated dimension. Under oligopoly, policy is more effective when markets are segmented than when they are integrated; with free entry this distinction is less clear, and in most cases the gains from policy are greater when markets are integrated. Despite these changes in ranking, the overall sensitivity of results with respect to equilibrium type is not as great as might have been feared from a reading of the theoretical literature. For example, there are relatively few cases in which moving from one type of equilibrium to another changes the sign of the welfare effect of the policy. The tariff simulations report four different tariff rates on nine industries for both oligopoly and free entry. This generates 72 cases for each of which results were derived under the four different equilibria; in 10 of the 72 cases there are sign differences between the equilibria. Export taxes were evaluated at three different rates, and in only 7 of the 54 cases are there sign changes as the experiments go across equilibria.

This paper has not, of course, investigated all possible dimensions of sensitivity analysis. For example, results may well be sensitive to choice of functional form. But the conclusion which emerges from the simulations is that trade models of this type provide a rather weak case for policy intervention. This is not because results are so sensitive to market structure that anything is possible, but rather because even if government gets the policy right, the maximum gains it can expect from it are quite small.

References

Baldwin, R., and P. R. Krugman. 1988. Market access and international competition: A simulation study of 16K random access memories. In *Empirical methods for international trade,* ed. R. Feenstra. Cambridge: MIT Press.

Deaton, A. S. 1975. The measurement of income and price elasticities. *European Economic Review* 6:261–73.

Dixit, A. K. 1988. Optimal trade and industrial policies for the US automobile industry. In *Empirical methods for international trade,* ed. R. Feenstra. Cambridge: MIT Press.

Dixit, A. K., and J. E. Stiglitz. 1977. Monopolistic competition and optimum product diversity. *American Economic Review* 67:297–308.

Eaton, J., and G. Grossman. 1986. Optimal trade and industrial policy under oligopoly. *Quarterly Journal of Economics* 101:383–406.

Horstmann, I., and J. Markusen. 1986. Up the average cost curve: Inefficient entry and the new protectionism. *Journal of International Economics* 20:225–47.

Houthakker, H. S. 1965. New evidence on demand elasticities. *Econometrica* 33:277–88.

Houthakker, H. S., and L. D. Taylor. 1970. *Consumer demand in the United States: Analysis and projections.* Cambridge: Harvard University Press.

Markusen, J. 1981. Trade and the gains from trade with imperfect competition. *Journal of International Economics* 11:531–51.

Markusen, J., and A. J. Venables. 1988. Trade policy with increasing returns and imperfect competition. *Journal of International Economics* 24:299–316.

Piggott, J. R., and J. Whalley. 1985. *UK tax policy and applied general equlibrium analysis.* Cambridge: Cambridge University Press.

Pratten, C. F. 1987. A survey of economies of scale. Department of Applied Economics, University of Cambridge. Manuscript.

Smith, A., and A. J. Venables. 1988. Completing the internal market in the European community: Some industry simulations. *European Economic Review* 32:1501–25.

Venables, A. J. 1985. Trade and trade policy with imperfect competition: The case of identical products and free entry. *Journal of International Economics* 19:1–19.

———. 1990. International capacity choice and national market games. *Journal of International Economics* 29:23–42.

Comment   David G. Tarr

The paper by Venables is interesting in a number of respects and represents another application of the model and extensive data set developed by Smith and Venables (1988) regarding the EC 1992 project. If properly interpreted, this work is a helpful first step in the process of assessing the consequences of 1992. My concern, however, is that the model and calibration do not allow Venables (or Smith and Venables in the related papers) to make the interpretations he does in three important areas: (1) the model is not a full Dixit-Stiglitz model, but rather closer to Armington, (2) the rates of trade protection reported are not trade protection, but rather a combination of trade protection and taste preferences, and (3) as a consequence of (2), the exercises which assess the liberalization of trade protection, especially market integration liberalizations such as 1992, are eliminating the taste preferences consumers have for national products along with the trade protection, attributing therefore too much to the trade liberalization. These will be discussed in turn.

The Model Is Closer to an Armington than to a Dixit-Stiglitz Model

Equation (1) of the paper simply does not follow from the assumptions of the author. It is claimed that products are differentiated by firm and model variety of the firm, and the Dixit-Stiglitz model is employed. We need to define some notation to investigate this. For a typical industry like automobiles, let

$x_{\alpha ij}$ = the output of variety α produced in country i and sold in country j,

$p_{\alpha ij}$ = the price of variety α produced in country i and sold in country j, and

$a_{\alpha ij}$ = a parameter in the utility function of consumers in country j reflecting taste preferences for variety α produced in country i.

Then, if we follow Dixit-Stiglitz, the preferences of consumers in country j can be characterized as CES and we have that their utility is

$$(1) \qquad y_j = \left(\sum_{i=1}^{I} \sum_{\alpha=1}^{n_i m_i} a_{\alpha ij} x_{\alpha ij}^{\rho} \right)^{1/\rho}, \, \rho < 1, \quad j = 1, \dots I,$$

where $\varepsilon = 1/(1 - \rho)$, and otherwise notation is in Venables.

I now ask how we can get from our equation (1), which is Dixit-Stiglitz preferences, to equation (1) of Venables? Make the following assumptions:

(A) $\qquad\qquad\qquad a_{\alpha ij} = a_{ij}$ for all α, i, and j, and

(B) $\qquad\qquad\qquad p_{\alpha ij} = p_{ij}$ for all α, i, and j.

David Tarr is a senior trade economist at the World Bank.
The views expressed are the author's and not necessarily those of the World Bank.

If the consumer in country j maximizes our utility function (1) subject to expenditure allocated to the good in question being fixed, it follows from assumptions A and B that

(C) $x_{\alpha ij} = x_{ij}$ for all α, i, and j.

That is, consumers in country j will buy an equal amount of each variety of the goods from country i. If we substitute (A) and (C) into (1) we arrive at equation (1) of Venables (and of Smith-Venables 1988).

To arrive at Venables's equation (1), however, we have developed a framework in which the price of Mercedes-Benz and Volkswagen are the same (B), and in which when consumers face equal prices for these cars they buy them in equal proportions (C). This is a long way from product variety within a country. The only significant product differentiation in Venables's equation (1) is by country of origin. In fact, except for the scalar factor, $n_i m_i$, which reflects love of variety, Venables's equation (1) is exactly the Armington specification, where products are differentiated by country of origin only. Thus, I suggest that this model is closer to an Armington model (without nesting) than to the Dixit-Stiglitz product variety model.[1]

Taste Differences Are Calibrated as Trade Protection

From equation (4) of Venables, we have that the ratio of sales of country i in country j to the sales of country j in country j can be written as

(2) $x_{ij}/x_{jj} = (p_{ij}/p_{jj})^{-\varepsilon}(a_{ij}/a_{jj})$.

Let $\bar{p}_{ij}$ be the border price of products from country i sold in country j and t_{ij} be the rate of protection applied on products from country i in country j; let t_{ij} be the combination of tariffs and nontariff-barrier equivalents. Rewrite (2), recognizing that it is the tariff-inclusive price that consumers pay for their products that enters the utility maximization problem (and $t_{jj} = 0$):

(3) $x_{ij}/x_{jj} = [\bar{p}_{ij}(1 + t_{ij})/p_{jj}]^{-\varepsilon}(a_{ij}/a_{jj})$

The usual calibration procedure involves a search for estimates of the rate of protection t_{ij}, which is difficult, and given these exogenous estimates of t_{ij}, the taste parameters a_{ij} are calibrated to assure initial equilibrium. In this paper, however, the t_{ij} are taken to equal 10 percent of all countries, which is assumed to equal transportation costs. Any further difference in the ratio of the sales of country i in country j to sales of the home country firms is attributed to trade distortions. That is, consumers in country j are assumed to display no taste differences among the products of any countries in the model; any market

---

1. Instead of using (A) and (B) to derive (C) given equation (1), it is possible to assume (A) and (C) from which (B) follows. These are equivalent procedures from the perspective of the interpretation of what type of model we have.

share differences beyond transportation costs are due to trade distortions. "Trade distortions" are, thus, endogenously calibrated from (3).

If Germans prefer strong beer and Americans prefer weak beer, there will be differences in the market shares of each country's producers in the two markets, independent of trade distortions. Thus, tables 2.3 and 2.4 of estimated trade distortions cannot be interpreted as such. The values are in fact a combination of taste differences and trade protection; without the usual external search for rates of trade protection, we have no way of knowing whether taste differences constitute almost all or almost none of the calculated values.

Eliminating Taste Preferences Is Interpreted as Trade Liberalization in These Models

Given the method by which trade protection is calibrated, when a trade liberalization exercise is conducted in this model, such as the market integration of 1992, the first thing that is done is to assume that the taste parameters (a_{ij}) are reduced or equalized in the markets that are liberalizing. This is interpreted as a reduction in protection. For small changes in protection, where significant differences in the a_{ij} remain, this is an acceptable exercise because we can assume that we have not exceeded any real rates of protection in the economy. For more significant simulated changes in protection, such as the 1992 changes, however, this procedure will eliminate taste changes as well. Thus, what Smith-Venables refer to as the "more conservative" estimates are probably closer to the truth.

Conclusion

I note also that the partial-equilibrium approach represented in this work leads to some obvious biases. For example, all 10 sectors in the Smith-Venables work on EC 92 expand. Since capital and labor must come from somewhere, obviously not all sectors can expand. One cannot simply apply a methodology like this across many industries and obtain an aggregate result. Thus, there is a need to do the kind of research suggested by these models in general equilibrium. Multilevel CES nesting is required, however, to incorporate the fact that the goods of individual countries in the European Community will become better substitutes after 1992, that is the issue is not simply one of lowering border protection. If product variety is to be incorporated, it could be done at the bottom level of the CES nest, along the lines of Krishna, Hogan, and Swagel in this volume. A properly interpreted version of the work of Smith and Venables will provide good intuition into these effects until results from more complicated general equilibrium studies are available.

3 Strategic Trade Policy in the European Car Market

Alasdair Smith

3.1 Introduction

The aim of this paper is to study the role of "strategic trade policy" in the European car market. This work derives from earlier partial-equilibrium modeling of trade policy in imperfectly competitive industries (Venables and Smith 1986; Smith and Venables 1988).

This is the third of a series of papers that adapts the earlier model to take account of the quantitative restrictions on imports in the European car market and allows not only for the effect on prices of such restrictions but also for the effect on the behavior of imperfectly competitive firms. The model is numerically calibrated to data on the European car market in 1988.

This model of the car market was used by Smith and Venables (1991) to study the ranking of policy instruments and to illustrate the interaction between quantitative restrictions and imperfect competition. The detailed implications of the model for the effects on likely policy changes in the European car market were discussed by Smith (1990).

These two earlier papers treated the industry as one with a given number of firms each of which produced a fixed number of different models of cars. Here I treat as endogenous the number of models produced by a firm. Then the trade

Alasdair Smith is professor of economics and dean of the School of European Studies at the University of Sussex and a research fellow in the international trade research program at the Centre for Economic Policy Research

The author is grateful for funding from the Economic and Social Research Council (grants no. B00232149 and R000231129) and from the Ford Foundation grant (no. 860–0312) supporting the Centre for Economic Policy Research program on Empirical Studies of Strategic Trade Policy and for the research assistance of Caroline Digby and Michael Gasiorek.

policy of one country (or one group of countries) can affect the number of models produced by firms located in other countries, and this in turn affects the outcome of competition between firms. This is one way of capturing the essential idea of strategic trade policy, in the sense of policy which changes the relative competitive strengths of home and foreign firms.

I investigate whether the nature of the strategic policy effects are sensitive to the specification of the model, and find that they are, and whether strategic policy effects are strong enough to overturn "conventional" wisdom about the welfare effects of trade policy, and find that they are not.

3.2   The Model

The formal model is fully presented by Smith (1990) and Smith and Venables (1991). The principal features are described below, but detailed derivations are not given. There is an imperfectly competitive industry producing differentiated products. Firms, which each produce several different models of car, see the demand for their products as depending on the price of the individual model and also on the overall price of cars. The Dixit-Stiglitz (1977) representation of consumer choice in markets with differentiated products allows us to write the demand per model in market j for cars produced by firm i as

$$(1) \qquad x_{ij} = (a_{ij}b_j)(p_{ij}/q_j)^{-\varepsilon}(q_j)^{-\mu},$$

where a_{ij} and b_j are shift parameters describing the size of the market, p_{ij} is the price in market j of a model of car produced by firm i, and q_j is an aggregate price index for cars in market j (and is a constant elasticity function of the prices p_{ij} of all models sold). Then ε is the elasticity of demand with respect to the relative price of the individual model of car reflecting the extent to which there is substitutability in demand between different product varieties, while μ is the aggregate elasticity of demand for cars.

The Dixit-Stiglitz formulation is convenient as it gives rise to a demand function in which demand is a constant elasticity function of two prices. It is based on the assumption that each individual consumer chooses to buy some of each of the products on the market. This is not as appealing a description of consumer choice of cars as the Lancaster (1979) approach, in which the consumer chooses one product whose price and characteristics come closest to that consumer's needs. Anderson, de Palma, and Thisse (1989) have presented conditions under which the Dixit-Stiglitz model describes the behavior of the aggregate market, even if individual consumers' behavior is described by the Lancaster approach.

Competition between firms is modeled as a two-stage game. In the first stage of the game, firms choose model numbers, taking account of the effect of their choices on the second-stage equilibrium, and the outcome is a Nash equilibrium in model numbers.

The second stage is Cournot competition (modified to take account of quantitative restrictions on imports) in output, given model numbers. Firms maximize profits, taking account of the impact of scale economies on marginal costs, of the effect of taxes, tariffs, and transport costs on the wedge between producer and consumer prices, and of the effect of elasticity of demand in different markets on their marginal revenues. National markets are assumed to be segmented, so that firms can set different prices in different markets. A producer with a large market share in a particular national market sees its own behavior as having a strong influence on the overall price of cars in that market and thus perceives a relatively inelastic demand for its product; this leads such firms to have higher price-cost margins. Specifically, the first-order condition for a firm selling in a market in which there are no quantitative restrictions on sales is the standard equation of marginal revenue and marginal cost,

$$(2) \qquad p_{ij}T_{ij}(1 - (1/e_{ij})) = mc_i,$$

where $p_{ij}T_{ij}$ is the producer price and mc_i is the firm's marginal cost. The term $1/e_{ij}$, the firm's perceived inverse demand elasticity, is a weighted average of the inverses of the two demand elasticities which appear in the demand function:

$$(3) \qquad 1/e_{ij} = (1/\varepsilon)(1 - s_{ij}) + (1/\mu)s_{ij},$$

where the weight s_{ij} is firm i's share in value terms of market j. This relation has the appealing feature of making firms perceive a less elastic demand for their product the larger their market share. A firm with a small market share takes almost no account of the elasticity of the aggregate market demand, while, at the other extreme, a monopoly perceives only the aggregate demand elasticity.

The model allows there to be a "voluntary" export restraint (VER) which limits the *share* that firms from one country may have in a particular national market (as Japanese firms are currently restricted in several European national markets. The model can alternatively allow there to be a restriction on the firms' overall market share in a group of national markets as a whole, as Japanese firms are in the near future to be restricted to a fixed share of the aggregate EC market).

Firms in markets that are not subject to sales restrictions are assumed to behave as Cournot competitors, and equations (2) and (3) apply. This assumption is also made about the behavior of the restricted firms in markets with sales restrictions. Where other firms are subject to restrictions on their market shares, however, an unrestricted firm is assumed to take account of the effect that a change in its sales will have on the sales of restricted firms. The effect of the share restriction on firms' behavior, derived in Smith and Venables (1991), is to replace in equation (3) above the unrestricted firm's actual value market share s_{ij} with the larger expression

$$(4) \qquad \tilde{s}_{ij} = s_{ij} + n_r s_{rj} \frac{m_i x_{ij}}{\sum_{k \notin R} m_k x_{kj}},$$

where n_r is the number of (equal-sized) firms subject to sales restraint in market j and s_{rj} the value market share of each, m_i the number of models produced by firm i, and R the set of restricted firms. Thus the second term in (4) is the product of the value market share of the restricted firms and the volume share taken by firm i of the sales of all the unrestricted firms. Clearly, firm i behaves as if its market share is larger than it actually is and perceives a more inelastic demand than it would in the absence of the VER. An extreme case is where all firms but firm i are subject to VERs, when (4) reduces to $\tilde{s}_{ij} = 1$. Because all other firms are constrained to fixed market shares, firm i can and will choose the perfectly collusive outcome. In the general case, the anticompetitive effect of the VER is less strong but still leads firms to set higher price-cost margins than they would in the absence of the VER.

Firms' cost functions are assumed to take the form

$$(5) \qquad\qquad C(x,m) = c_1 + c_2 m + c_3 m x_4^c,$$

where x is output per model, and m is the number of models. The values of the parameters c_1, c_2, and c_c are permitted to vary between firms, but c_4 is assumed to be a positive number less than unity and constant across firms. This function displays economies of scale in two dimensions: defining variable cost as the element in cost which varies with output per model, average variable cost is a decreasing function of output per model, while the fixed cost per model is a decreasing function of the number of models.

The model is solved backwards: a solution for the second-stage game is derived from given model numbers, as described above, and then a Nash equilibrium in model numbers is found, taking into account the effects of model number choices on the second-stage equilibrium. An analytical description of the determination of model numbers has not been derived: the equilibrium is found numerically.

3.3 Data and Model Calibration

The model is calibrated to data for the world car market in 1988. The world is divided into eight markets: France, West Germany, Italy, the United Kingdom, Iberia (Spain and Portugal), the rest of the European Community (RoEC; an aggregation of Benelux, Ireland, Greece, and Denmark), EFTA, and the rest of the world (RoW). This level of country disaggregation is needed in order to model the differences in trade policy in 1988 between different members of the European Community and to allow for the fact that the Iberian countries were still in the process of harmonizing their trade policy with the common external tariff of the Community.

The producers are divided into eight groups: French (two producers, Peugeot and Renault), Volkswagen (VW), Fiat, Rover, the U.S. multinationals in Europe (Ford and General Motors [GM] in Europe, who are treated as entirely independent of their American parents), the "specialist" producers (Mercedes,

BMW, Volvo, Saab, Jaguar, and Porsche), the Japanese, and the rest of the world (who are mainly the North American producers). This level of producer disaggregation allows the model to capture the strong differences which exist in national sales patterns. Within each group, firms are assumed to be identical. In the case of the French and the Americans in Europe, this is very close to reality: in each pair the firms are of roughly equal size and have similar sales patterns. The specialists and the Japanese are more heterogenous; calculation of Herfindahl indices suggests it is appropriate to assume the existence of three equal-sized specialist manufacturers and four equal-sized Japanese firms.

Table 3.1 summarizes the shape of the European car market in 1988. The top two sections of the table show sales in the eight markets and the distribution of those sales by producer group, based on registration data in the *Automotive Industry Data 1989 Car Yearbook* (1990). Both the rest of the world market and the sales in Europe by non-Japanese non-European producers—(Other (N) in table 3.1)—are included only to close the model and no attention has been given to accurate modeling of the non-European markets. Therefore, in the discussion of the effects of policy changes, the effects both on "other" producers and in the rest of the world market are ignored. There is no attempt to explain in this paper the model-number choices of Rover or the European "specialist" producers (so they do not enjoy "strategic" policy effects), and they are aggregated in tables as Other (E) even though they are treated as separate groups in the numerical modeling.

The shares of Japanese producers in the different markets display the effects of trade restrictions. In our base year of 1988, there were restrictions on imports from Japan to France, Italy, the United Kingdom, Portugal, and Spain. Since 1977, Japanese imports were restricted to 3 percent of the French market

Table 3.1   **The European Car Market, 1988**

	France	Germany	Italy	United Kingdom	RoEC	Iberia	EFTA	RoW
Market sales total (million) cars								
	2.2	2.8	2.2	2.2	1.1	1.3	1.2	17.2
Market shares (%):								
French	63.2	6.7	14.8	12.6	18.3	38.0	9.3	2.6
VW	8.6	29.4	11.7	5.9	13.0	17.5	14.2	1.6
Fiat	7.2	4.7	59.9	3.7	5.3	9.7	5.2	0.0
Ford/GM	11.3	25.4	6.9	40.1	22.5	26.9	19.2	0.6
Japanese	3.0	15.2	0.9	11.4	26.6	2.1	31.9	39.0
Other (E)	5.5	17.9	4.5	22.9	9.6	5.2	17.7	2.8
Other (N)	1.3	0.8	1.2	3.4	4.6	0.6	2.5	53.4
Total	100.0	100.0	100.0	100.0	100.0	100.0	100.0	100.0
Estimated sales value (billion ECU)								
	26.2	28.9	25.2	25.3	17.1	16.2		
EC total			138.9					

and 11 percent of the U.K. market. (The 11.4 percent Japanese share of the U.K. market shown in table 3.1 includes a small number of U.K.-produced cars, but in the model all "Japanese" cars are treated as imports.) Italy, Spain, and Portugal have long-standing and tight limits on Japanese imports. Both the Italian and Iberian restrictions are modeled, like the French and U.K. restrictions, as limiting Japanese market shares. This is not strictly accurate, but the levels to which Japanese imports are restricted in these markets are so low that the distinction between levels and shares is of little significance. In other EC markets (including Germany) there are no explicit restraints on Japanese sales, and we have assumed no VERs in Germany or the RoEC.

Calibration of the model to this data requires assumptions about cost and demand elasticities and about taxes, tariffs, and transport costs. As in the previous work with this model, a value of 1.5 is chosen for μ, the aggregate industry elasticity of demand, and a value of 4 for ε, the elasticity of demand for an individual model of car. For justification of these elasticity choices and further details on taxes, tariffs, and transport costs, see Smith (1990).

In earlier work (Venables and Smith 1986; Smith and Venables 1988), variation in numbers of models per firm was used as a device to account for the difference in the scale of different firms. In the case of the car industry, however, it is possible to give a concrete interpretation. The Ludvigsen study for the European Commission (Ludvigsen Associates Limited 1988) centered its description of scale economies on the concept of a "platform," essentially a floor plan on which a family of cars can be based. The Ludvigsen information on the numbers of platforms per producer gives the model numbers shown in table 3.2 (where, however, the model numbers for Japanese producers are simply assumed). Ludvigsen provides information about the relation between variable costs and scale and output per platform that suggests that average variable cost declines by 5 percent for every doubling of output per platform, and this property is satisfied by choosing $c_4 = 0.925$ for all firms. Ludvigsen provides much sketchier information about fixed costs, and the rest of the parameters of the cost function are calibrated in a way described below.

Ludvigsen also provides some information on the prices of cars of different types in different markets. German market prices are used as the base for calibrating prices, on the grounds that, of the markets for which Ludvigsen provides price data, this is the least distorted by taxes and protection. Assuming

Table 3.2	The European Car Market, 1988: Production and Sales			
	Sales (million)	Models per Firm	Firm Numbers	Sales per Model (thousand)
French	3.443	7	2	245
VW	2.205	7	1	315
Fiat	1.929	6	1	321
Ford/GM	2.935	5	2	293
Japanese	8.190	6	4	341

that the distribution of cars of different types (utility, small, lower-medium, etc.) in each firm's output is the same as in the firm's German sales gives a price for each producer group's "typical" car in Germany, then a price in each of the other markets is derived from the model. These prices are reflected in the estimated sales values reported in the third section of table 3.1.

The calibration of the model then consists of the choice of firm-specific marginal cost parameters c_3 to reproduce the German prices and, in the absence of VERs, the choice of parameters to scale the demand functions to observed sales, that is to say, to explain the pattern of sales displayed in table 3.1. However, in markets where VERs are in operation we have no observations on Japanese market shares in the absence of constraints and therefore infer these demand parameters from information about unrestricted markets, as described in detail in Smith (1990).

Finally, the parameters c_2 are calibrated to make the actual model numbers shown in table 3.2 optimal for the French, German, Italian, "American-European," and Japanese producers. (The peculiar features or the lack of information about the other producers made it unreasonable to assume that model numbers were chosen by these firms in the same way as by the mass-market producers.) For each producer a range of possible values of c_2 was found by simulating new equilibria in which that producer had one more and one fewer model than in the base case and calculating the values of the cost parameter consistent with the base case being optimal. (In all cases, the profit function was locally concave in model numbers, so the base could be calibrated as an optimum.)

The results of this calibration do not allow the choice of the same value of c_2 for all firms (nor do they allow c_2 to be chosen proportionally to the firm-specific marginal cost factors c_3). However, from the ranges of values compatible with the base it was possible to choose values implying a cost of 400 million ECU per year per model for French and Japanese producers and of 475 million ECU per year for all others. For all firms but the Japanese these parameters imply that the cost associated with model numbers ($c_2 m$) are in the range of 26–28 percent of variable cost, and this ratio is not inconsistent with the vague information given by Ludvigsen on these matters. (For the Japanese firms, the proportion is 18.5 percent.) There is, of course, an element of arbitrariness about these choices, and the implications of this arbitrariness are explored below.

The values of c_1 play no role in the policy simulations below, since changes in firm numbers are not considered. If such changes were permitted, it would be natural to choose c_1 to make the base a zero-profit free-entry equilibrium.

3.4   VERs as a Strategic Trade Policy for the European Community

In this section, I address the question of whether the national VERs on Japanese imports can be seen, from the viewpoint of the European Community as a whole, as an effective strategic trade policy.

Table 3.3 National VERs, Model Numbers Fixed

	France	Germany	Italy	United Kingdom	RoEC	Iberia	EC Total	EFTA
Japanese market shares								
Initial	19.1	20.4	21.5	22.2	34.1	16.1	21.5	
Final	3.0	19.4	0.9	11.4	32.7	2.1	10.9	
Welfare changes (million ECU per year)								
Consumer surplus	−2,345.2	32.0	−3,873.2	−1,446.4	−16.0	−1,276.8	−8,925.6	−14.1
Tax revenue	−256.5	1.9	−322.7	−144.7	−2.9	−179.1	−904.0	−1.2
CET revenue	6.4	0.0	8.9	10.3	0.3	26.9	52.8	0.0

	French	VW	Fiat	Ford/GM	Other(E)	EC Total[a]	Japanese
Profits	1,271.2	354.9	1,315.4	564.2	379.5	3,603.1	−1,529.6

Total[b]   −6,173.1
Total (excluding tax)[c]   −5,269.1

[a] Equals sum of profits for French, VW, Fiat, and Other(E) plus one-half of profits for Ford/GM.
[b] Equals sum of EC total consumer surplus, tax revenue, CET revenue, and profits.
[c] Equals sum of EC total consumer surplus, CET revenue, and profits.

Tables 3.3 and 3.4 show the effects of the restraints on Japanese imports under alternative assumptions about variation in firms' model numbers. The base case on which the model is calibrated is one with import restrictions in place in France, Italy, the United Kingdom, and Iberia. However, for expositional convenience the tables present the simulation results as the imposition of such restrictions. Table 3.4 shows the effects of moving from the simulated equilibrium with no import restrictions back to the base equilibrium with import restrictions. Table 3.3 shows the same change but with firms' model numbers fixed at the level of the no-restriction simulation. Thus table 3.3 has no "strategic trade policy" effects.

The dramatic reductions in the market share of Japanese producers in table 3.3 are associated with large reductions in Japanese sales and associated price increases in the restricted markets. Non-Japanese firms raise their prices a little as their market power increases. In the unrestricted markets there are only small redistributions of market share, as Japanese firms' marginal costs rise a little and non-Japanese firms' marginal costs and prices fall a little. The effects on firms' profits and on consumer surplus are shown in the lower part of table 3.3: large reductions in consumer surplus in the restricted markets, large increases in the profits of European producers, especially those with large market shares in the most restricted markets. There are also changes in tax revenue (which are separately shown in the table as sales tax revenue and revenue from the common external tariff [CET] of the European Community).

There are ambiguities in the summation of the welfare effects of these changes. The multinationality of production makes it undesirable to count, say, the profits, of Peugeot and Renault as gains to France, since some of these profits may go to workers and managers in Spain and the United Kingdom. At the level of the European Community as a whole, however, this problem exists only for Ford and GM. Arbitrarily, I count half of their profit change as accruing to the European Community. Whether tax revenue should be counted as a gain depends on whether one sees the taxes as creating or correcting distortions, but we can ignore this problem since the treatment of tax revenue never makes a qualitative difference to results.

In brief, table 3.3 shows the welfare losses to European consumers from the import restrictions greatly outweighing the welfare gains to European producers. There are also negative effects on Japanese profits. The results are derived in a model in which imperfect competition is given a key role, and the implications of the interaction between imperfect competition and quantitative import restrictions are spelled out in Smith and Venables (1991), but the general shape of the results is not dissimilar to those that would be derived in a conventional model of perfect competition.

Table 3.4 incorporates strategic effects. The imposition of the VERs leads to an increase in model numbers by one each by the two French producers, the two "American-European" producers, and VW, while each of the Japanese producers reduces its model numbers by two. There is a marked effect on con-

Table 3.4   National VERs, Model Numbers Variable

	France	Germany	Italy	United Kingdom	RoEC	Iberia	EC Total	EFTA
Japanese market shares								
Initial	19.1	20.4	21.5	22.2	34.1	16.1	21.5	21.5
Final	3.0	15.2	0.9	11.4	26.6	2.1	9.3	9.3
Welfare changes (million ECU per year)								
Consumer surplus	−1,399.4	241.9	−3,340.8	−717.0	−90.9	−662.9	−5,969.1	−132.3
Tax revenue	−153.1	14.8	−278.4	−71.7	−16.2	−93.0	−597.6	−11.0
CET revenue	3.9	−0.3	7.6	5.4	1.2	14.1	31.9	0.0

	French	VW	Fiat	Ford/GM	Other(E)	EC Total[a]	Japanese
Profits	996.4	323.1	1,077.0	444.6	308.9	2,927.7	−1,655.8
Total[b]						−3,607.1	
Total (excluding tax)[c]						−3,009.5	

[a] Equals sum of profits for French, VW, Fiat, and Other(E) plus one-half of profits for Ford/GM.
[b] Equals sum of EC total consumer surplus, tax revenue, CET revenue, and profits.
[c] Equals sum of EC total consumer surplus, CET revenue, and profits.

sumer welfare: the increase in model variety combined with price increases that are generally lower than when model numbers are fixed reduces the loss in consumer welfare to 6,000 million ECU per year in table 3.4, compared with 9,000 million in table 3.3. However, not only is this loss still in excess of the gains to European producers, the producers' gains are actually lower in table 3.4 than in table 3.3. The VERs are counterproductive as a strategic trade policy in shifting profits toward European producers.

The reason for this is easy to see. The change in model numbers is optimal for each individual producer, taking the other producers' model numbers as given, but the change in all producers' model numbers is profit-reducing, as intensified competition among European producers more than outweighs the beneficial effects of the reduction in Japanese competition. This is an example of the problem identified by Dixit (1984) of the weakening of the strategic case for import restrictions as the number of "home" firms increases.

When we look at policy from an EC point of view it might seem more natural to look at an EC-wide strategic trade policy rather than the EC-wide effects of national trade policies. I have shown results for the latter in this section because the national trade policies are the actual policies currently in place, but policy simulations for an EC-wide VER have been carried out. There are significant differences in the cross-country distribution of effects: EC-wide restrictions impose larger costs on consumers in markets unaffected by present national restrictions and lower costs on consumers in markets where tight national restrictions are replaced by a looser EC-wide restriction, and they give greater benefits to producers whose output is spread across the EC markets and less to those whose sales are concentrated in the presently restricted national markets. However, at the EC level the welfare results are remarkably similar to those reported in tables 3.3 and 3.4, so the details are not reported here.

3.5   A National VER as Strategic Trade Policy

Tables 3.5 and 3.6 explore the effectiveness of a VER for a single country, France. As in the previous section, the tables present the results in the form of the effects of the imposition of the VER. Table 3.5 shows the effects of imposing a VER on Japanese imports into France, with other national VERs in place and with producers' model numbers fixed at the equilibrium level with no French VER. Table 3.6 looks at the same policy experiment, but now with producers' model numbers variable (so that the endpoint of the policy experiment, as in table 3.4, is the base on which the model was calibrated).

Table 3.5 shows the French VER imposing costs on consumers greatly in excess of the gains to French producers, indeed greatly in excess of the gains to all European producers. Table 3.6 introduces the strategic effects: the imposition of the French VER has the effect of reducing Japanese model numbers by one per producer and raising VW's model numbers by one.

It is a little surprising that the producer which expands its model range as a

Table 3.5　　French VER, Model Numbers Fixed

	France	Germany	Italy	United Kingdom	RoEC	Iberia	EC Total	EFTA
Japanese market shares								
Initial	16.0	17.3	0.9	11.4	29.6	2.1		12.5
Final	3.0	17.1	0.9	11.4	29.2	2.1		10.0
Welfare changes (million ECU per year)								
Consumer surplus	−2,002.9	4.5	29.9	29.8	−4.6	21.5	−1,921.8	−4.4
Tax revenue	−219.1	0.3	2.5	3.0	−0.8	3.0	−211.1	−0.4
CET revenue	5.1	0.1	0.0	−0.2	0.0	−0.2	4.8	0.0

	French	VW	Fiat	Ford/GM	Other(E)	EC Total[a]	Japanese
Profits	660.2	57.0	45.2	84.4	53.1	857.7	−315.2
Total[b]						−1,270.4	
Total (excluding tax)[c]						−1,059.3	

[a]Equals sum of profits for French, VW, Fiat, and Other(E) plus one-half of profits for Ford/GM.
[b]Equals sum of EC total consumer surplus, tax revenue, CET revenue, and profits.
[c]Equals sum of EC total consumer surplus, CET revenue, and profits.

Table 3.6   French VER, Model Numbers Variable

	France	Germany	Italy	United Kingdom	RoEC	Iberia	EC Total	EFTA
Japanese market shares								
Initial	16.0	17.3	0.9	11.4	29.6	2.1	12.5	
Final	3.0	15.2	0.9	11.4	26.6	2.1	9.3	
Welfare changes (million ECU per year)								
Consumer surplus	−1,898.6	16.7	196.7	64.5	−162.8	130.0	−1,653.5	−121.6
Tax revenue	−207.7	1.0	16.4	6.5	−28.9	18.2	−194.5	−10.1
CET revenue	5.0	0.1	−0.4	−0.1	1.4	−1.9	4.1	0.0

	French	VW	Fiat	Ford/GM	Other(E)	EC Total[a]	Japanese
Profits	641.6	147.5	−9.4	86.2	113.4	936.2	−365.8

Total[b]	−907.7
Total (excluding tax)[c]	−713.2

[a]Equals sum of profits for French, VW, Fiat, and Other(E) plus one-half of profits for Ford/GM.
[b]Equals sum of EC total consumer surplus, tax revenue, CET revenue, and profits.
[c]Equals sum of EC total consumer surplus, CET revenue, and profits.

result of the French VER should be a German producer rather than a French producer, but given the levels of the parameter c_2 chosen in the calibration, this turns out to be the (unique) equilibrium.

The first point to be made, then, is that there is no guarantee in a many-country world that the benefits of a strategic trade policy imposed by one country will accrue to that country's own producers.

Second, the location of the strategic effects are quite sensitive to the values of c_2 chosen in the calibration. The assumption that the base is an equilibrium gave us a range of values from which to choose c_2 for each producer, but the actual choice was arbitrary. The location of the strategic effects is therefore sensitive to an aspect of model specification on which we are ill informed.

Finally, even if we were to pretend that VW is a French firm, table 3.6 makes no case for a French VER as a strategic trade policy. The changes in model numbers as the Japanese producers contract and VW expands reduces the cost of the VER to French consumers from 2,000 million ECU per year to 1,900, but it raises the effect on VW's profits only from 57 to 147 million ECU, and all of the profit gains are still far short of the losses to consumers.

3.6   Conclusions

When numerically calibrated models are used to analyze economic policy, data are used only to calibrate and not to test the model. Thus much depends on the prior specification of the model, and it is not clear how much confidence one should have in the detailed results. At best, the numerical results presented in this paper should be taken as illustrations of possible orders of magnitude associated with the effects discussed in the theoretical model rather than as precise numerical predictions.

Concern about sensitivity to prior specification and to the parameter values used in the calibration can be fully allayed by very systematic sensitivity analysis. I have not conducted a systematic sensitivity analysis with respect to model specification, but we have seen that the general nature of the results is not greatly altered by changing the crucial assumption about whether firms' model numbers are exogenous or endogenous. I have undertaken only very limited sensitivity analysis with respect to model parameters. The details are not reported here, but again the conclusion is that the general shape of the result remains unchanged as parameter values change.

However, one crucial aspect of the results discussed in this paper does depend on model specification: how firms' model numbers change in response to policy changes turns out to be very sensitive to the "cost per model" parameter in firms' cost functions. Thus both the location and the very existence of the "strategic trade policy" effects in this model depend sensitively on a modeling choice that has to be made with a degree of arbitrariness at the calibration stage.

Even leaving aside the issue of sensitivity, the results presented here cast doubt on the case for strategic trade policy. The effects on increased competition among "home" firms may wipe out the expected benefits of a strengthened strategic position in competition with "foreign" firms. In a many-country world with multilateral trade flows, the beneficiary of one country's strategic trade policy may be another country's producer. Finally, in the cases discussed in this paper, the "strategic" effects of trade policy are greatly outweighed by more traditional effects.

References

Anderson, Simon P., André de Palma, and Jacques-François Thisse. 1989. Demand for differentiated products, discrete choice models, and the characteristics approach. *Review of Economic Studies* 56:21–35.
Automobile Industry Data 1989 Car Yearbook. 1990. Lichfield (Eng.): Automotive Industry Data Ltd.
Dixit, Avinash. 1984. International trade policy for oligopolistic industries. *Economic Journal* 94 (Supplement): 1–16.
Dixit, Avinash, and Joseph Stiglitz. 1977. Monopolistic competition and optimum product diversity. *American Economic Review* 67 (3): 297–308.
Lancaster, Kelvin. 1979. *Variety, equity and efficiency.* New York: Columbia University Press.
Ludvigsen Associates Limited. 1988. *The EC92 automobile sector.* Commission of the European Communities, Research on the Cost of Non-Europe, Basic Findings, vol. 11. Luxembourg: European Communities Publications Office.
Smith, Alasdair. 1990. The market for cars in the enlarged European Community. In *Unity with diversity in the European Community: The Community's southern frontier,* ed. Christopher Bliss and Jorge Braga de Macedo, 78–103. Cambridge: Cambridge University Press.
Smith, Alasdair, and Anthony J. Venables. 1988. Completing the internal market in the European Community: Some industry simulations. *European Economic Review* 32 (7): 1501–25.
———. 1991. Counting the cost of voluntary export restraints in the European car market. In *International Trade and Trade Policy,* ed. Elhanan Helpman and Assaf Razin, 187–220. Cambridge: MIT Press.
Venables, Anthony J., and Alasdair Smith. 1986. Trade and industrial policy under imperfect competition. *Economic Policy* 1 (3): 622–72.

Comment   James Levinsohn

The European car market is complex. There are several European producers, a few big American players producing in Europe, and of course Japanese imports. The menu of plausible trade policies to be investigated is long and also complex. For example, quotas on Japanese imports might be set individually

James Levinsohn is professor of economics at the University of Michigan.

for each European country, or there might be a quota on total European imports from Japan. The quota might be in value terms, or it might be in terms of physical units. Many European countries have very disparate domestic tax structures that in effect act as trade barriers. These seemingly domestic policies are also candidates for trade policy reform in the European automobile market. In short, modeling trade policy for the European car market is tricky business. Alasdair Smith does a very admirable job coming up with answers to some very relevant and very hard questions.

There are many standards by which the results of this paper might be judged. The most compelling of these, though, is to ask how one could improve on the paper *conditional on having to actually come up with answers.* There are plenty of detailed econometric methodologies to estimate demand and oligopoly pricing in the automobile market. Could these methodologies be readily applied to a market characterized by the many countries and potential policies in the European market? Probably not. When the questions addressed become as complex as those Smith poses in this paper, empirical effects are unlikely to get beyond the simulation methodology.

I would like to address two issues in the remainder of my comments. First, if the complexity of the issues addressed forces the researcher to use a simulation methodology, are there margins on which to improve? Second, even in the perfect simulation model, how much trust should we place in the results?

Smith is one of the pioneers in modeling trade policies with imperfect competition. Our search for margins on which to improve is brief since the job is done right. There are, though, two possible improvements. First, many of the policies that are analyzed in the paper are related to the broad changes associated with 1992. Pan-European quotas are an example. The policies associated with 1992 are not likely to come as surprises. By 1992, only economists with good memories will remember how many "1992" conferences they attended in the four years preceding that date. When broad changes in the economic environment are expected far in advance, thinking firms will act to preclude adverse effects that the changes might bring. Japanese auto firms are no exception, and modeling preemptive behavior in the simulation model would be nice. Specifically, direct foreign investment by Japanese firms in Europe is important and might be profitably added to the model. This is especially so if, as in the United States, Japanese production via direct foreign investment does not count against any quota. Also, if a quota is to be based on the prequota market share, predatory pricing becomes an important consideration. This entails an increase in European consumer surplus that, it seems, could be important when analyzing the welfare effects of policies.

Second, the Dixit-Stiglitz utility function seems a strange approach to modeling automobile demand. While it provides a nice representation of preferences when confronted with a menu at a Chinese restaurant, the love-of-variety approach is probably not appropriate to modeling the demand for automobiles. Rather, the Lancasterian approach in which consumers buy one unit of the good and choose the unit nearest their ideal variety seems more appropriate. The demand and oligopoly-pricing equations that fall out of this approach are admittedly more complicated than those of the Dixit-Stiglitz approach, but since the model is simulated instead of estimated, this problem is not insurmountable.

Smith's simulation model is very complete and carefully constructed. Suppose he were to somehow also adopt a Lancasterian approach while simultaneously modeling the model-firm behavior resulting from the expectation of 1992. How much trust should we place in the answers that this model would provide? Put another way, what can we learn from even the very best that the simulation methodology has to offer? Here I am skeptical about the marginal product of simulation studies. My reasons are twofold.

The inputs to the simulation model—elasticities, costs, as well as other parameters estimated elsewhere—have standard errors associated with them. When the inputs to the simulation model have standard errors, so should the outputs. The multiplicative nature of probabilities is such that even if we are reasonably confident about the point estimates of several inputs, the solutions to the simulation model will often have, by econometric standards, huge standard errors. Varying one parameter at a time and re-solving the model for each parameter value, as is often done in sensitivity analysis for simulation models, is not enough. If the solutions of simulation models are to be credible, standard errors should accompany the solution values.

If the above reason for some healthy skepticism is basically a statistical argument, the other cause of skepticism is an economic story. Myriad recent theoretical papers have investigated how trade policy works in imperfectly competitive markets. A key lesson that has been learned is that the effects of a given trade policy frequently hinge critically on firms' modes of market conduct. This is troubling since the mode of market conduct is seldom observable. The policies investigated by Smith in this paper are also sensitive to market conduct. In this case, Cournot behavior is assumed. Since signs, not just magnitudes, of the effects of policy often depend on the mode of market conduct, it would be nice to see reference to some estimates of the mode of conduct in the European auto industry. If such estimates do not already exist, this is one parameter that especially seems worth estimating.

The bottom line is that once we constrain ourselves to coming up with answers to very complex questions (in a reasonable amount of time), we perhaps lock ourselves into a methodology which will not allow terribly precise estimates. An alternative is to ask simpler questions and get more precise answers. This trade-off is a judgment call. Having decided on asking the big-picture questions, Smith does a very nice job coming up with the best answers that his methodology will allow.

4   Deregulation of Scandinavian Airlines: A Case Study of the Oslo–Stockholm Route

Victor D. Norman and Siri P. Strandenes

As part of the 1992 program, the national preferences inherent in the airline policies of most EC countries will gradually be abandoned. This will be accompanied by general deregulation of air services within the European Community, although the extent and nature of deregulation remains uncertain. The Scandinavian countries are likely to match such a program, whether or not Sweden and Norway become part of the internal market. The purpose of the present paper is to assess the possible welfare effects for the Scandinavian countries of deregulation. We restrict the analysis to inter-Scandinavian routes and use the Oslo–Stockholm route as a case study.

The Oslo–Stockholm leg is suitable for several reasons. First, it is at present a virtual Scandinavian Airlines (SAS) monopoly. Finnair has one flight in each direction per day, but as this is an Oslo-Stockholm-Helsinki flight, a majority of the passengers have Helsinki as point of origin or destination. Aeroflot also has connecting flights, but only on a daily basis. The remaining flights—on the average nine per day—are all SAS flights, giving SAS 90–95 percent of the market. Moreover, the SAS monopoly is not a natural one—it is a direct consequence of the consortium agreement between the three Scandinavian governments, which reserves flights between the Scandinavian countries for SAS. Thus, deregulation is likely to have an impact on the route. Second, the traffic is large enough to make entry likely if permitted. Third, the route can

Victor D. Norman is professor of international economics at the Norwegian School of Economics and Business Administration, Bergen. Siri P. Strandenes is associate professor of shipping economics at the Norwegian School of Economics and Business Administration, Bergen.

The research for this paper was financed by a grant from the Nordic Economic Research Council and support from the NBER/CEPR strategic trade policy project. The authors thank SAS for providing some of the data used in the study and for public comments on an earlier draft of the paper. The authors are grateful to Geir Asheim, Sonja Daltung, David Newbery, Paul Seabright, and Lars Sørgard for valuable comments and ideas.

be studied in isolation, as neither Oslo nor Stockholm are natural transfer points for passengers from the other city.

In the paper, we analyze the effects of deregulation using a numerical simulation model in which consumer demand for air transportation depends both on price and flight frequency and in which there is oligopolistic interaction between airlines. The route is initially considered as a pure SAS monopoly (i.e., we ignore the Finnair and Aeroflot flights), so the model parameters are found by calibrating the model to initial data and first-order conditions for a profit-maximizing monopolist. We use the model to simulate the effects of entry, assuming that a many-firm equilibrium will be perfectly symmetric (i.e., firms will have equal numbers of flights and charge the same price). The oligopoly equilibrium is assumed to reflect a Bertrand equilibrium in prices and a Cournot equilibrium in the number of flights. Methodologically, the study is related to recent simulation studies of trade and trade policy under imperfect competition—see, e.g., Smith and Venables (1986), Baldwin and Krugman (1987), Baldwin and Flam (1989), and the surveys in Helpman and Krugman (1989) and Norman (1989).

We know of no comparable simulation studies of air transportation. Prior to the 1978 deregulation of air services in the United States, however, Douglas and Miller (1974) did a careful study of the effects of regulation, using an approach with points of similarity to our study. They modeled city-pair markets as Cournot oligopolies and studied the effects of nonprice competition (competition in capacity offered) given publicly regulated airfares. They found, not surprisingly, that nonprice competition eliminates pure rents (through overcapacity). In an extension, they also looked at the trade-off between frequency and price, using queuing theory.

Other relevant studies are Jordan (1970) and DeVaney (1975). DeVaney looked at the effects of entry given alternative assumptions regarding scheduling decisions. Jordan looked at airline regulation as an endogenous regulatory regime.

Finally, the present study builds on the experience of deregulation in the United States. For a summary of the U.S. experience and a discussion of the issues involved in European deregulation, see McGowan and Seabright (1989) and Strandenes (1987).

4.1 The Simulation Model

4.1.1 Demand

To study the route, we use a highly stylized model of the demand for air transportation. Suppose the consumer can choose among n flights per day, equally spaced over the time interval $(0,T)$. Thus, the time interval between flights is $I = T/n$. Suppose that a potential passenger has a gross value, v, associated with the flight and that he has a desired departure time, z. His net value

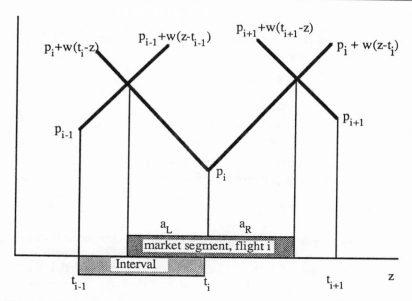

Fig. 4.1   Flight market segment

is assumed to be the value of the flight less the opportunity cost of the time difference between his desired departure time and the actual departure time of his flight, i.e., $(v - w|t - z|)$, where w is his unit opportunity cost of time. His consumer surplus is the net value less the price of the ticket.

We assume that the distribution of desired departure times is uniform over the time interval $(0,T)$ and independent of the distribution of gross values across potential passengers.[1] Let $N(v)$ denote the cumulative density function over gross values, so $N(v)$ can be interpreted as the number of passengers with gross values $\geq v$. The density of consumers with values $\geq v$ at a particular desired departure time is then simply $N(v)/T$.

Within this demand framework, consider the demand for flight number i, with departure time t_i and ticket price p_i. Figure 4.1 may be useful. Flight i competes with neighboring flights, $i - 1$ and $i + 1$, with departures times t_{i-1} $= t_i - I$. A passenger will choose flight i if the price plus the imputed waiting-time cost is lower for that flight than for neighboring flights. Passengers with $z < t_{i-1}$ will always (in a symmetric equilibrium) prefer flight $i - 1$, and passengers with $z > t_{i+1}$ will always prefer flight $i + 1$, so we need only consider potential passengers with $t_{i-1} \leq z \leq t_{i+1}$. Those with $t_{i-1} \leq z \leq t_i$ will prefer

---

1. If the distribution of desired departure times is nonuniform, an appropriate transformation of the time axis can always be used to make it uniform. Such an interpretation will, however, imply that the opportunity cost of time will vary with the time of day and proportionally with the density of traffic.

flight i if and only if $p_i + w(t_i - z) < p_{i-1} + w(z - t_{i-1})$. Thus, flight i will capture all potential passengers with desired departure times between $t_i - a_L$ and t_p where a_L is given by

$$p_i + w\,a_L = p_{i-1} + w\,(I - a_L),$$

i.e., by

(1) $$a_L = \frac{I}{2} + \frac{p_{i-1} - p_i}{2w}.$$

Similarly, flight i will capture all potential passengers with desired departure times between t_i and $t_i + a_R$, where a_R is given by

(2) $$a_R = \frac{I}{2} + \frac{p_{i+1} - p_i}{2w}.$$

Thus, the market segment for flight i will be potential passengers with desired departure times, $t_{i-1} - a_L < z < t_i + a_R$. A potential passenger with a particular desired departure time within this interval will actually purchase a ticket if the gross flight value exceeds the price plus the waiting-time cost. The demand for flight i will therefore be

(3) $$x_i = \frac{1}{T} \int\limits_{p_i}^{p_i + wa_L} N(v)dv + \frac{1}{T} \int\limits_{p_i}^{p_i + wa_R} N(v)dv,$$

or, using averages as approximations,

(4) $$x_i \approx \frac{1}{T}\left[a_L\, N\!\left(p_i + w\,\frac{a_L}{2}\right) + a_R\, N\!\left(p_i + w\,\frac{a_R}{2}\right)\right].$$

Restricting ourselves to symmetric cases, where $p_{i-1} = p_{i+1} = p_c$ say, we have

(5) $$a_L = a_R = \frac{I}{2} + \frac{p_c - p_i}{2w,}$$

which gives the demand function

(6) $$x_i = \frac{1}{T}\left(I + \frac{p_c - p_i}{w}\right) N\!\left(p_i + w\!\left(\frac{I}{4} + \frac{p_c - p_i}{4w}\right)\right).$$

In a fully symmetric equilibrium, where $p_i = p_c = p$, this reduces to, using $I = (T/n)$,

(7) $$x_i = \frac{N\!\left(p + wT/4n\right)}{n}.$$

4.1.2   The Market Game

In the market, there are a number of identical airlines—i.e., airlines with identical cost functions and equal numbers of flights. The flights are scheduled in such a way that no airline has neighboring flights (except, of course, in the monopoly case).[2] The market game is assumed to be a simultaneous Bertrand pricing game and Cournot capacity game: The firms set prices assuming that the prices of competing airlines are fixed and decide on the number of flights assuming that the number of competing flights is given.

One could, perhaps, argue that the market should be modeled as a two-stage game, in which the airlines in stage 1 decide on the number of departures (as a Cournot game) and in stage 2 decide on prices (as a Bertrand game). In a later version of the paper, we may do that. It should be noted, however, that there is nothing in the technology or the institutional arrangements that suggests that capacities must be decided prior to pricing decisions—airlines have great flexibility, even in the short term, with respect to prices, capacities, and schedules. Thus, a simultaneous price/quantity framework seems as reasonable as a two-stage game.

Firm j has n_j departures, selling x_j seats on each flight, at price p_j. Its profits are therefore

$$(8) \qquad \pi_j = n_j p_j x_j - b(x_j, n_j),$$

where $b(x,n)$ is the total cost associated with n flights with x passengers per flight. Taking the prices of competing (neighboring) flights as given and taking the number of departures of other airlines as given, the firm chooses price and schedules departures so as to maximize (8). The first-order conditions are

$$(9) \qquad \frac{\partial \pi_j}{\partial p_j} = n_j \left[x_j + \left(p_j - \frac{b_x}{n_j} \right) \frac{\partial x_j}{\partial p_j} \right] = 0,$$

$$(10) \qquad \frac{\partial \pi_j}{\partial n_j} = p_j x_j + n_j \left(p_j - \frac{b_x}{n_j} \right) \frac{\partial x_j}{\partial n_j} - b_n = 0,$$

where b_x and b_n denote partial derivatives. The derivatives $(\partial x / \partial p_j)$ and $(\partial x / \partial n_j)$ are obtained from the demand function (6): the (Bertrand) price derivative of demand for a particular flight offered by company j is

$$(11) \qquad \frac{\partial x_j}{\partial p_j} = \frac{N}{wT} + \frac{1}{T}(I + \frac{P_c - P_j}{w}) N'[1 - \frac{1}{4}].$$

2. Note that we do not go into the complex issue of optimum scheduling, beyond observing that any scheduling equilibrium (if it exists) must involve alternating departures. In particular, we do not look at the issue of Hotelling-type clustering. It is not clear, from the experience of U.S. deregulation, that competition leads to clustering over and beyond what follows from peak-hour demand, but the issue deserves careful analysis. For a discussion, see McGowan and Seabright (1989).

In a symmetric equilibrium, with $p_j = p_c = p$, this can be written as

(12)
$$\frac{\partial x_j}{\partial p_j} = -\frac{N}{wT}\left(1 - w\frac{3}{4}I\frac{N'}{N}\right),$$

or

(13)
$$\frac{\partial x_j}{\partial p_j} = -\frac{N}{wT}\left[1 - \left(\frac{3/4wI}{p + 1/4wI}\right)\left(\frac{N'v}{N}\right)\right],$$

where the elasticity $[(N'v)/N]$ is evaluated at $v = [p + w(I/4)]$; i.e., at the effective cost of the trip to the average passenger. We treat the elasticity $[(N'v)/N]$ as a constant, $-e$. Using this, and recalling that $x_j = (N/n)$ and $I = (T/n)$, the price elasticity can be written as

(14)
$$\frac{\partial x_j}{\partial p_j}\frac{P_j}{x_j} = -\left[1 + \left(\frac{3/4wI}{p + 1/4\ wI}\right)e\right]\left(\frac{p}{wI}\right).$$

This reflects two price effects. One is the loss of market segment when the price is raised: passengers indifferent between our flight and a neighboring flight will choose the latter when our price increases. The other is the loss of passengers initially indifferent between traveling and not traveling.

The (Cournot) elasticity of demand per flight with respect to the number of flights is found in a similar way. It is most easily found from the symmetric demand function (7), keeping in mind that $n = \Sigma\ n_j$. It gives

(15)
$$\frac{\partial x_j}{\partial n_j} = -\frac{N}{n^2}\left[1 + \left(\frac{wT}{4n}\right)\frac{N'}{N}\right].$$

But we know that $(T/n) = I$. Using this, $x_j = (N/n)$, and $v = [p + w(I/4)]$, (15) can be written in elasticity form as

(16)
$$\frac{\partial x_j}{\partial n_j}\frac{n_j}{x_j} = -\frac{n_j}{n}\left[1 - (\frac{wI/4}{p + wI/4})e\right].$$

Again, this reflects two forces. One is the direct effect of spreading a given total number of passengers across more flights: A one percent increase in the number of flights will, for a given total number of passengers, mean one percent fewer passengers per flight. The other is the indirect effect through the effective cost of traveling: More flights mean less waiting time and thus lower total travel costs. This indirect effect thus contributes to larger total demand and will dampen—and possibly reverse—the direct effect.

Substituting the elasticities (14) and (16) into the first-order conditions (9) and (10), we find the Bertrand/Cournot equilibrium in prices and departures when (9) and (10) hold for all firms simultaneously.

4.2   Data and Calibration

The model is parameterized through what is now the standard procedure for numerical imperfect-competition models: A few key parameters are set exogenously; the rest are found by calibrating the model to actual data for some base period. In our case, we set the price elasticities of demand and the marginal passenger costs exogenously and find the remaining parameters by calibrating the model to 1989 data for demand and prices and estimates of marginal and total costs.

4.2.1   Demand and Prices

In the numerical implementation, we distinguish between Euroclass (full fare) and tourist (discount fare) passengers. SAS provided data for a representative week (in September 1989) on the number of passengers in each direction and in each class for each day of the week. From the SAS timetable we have data on the number of flights and the aircraft used (mostly DC9; on two daily flights in each direction MD80 or the slightly larger MD87). On the basis of this information we have constructed a "representative" day of the week with nine flights in each direction, each carrying 52 Euroclass and 21 tourist class passengers.

We do not have data on actual prices paid, but we know the full fare (NOK 1,260, or $177, one way). We assume that 80 percent of the Euroclass passengers pay the full fare, while the remainder travel on discounts averaging 50 percent. For the tourist-class passengers, we have—arbitrarily—set the average discount at 50 percent. In computing average prices for the two classes, we have also deducted 7.5 percent for travel agency commissions, assuming (if the tickets are sold directly by SAS) that the commission reflects real costs associated with sales and ticketing. The prices are converted to dollars using the official SAS exchange rate of NOK 7.11 per dollar.

4.2.2   Costs

We do not have data for actual costs for the Oslo-Stockholm route,[3] so we have had to rely on ad hoc estimates and cost data reported in the literature. Marginal passengers costs are likely to be quite low. Safety regulations fix the minimum crew, and this minimum is usually sufficient even for a full plane. Fuel consumption depends on the weight of the plane, but the number of passengers has little impact on the total weight. The most important passenger-related costs are therefore catering expenses (very small on a short flight) and airport fees. In the base-case simulations reported in this paper, we arbitrarily set marginal passenger cost at $25. In the sensitivity analyses, we will see how the results are affected if instead marginal passenger costs are $20 or $30.

---

3. We asked SAS for cost data, but the company found such information to be too sensitive to give out.

As for the total cost per flight, there are several studies which give relevant data. We rely on two sources. Oster and McKey (1984) report actual 1982 costs for a 200-mile flight for three airlines—Southern, United, and Piedmont—using a Boeing 737, i.e., a plane very similar to the DC9 used by SAS and a distance very close to Oslo–Stockholm (249 miles). McGowan and Seabright (1989) report representative costs per available seat miles (ASM) for different planes. They also report, based on official industry sources, costs per tonkilometers performed for different airlines and a breakdown of those costs. Based on these, we make three alternative estimates, shown in table 4.1, of total costs for a representative Oslo-Stockholm flight.

The first alternative is based on the average direct cost per ASM for three of the planes reported in McGowan and Seabright—DC9–10, Boeing 737–200, and Boeing 737–300. None of these are used on the route today (SAS uses larger, newer versions of the DC9), but they should be representative of planes which could be used. We convert this into total cost per ASM using the actual SAS figures for direct costs as a percentage of total costs, then multiply by the distance (249 miles) and the number of seats (110) to get a total cost estimate. As the reported figures are for 1988, we add an arbitrary 5 percent to account for cost increases since then. This procedure gives a cost estimate of $3,241.

The second alternative is based on the McGowan and Seabright figure of $1.69 for SAS 1987 total costs per tonkilometer. It should be noted that the SAS figure is very much higher than the corresponding figures for other airlines. For U.S. airlines, they report costs of $0.68–$0.89, and for the two other European airlines in their sample (Alitalia and British Airways), the costs are

Table 4.1   **Alternative Total Cost Estimates**

	Estimate
Based on 1988 direct costs per available seat miles (ASM)	
Direct costs per ASM (¢)	4.26[a]
Indirect SAS costs (% of total costs)	62.2
Estimated total costs per ASM (¢)	11.27
Estimated total costs, 110 seats, 249 miles ($)	3,087
Adjusted for 5 percent cost increase since 1988 ($)	3,241
Based on 1987 costs per tonkilometers performed	
Average SAS cost per tonkilometer ($)	1.67
Estimated tonkilometers, 73 passengers, 100 kilos, 249 miles	2.945
Estimated total costs, 73 passengers, 249 miles ($)	4.918
Adjusted for 10 percent cost increase since 1987 ($)	5.409
Based on 1982 costs for United	
Total United costs, 200 miles, Boeing 737 ($)	3.600
Adjusted to 249 miles ($)	4.482
Adjusted for 35 percent cost increase since 1982	6.051

Sources: McGowan and Seabright (1989); Oster and McKey (1984).

[a]For 125 seats: obtained as average of values for DC 9-10 (92 seats, 5.92¢ per ASM), Boeing 737-200 (133 seats, 3.92¢ per ASM), and Boeing 737-300 (149 seats, 2.94¢ per ASM).

$0.80 and $0.83, respectively. To some extent the difference can be explained by the shorter hauls of the SAS network. Still, the figures may suggest that the SAS figures include costs not directly related to air transportation or that there is substantial inefficiency in SAS operations. We convert the SAS costs per tonkilometer to total costs for the route by using the actual (average) number of passengers and assuming an average weight (including baggage) of 100 kilos per passenger. Adding an arbitrary 10 percent to account for cost increases since 1987, this method yields a total cost estimate of $5,409.

The third method is based on the actual 1982 total cost figures for U.S. airlines reported by Oster and McKey. This was before the full effects of U.S. deregulation had been felt; significantly, their figures show that the established carrier (United) had very much higher costs than the other two. We use the United figure, assume that costs rise proportionally with distance, and add 35 percent for cost increases since 1982. That gives a total cost estimate as high as $6,051.

Of the three estimates, it is likely that the first is an underestimate and the last is an overestimate. The first method is likely to lead to an underestimate because (a) the aircraft used represent an older and cheaper generation than the planes actually used by SAS and (b) costs per ASM are lower for long than for short hauls, and the Oslo–Stockholm route is probably shorter than the average route for which these aircraft are used. The third method is likely to overestimate because (a) the 1982 United costs were much higher than the costs of the other carriers and (b) costs do not, as we have assumed, rise proportionally with distance.

In the simulations, we take a total cost of $4,800 as our base case. This is close to the average ($4,900) of the estimates obtained from the three alternative approaches. Because of the divergence, however, we also calibrate and simulate the model for the higher cost figures of $5,800 and $6,800. The last of these is included, even though it is outside the cost range indicated in table 4.1, because SAS—in a public reaction to an earlier draft of this paper—indicated that its actual costs for the route are that high.[4]

4.2.3   Calibration

Knowing prices, departures, passengers per flight, and costs, the remaining unknowns are the demand function parameters (the elasticities of the $N(v)$ functions and the shadow wage rates). The demand-side parameters are calibrated to satisfy the first-order conditions for a profit-maximizing monopolist. There are three relevant conditions: the marginal revenue = marginal cost conditions for the pricing of Euroclass and tourist class seats, respectively, and the condition that the monopolist have a profit-maximizing number of flights. The

---

4. SAS stated that our estimate of $4,800 was 30 percent below the actual costs of the company for the Oslo–Stockholm route, i.e., that actual costs are around $6,800. We suspect, however, that such a figure includes allocated fixed costs for the SAS system as a whole.

first two conditions determine the price elasticity of demand for a particular flight, equal to the ratio of price to (price − marginal cost); with a marginal cost of $25, the implied price elasticities are, respectively, 1.2 and 1.5 for Euro- and tourist class. From equation (14), we see that given the price elasticity, we can solve for e or w as function of the other. The optimum condition with respect to the number of flights involves passengers per flight, prices, marginal passenger costs, and the marginal cost per flight—all of which we know. In addition, it involves e and w for each of the two classes. All told, therefore, we have three equations to solve for e and w in each of the two classes. The missing equation is obtained by assuming that the shadow wage for tourist-class passengers is 40 percent of the Euroclass shadow wage. Using this and solving the full set of equations, we get shadow wages of $57 in the Euroclass segment and $23 in tourist class, and elasticities of the $N(v)$ functions of 1.36 and 1.67, respectively. The full set of data and calibrated parameter values for the base case is shown in table 4.2.

4.3   Simulation Results

We use the model to simulate the effects of entry. An oligopoly equilibrium is assumed to be perfectly symmetric, so SAS and new entrants will have equal numbers of flights and charge the same price. We do not try to analyze entry barriers (fixed costs or artificial barriers) but simply look at equilibria with different numbers of firms. In the calculations, we take account of integer constraints on the number of flights offered by each carrier, so the number of flights is determined by the maximum number of flights per carrier consistent with positive marginal profitability of new flights. We also take into account capacity constraints on each flight. We, arbitrarily, assume that the average load factor cannot exceed 80 percent and include a shadow price of capacity in the pricing equation to account for this constraint. In all the oligopoly cases, the capacity constraint is binding.

Table 4.2   **Data Set and Calibrated Coefficients**

	Total	Euro class	Tourist Class
Stylized data			
Number of flights	9		
Passengers per flight	73	52	21
Price ($)		148	74
Marginal passenger cost ($)	25		
Total cost per flight ($)	4,800		
Calibrated coefficients			
Price elasticity of demand		1.20	1.51
Marginal cost per flight ($)	2,975		
Shadow wage ($ per hour)		57	23
Elasticity $(-(N'v)/N)$		1.36	1.67

Table 4.3   **Summary of Results**

	SAS Monopoly	Duopoly	Three-firm Oligopoly	Four-firm Oligopoly
Consumer gains				
Number of flights	9	12	15	16
Change in average price (%)		−29.7	−39.5	−42.1
Change in number of passengers (%)		60.7	100.9	114.3
Change in consumer surplus ($ per day)		38,143	55,748	61,047
Change in consumer surplus (% of initial consumer expenditure)		45.8	67.0	73.3
Producer losses				
Change in SAS profits ($ per day)		−24,050	−32,200	−34,923
Change in foreign airline profits ($ per day)		16,000	15,700	15,382
Sum of producer losses ($ per day)		8,050	16,500	19,540
Welfare changes (% of total initial consumer expenditure)				
World		36.1	47.1	49.9
Scandinavia		16.9	28.3	31.4
Norway		14.7	22.4	24.7
Sweden		10.5	16.9	18.7
Denmark		−8.3	−11.1	−12.0

The main results are shown in table 4.3. The welfare effects for Scandinavia are calculated assuming that 50 percent of the passengers on the route are Norwegians and 50 percent Swedes and using the ownership shares in SAS (Norway and Denmark 2/7 each, Sweden 3/7). It is assumed that new entrants are from outside Scandinavia.

As we can see, the simulations indicate very substantial gains from entry—particularly from entry by one firm (giving a consumer gain of 45.8 percent and an efficiency gain of 36.1 percent of initial consumer expenditure). The simulations also indicate significant profit shifts, however: More than half of the net gain will accrue to the new entrant, so if the new firm is non-Scandinavian, more than half the net gain will "leak out."

4.3.1   Sensitivity: Bertrand versus Cournot

To see whether our assumption that the oligopoly equilibrium involves Bertrand price competition is important, we also simulate the effects of entry assuming Cournot competition in the number of seats offered on each flight. A comparison of the Bertrand and Cournot duopoly solutions is given in table 4.4.

As is seen, the simulated equilibria are virtually identical, except as regards the degree of price discrimination between Euroclass and tourist-class passengers: As should be expected, Cournot competition (being less aggressive than Bertrand) involves greater price discrimination; consequently, the relative price of Euroclass tickets falls more in the case of Bertrand than in the Cournot case.

Table 4.4   **Cournot versus Bertrand Duopoly**

	Bertrand Duopoly	Cournot Duopoly
Consumer gains		
Number of flights	12	12
Change in average price (%)	−29.7	−29.6
Change in Euroclass price (%)	−37.2	−36.8
Change in tourist-class price (%)	−1.7	−3.7
Change in number of passengers (%)	60.7	60.7
Change in consumer surplus ($ per day)	38,143	37,939
Change in consumer surplus (% of initial consumer expenditure)	45.8	45.6
Producer losses		
Change in SAS profits ($ per day)	−24,050	−24,015
Change in foreign airline profits ($ per day)	16,000	16,035
Sum of producer losses ($ per day)	8,050	7,979
Welfare changes (% of total initial consumer expenditure)		
World	36.1	36.0
Scandinavia	16.9	16.7
Norway	14.7	14.5
Sweden	10.5	10.4
Denmark	−8.3	−8.2

4.3.2   Sensitivity: Cost Parameters

To see how sensitive the results are with respect to our cost estimates, for the duopoly cases, we also simulate the effects assuming higher total costs and higher marginal passenger costs. For total costs, the base case is total costs of $4,800 per flight (at the initial load factor); as alternatives, we also look at total costs of $5,800 and $6,800. For marginal passenger costs, we assume $20 and $30 as alternatives to the base-case assumption of $25. The results are shown in table 4.5. As is seen, the general conclusions are not very sensitive to the underlying cost assumptions.

4.3.3   Sensitivity: Initial Regulation

The last simulation experiment we carry out relates to the initial equilibrium for the route. We assume that SAS initially behaves as an unregulated monopolist. In fact, SAS is subject to government regulation, in the sense that both prices and schedules have to be approved by Norwegian and Swedish authorities. It is unclear whether, or to what extent, regulation is binding. Insofar as our calibrated coefficients seem "reasonable," the regulatory constraints cannot be severe.

To see how important initial regulation may be, however, we also calibrate the model assuming binding regulatory constraints on SAS initially. Specifically, we have assumed a 10 percent wedge between marginal revenue and marginal cost both with respect to pricing and frequency—in other words,

Table 4.5   **Sensitivity Analysis: Total and Marginal Cost**

Total Cost ($)		Marginal Passenger Cost ($)		
		20	25	30
4,800	Departures	14	12	12
	Price change (%)	−35.8	−29.7	−30.3
	Consumer surplus change (%)	62.5	45.8	44.8
	World welfare change (%)	49.0	36.1	33.1
	Scandinavian welfare change (%)	31.7	16.9	14.9
5,800	Departures	12	10	10
	Price change (%)	−26.9	−19.4	−19.4
	Consumer surplus change (%)	46.9	28.6	28.6
	World welfare change (%)	39.2	25.1	24.2
	Scandinavian welfare change (%)	24.4	8.2	7.7
6,800	Departures	10	10	8
	Price change (%)	−18.5	−18.3	−8.9
	Consumer surplus change (%)	27.9	27.6	8.8
	World welfare change (%)	25.3	24.3	10.2
	Scandinavian welfare change (%)	13.4	12.7	−3.7

Note: Changes in consumer surplus and welfare are expressed as percentages of initial consumer expenditures.

regulation forces SAS to offer so many more seats on each flight, and so many more departures, that marginal revenue is uniformly 10 percent below marginal cost. The implication is that the initial average price is some 15 percent below the monopoly price, and SAS initially would have liked to offer only seven departures per day (compared to the actual figure of nine departures).

The results are shown in table 4.6. Note again the robustness of the general results: The effects of competition will be very similar whether the initial equilibrium is interpreted as one of regulated or unregulated monopoly.

4.3.4   Other Sensitivity Tests

We have also carried out two other sensitivity tests. Details of those tests will not be reported here, but let us point out the general conclusions. One test concerns initial prices. In the experiments reported above, the model is calibrated to an average discount fare of 50 percent of the Euroclass fare. Alternatively, we have carried out calibration and simulations assuming an average discount fare of 30 percent. The corresponding simulations give slightly *higher* welfare gains from competition. The reason is that a lower initial tourist-class fare implies a higher elasticity of demand in the tourist-class segment and thus a large efficiency loss from monopoly.

The other sensitivity test concerns the form of the demand function. Instead of assuming a loglinear $N(v)$ function, we have calibrated the model and carried out simulation experiments using a linear $N(v)$ function. By itself, a linear function would reduce the value of extra flights and should therefore give

Table 4.6   Importance of Initial Regulation

	Initially Unregulated			Initially Regulated		
	Total	Euroclass	Tourist class	Total	Euroclass	Tourist class
Calibrated coefficients						
e (elasticity of N (v))		1.36	1.67		1.30	1.56
w (shadow wage)		57	23		45	18
Unregulated monopoly compared to Initial equilibrium						
Price change (%)				15.5	16.2	12.7
Demand change (%)				−18.6	−18.8	−18.3
Consumer surplus change (%)				−16.6	−17.2	−13.5
Scandinavian welfare change (%)				−11.8		
Duopoly compared to initial equilibrium						
Price change (%)	−29.7	−37.2	−1.7	−30.8	−38.6	−0.5
Demand change (%)	60.7	82.5	6.9	60.7	83.8	3.7
Consumer surplus change (%)	45.8	54.2	4.5	46.4	55.3	2.5
Scandinavian welfare change (%)	16.9			16.6		

Note: Changes in consumer surplus and welfare are expressed as percentages of initial consumer expenditure.

smaller efficiency gains from competition. That is offset by the calibration procedure, however. Since the model has to support the actual, initial number of flights, a functional form which gives lower value to extra flights must give higher calibrated opportunity time costs. It is not *a priori* clear, therefore, how the choice of functional form would affect the simulated efficiency gains. In fact, it hardly matters: The order of magnitude of the welfare gains are the same for the loglinear and linear functions.

4.4   Conclusions and Extensions

The analysis indicates that there would be very significant effects of entry into the Oslo–Stockholm market. Prices could fall dramatically, and there could be some (more modest) increase in flight frequency. Consumer gains would, not surprisingly, outweigh SAS losses. Moreover, and perhaps more surprisingly, even though there would be a significant shift of profits from SAS to new entrants, the net welfare effect on Scandinavia would be positive and significant even if the entrants came from outside Scandinavia.

The analysis also indicates that these conclusions are robust, both with respect to the average and marginal costs of the firms and to the nature of the market game. In particular, it does not seem to matter greatly whether a future oligopoly equilibrium involves price or quantity competition.

The reason the two equilibria are virtually identical is that the capacity constraint on each flight is binding in all our simulated equilibria. That suggests that it may be worthwhile to incorporate optimum choice of aircraft (size) into the simulations. That is one natural extension of our work.

Another natural extension is to look at entry and exit games. We have not looked at the likelihood of entry at all. To see whether deregulation *will* make new firms enter, one should analyze the optimum behavior of SAS vis-à-vis potential entrants and look at the welfare implications of such behavior. Nor have we looked at the sustainability of an oligopolistic equilibrium. Given the U.S. deregulation experience, it would be worthwhile to study strategic interaction between firms in a setting where each knows that exit is an option. Our simulation model seems suitable to such experiments. To carry them out, however, we would need estimates of fixed costs associated with maintaining the route.

References

Baldwin, R., and H. Flam. 1989. Strategic trade policy in the market for 30–40 seat commuter aircraft. *Weltwirtschaftlisches Archiv* 125(3): 485–500.

Baldwin, R., and P. R. Krugman. 1987. Market access and competition: A simulation study of 16K random access memories. In *Empirical methods in international trade,* ed. R. Feenstra. Cambridge: MIT Press.

DeVaney, A. S. 1975. The effect of price and entry regulation on airline output, capacity and efficiency. *Bell Journal of Economics* 6(1):327–45.

Douglas, G. W., and J. C. Miller, Jr. 1974. *Economic regulation of domestic air transport: Theory and policy.* Washington, D.C.: Brookings Institution.

Helpman, E., and P. R. Krugman. 1989. *Trade policy and market structure.* Cambridge: MIT Press.

Jordan, W. A. 1970. *Airline regulation in America: Effects and imperfections.* Baltimore: John Hopkins University Press.

McGowan, F., and P. Seabright. 1989. Deregulating European airlines. *Economic Policy* no. 9 (October): 283–344.

Norman, V. (1989). Trade policy under imperfect competition: Theoretical ambiguities—Empirical regularities? *European Economic Review* 33:473–79.

Oster, C. V., Jr., and A. McKey. 1984. The cost structure of short-haul air service. In *Deregulation and the new airline entrepreneurs,* ed. John R. Meyer and Clinton V. Oster, Jr. Cambridge: MIT Press.

Smith, A., and A. J. Venables. 1986. Trade and industrial policy under imperfect competition. *Economic Policy* 1(3): 622–72.

Strandenes, Siri Pettersen. 1987. Scandinavian airline industry. Market structure and competition. *Report no. 21/87.* Bergen: Centre for Applied Research.

5 Industrial Policy in the Transport Aircraft Industry

Gernot Klepper

5.1 Introduction

Large commercial aircraft production is one of the areas in which the United States accuses European governments of unfair trade practices. Airbus Industrie is undoubtedly heavily supported by subsidies from all participating countries. From 1970 up to today, at least $11–$12 billion (U.S.) has been paid by European governments—some American estimates of that support come to as much as $20 billion (U.S.)—and the development of the A330/340 will require several billion dollars more in the next few years. The cause for these payments was the decision of European governments in the late 1960s to support the entry of a European competitor in the market for large transport aircraft.

Up to now these subsidies have been predominantly paid to finance start-up investments of the now-existing and planned fleet of aircraft—the A300, A310, A320, A330, A340, most likely the A321, and possibly a military freighter. This situation might change in the future, because the German government has agreed to grant production subsidies under specific circumstances. By the end of 1989 Daimler-Benz had merged with MBB, the German partners of Airbus Industrie, and a precondition of Daimler-Benz's acquiring the risky commercial aircraft business was a long-term exchange rate guarantee from the German government. Since aircraft are sold in U.S. dollars worldwide, this could amount to a sizable production subsidy if the DM/dollar exchange rate stays below 1.80 for a considerable time, e.g., in 1990 some 240 million DM will be paid to German Airbus.

This government-supported market entry and the exchange rate guarantees make it an interesting goal to analyze the strategic trade policy issue of European government intervention. One aspect of this competition between Euro-

Gernot Klepper is a researcher at the Kiel Institute of World Economics and a research fellow of the Centre for Economic Policy Research.

pean and American producers was examined by Baldwin and Krugman (1988), who developed a simulation model for the entry of the Airbus A300 in the market for medium- to long-range wide-bodied jet aircraft. The A300 was the first aircraft to be launched by Airbus, and it entered a market segment—a "window," as it is called in the industry—which had appeared in the 1970s due to the strong expansion of air traffic. At that time, Airbus was in an ambiguous situation: it was a new entrant to the overall market for large transport aircraft competing with well-established firms, but it was the first to enter the market segment for which the A300 was designed, whereas deliveries of Boeing's new 767 started six years later.

Baldwin and Krugman explained this situation of being a first-mover and at the same time having little chance to make profits on the A300 by cost differences between Airbus and Boeing—that is, Airbus had an approximately 17 percent higher unit cost at the same scale of production (1988, 25). This apparent cost disadvantage has been attributed by company officials to accumulated learning effects in the production of other aircraft types. They claim that such economies of scope account for Airbus's lack of success, hence the decision to develop the A320/321 and A330/340 in order to supply a complete family of aircraft. One purpose of this paper is to look at the effects of the market entry of Airbus by taking into account the complete family of aircraft.

The simulation model of Baldwin and Krugman uses government support that essentially supports the fixed costs of start-up investments and thus enables the firm to accept a lower than average profitability or even losses. Direct production subsidies, which have been minor in the past, seem to have become more important with the devaluation of the dollar. If the dollar stays at the fall 1990 level there will be substantial subsidies to be paid, at least by the German government. The comparative advantage of the American civil aircraft industry will deteriorate, and political pressures on the U.S. government to retaliate against such policies will increase. The already ongoing dispute about aircraft subsidies will most likely intensify. How such European subsidization of sales and potential American retaliation might affect competition among aircraft producers as well as welfare in the different regions is another topic to be looked at in this paper.

This paper uses the conceptual ideas of Spence (1981) and Baldwin and Krugman (1988) to model the long-term impact of dynamic learning effects on competition. The same approach has also been used by Baldwin and Flam (1989) in a simulation study of the commuter aircraft market. The present effort deviates in its calibration philosophy. Commonly, producer cost differences are calibrated according to market shares: a producer with a large market share is presumed to have lower costs. The source of such cost differences remains unexplained. In this paper, it is assumed that technical know-how is available equally to all producers and that factor prices do not deviate greatly between Europe and North America. The question then is, can the existing market shares and those which are expected for the coming years be reasonably explained without factor price or technological differences?

We show that this is possible by accounting for different times of market entry in the three market segments by two producers: a newcomer and an incumbent. Yet, if the model is calibrated to such a situation, the claim of Airbus officials that Airbus will become profitable as soon as it can supply a complete family of aircraft can not be supported by the simulations.

The paper starts with a short introduction to the specific features of the market for transport aircraft. It is followed by the presentation of the calibration model and a discussion of the calibration procedure. The welfare effects of Airbus market entry are assessed by comparing the existing duopoly to a potential American monopoly and to a potential American duopoly. Then the allocation and welfare effects of an ad valorem subsidy to Airbus are simulated. Finally, the impact of potential retaliation by the American administration on competition among European and American producers is analyzed.

5.2 Industry Characteristics

Today there are three large producers of large transport aircraft: Boeing (over 50 percent market share), Airbus (30–35 percent), and McDonnell Douglas (10–15 percent). Other civil aircraft forms a relatively minor part of the industry in terms of value. In the United States, large transport aircraft covers about 70 percent of all civil aircraft industry shipments. Light transport aircraft, helicopters, business aircraft, and other aircraft account for the rest (U.S. Department of Commerce 1986). The three large producers are embedded in a network of subcontractors that supply aircraft parts. Most important, the engines, amounting to 20–30 percent of the value of an aircraft, are developed by outside companies. Avionics, systems, and components (brakes, tires, etc.) are often subcontracted as well.

The market is small in terms of number of aircraft sold, but each aircraft is an expensive product. Every year, 400 to 500 large transport aircraft are expected to be sold, allowing for some yearly fluctuation. Aircraft prices range from $25 to $30 million for a Boeing 737, to $30 to $32 million for an A320, to around $120 million for a Boeing 747. The relatively small number of aircraft sold goes hand in hand with a long product cycle: it takes five to six years from launch to first delivery. Then an aircraft has a product cycle of at least 20–25 years, during which it may be upgraded to new technological standards.

Large transport aircraft have a complex production technology that results in strong learning effects. An essential part of learning appears in the assembly of an aircraft, which requires craftsmanship and the careful timing of thousands of activities. Such experience is embodied in the work force and accumulates with the number of aircraft that have been produced. There is worldwide consensus that aircraft production exhibits a learning elasticity of 0.2; that is, production costs decrease by 20 percent with a doubling of output (Berg and Tielke-Hosemann 1987; U.S. Department of Commerce 1986; see fig. 5A.1 in the appendix for some empirical examples). Whereas start-up investments and R&D are costly in absolute terms, the economies of scale are dominated by learning effects which amount to 90 percent of the overall economies of scale. Some production stages are not specific to a particular type of aircraft, so that learning effects which are realized in the production of a generic aircraft can influence the marginal cost of producing another generic aircraft. Such cross-effects are strong for updated versions of an aircraft, the so-called derivatives. These effects can be captured by economies of scope. Industry characteristics can then be summarized as (i) static economies of scale (R&D and start-up investment), (ii) dynamic economies of scale (learning in production), and (iii) economies of scope (cross-effects of learning).

5.2.1 Competition

Aircraft producers compete in essentially two ways. There is first the long-run decision about product choice and capacity. The demand in each segment even over a long time horizon is small in terms of the number of aircraft: 3,000 to 4,000 units each in the short- and medium-range markets and around 2,000 units in the long-range market are the expected market sizes over the next 20 years. Since learning effects are embodied in the work force, capacity choice becomes the crucial long-run decision variable.

There is, of course, limited information about future demand. Market forecasts by the large producers over the next 20 years, however, do not differ greatly, suggesting that the game is played under identical expectations. Figure 5.1 illustrates the different types of aircraft that are currently offered by the three producers, according to range and seating capacity. In each of the market segments—short-range narrow-bodied, short- and medium-range wide-bodied, and long-range aircraft—Airbus and Boeing offer competing generic aircraft, with possible derivatives.

Once capacity is determined, aircraft producers have limited choice over short-run output levels. They essentially produce at full capacity; that is, their time profile of deliveries is determined. A decision to increase capacity is then comparable to a new start on the learning curve.[1] The producers then bargain with airlines in their day-to-day marketing activities over the price of aircraft. Airlines seem to make extensive use of repeated negotiations with the suppliers of an aircraft for a specific market segment. Competition takes the form of a price game at given capacity levels, where the outcome of the long-run quantity game then becomes a restriction in the short-run price game. If demand turns out to be larger than expected, firms will produce at their capacity limit and choose prices which maximize profits. For unexpectedly low demand, the

---

1. This is supported by the evidence about capacity expansions in Boeing's production plants, which did at first result in very little output effects but in embarrassing quality problems.

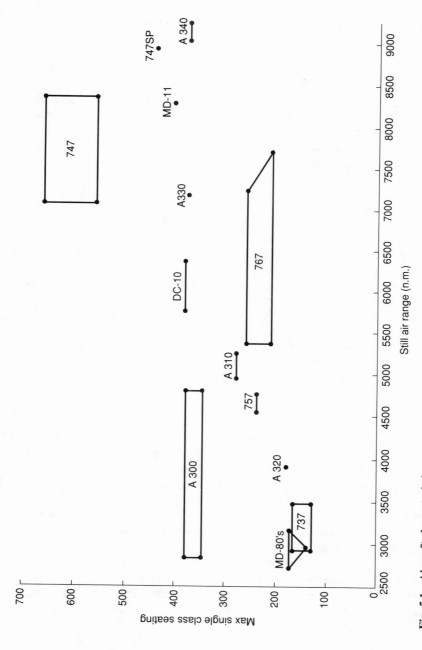

Fig. 5.1 Aircraft characteristics
Source: Hofton (1987)

price game may drive prices down to marginal cost levels. In extreme cases, "white tails" are produced; that is, aircraft are produced without a customer in sight.

5.2.2   Market Entry

Entry in a market such as the one for large transport aircraft is an expensive and time-consuming effort. Dynamic and static economies of scale together with economies of scope give incumbent firms a considerable competitive advantage. It is therefore not surprising that the market entry of Airbus was accompanied by the heavy involvement of European governments. After several commercially unsuccessful projects, European aircraft producers were not willing to take yet another gamble.

When in the 1960s European aerospace firms were considering entering the market for large transport with a new generation of aircraft, this market was almost completely dominated by the three American producers—Boeing, McDonnell Douglas, and Lockheed. Previously produced European aircraft had not been successful commercially, and the belief was that no non-American producer could compete in size with the three firms. In this situation, market entry can be viewed as the first stage of a three-stage decision process. First, commitment by European governments to subsidize the launch of a new aircraft was necessary since, apparently, financing on capital markets without state support was not possible. Second, firms had to decide which market segment to enter, and they had to choose a capacity which would allow them to capture the learning effects of large-scale production and at the same time keep prices at a profitable level. Finally, once the first two decisions were made, firms had to compete with the other producers in the day-to-day business of selling their product.

The first decision must be made under great uncertainty, and not only economic but also political arguments govern this process. Industrial policy aspects such as civil-military interaction in the aerospace industry were important. From the perspective of European firms, government support turned out to be essential. Not only is the financial burden for the launch of a completely new aircraft high, but the commitment by governments to support market entry could also prevent incumbent firms from starting a price war in the hope of stripping the entrant of its financial resources (Brander and Spencer 1983). When the Bonner Protokoll of September 1967 gave British, French, and German governmental support to the launch of the A300 (Berg and Tielke-Hosemann 1987, 1988), the first-stage was considered finished.

Once the A300 came to the market in 1974, airlines were not enthusiastic about buying a new aircraft from a new producer. Parts, maintenance, training, etc., did not fit the products of Boeing, Lockheed, or McDonnell Douglas. Although the A300 was designed to close the window for a high-capacity short- to medium-range transport aircraft and this window surely existed, the market opportunities in this segment were unclear. Lockheed and McDonnell

Douglas were already engaged in head-to-head competition with their L1011 and DC-10. The low prices of these two aircraft could make them competitive even in the shorter-range market segment of the A300. It became clear that Airbus had to supply a complete family of aircraft in order to stay in the market in the long run. This also meant a new commitment by the participating governments to finance new types of aircraft, since the A300 and later the A310 were not even close to their break-even points.

The political decision in the 1960s to support a European civil aircraft industry by subsidizing the development of one new aircraft, the A300, has over time turned into the need to subsidize the market entry of a producer of a complete family of aircraft. Subsidies and guarantees are given today for the development and launch of the A330 and the A340, but this is not necessarily the last step. Airbus has not yet internalized learning and scale effects in the same way as the established producers. The cost disadvantage of later market entry still exists. Airbus competes in market segments in which Boeing has already realized large learning effects and is able to produce at lower marginal cost.

Such a situation invites governments not only to support market entry but to subsidize the domestic firm in order to capture rents from the foreign firm. Brander and Spencer (1985) have shown that in a Cournot-Nash game subsidies paid by one government to its domestic producer who is selling its products in a third country increases profits and welfare. Can Europe gain by not only supporting market entry but also subsidizing the production of its domestic producer? In the past such subsidies have not been paid in significant amounts, but recently, at least by the German government, considerable price support has been given. This development and the impact of potential retaliation by the American government will be included in the simulation exercises.

5.3   The Model

For the purposes of this paper the political decision to support market entry is taken as given. Up to now this support has taken the form of financing the launch investment. Such fixed-cost subsidies do not affect the capacity decisions of the producers. Government support, therefore, only makes credible that the entrant will stay in the market even if entry is not profitable over the planning horizon. Entry-deterring pricing strategies by the incumbent producer are therefore not rational. With entry "exogenously" given, the game amounts to a Cournot-Nash game in capacity over the planning horizon. The possibility that European governments will pay and may already have paid production subsidies is taken up later. Past production subsidies and marketing aid are small compared to the subsidization of the launch investment (Coopers & Lybrand 1988). The amount of production subsidies to be paid in the future is unknown, since these subsides are made dependent on exchange rate developments.

The short-run price game naturally can not be empirically investigated, since it depends on the actual development of demand in the future. Historical examples show that aircraft prices fluctuate with demand; in 1979–83 rebates of up to 20 percent were not uncommon, according to airline officials. Apart from such demand fluctuations, real aircraft prices tend to remain constant over a product cycle. Our focus will be exclusively on the capacity game played between two producers, which one could imagine as being Airbus Industrie and Boeing. McDonnell Douglas is left out of the model, since it has not developed a really new aircraft and seems to function more as a competitive fringe. Until the Pentagon issued a large order for military tanker aircraft recently, there had been doubts whether McDonnell Douglas would stay in the civil market at all.

The model represents a stylized picture of the industry. In particular the production network of a large number of subcontractors is ignored. The producers are modeled as decision units and production units. This approach implicitly assumes that subcontractors have production technologies similar to those of the main firm, i.e., that they experience similar learning effects. An alternative model would only investigate the value added inside the two main producers and assume that intermediate products are bought from a competitive market, a less realistic assumption.

5.3.1 Supply Decision

Since an important part of the economies of scale of aircraft production are incorporated in the learning of the work force over time, a producer must essentially decide what the production capacity for a particular aircraft will be. In this model, entry times are treated as exogenous and correspond to the history of launches and the announced launch dates for the A330 and A340. At the beginning of the model's planning period each producer has to determine the capacity for every type of aircraft, whereby the cost function at that time is determined by the learning effect which has been accumulated in the past. This is done by choosing the rate of production for each aircraft. Profit maximization then requires balancing between large production rates with lower costs and sufficiently high prices which require low production rates.

In reality this will be a sequential decision with updates as time goes on and external parameters such as demand change. Nevertheless, capacity decisions do have a long-run character even if they are not made once and for all. A producer i therefore faces for a given capacity a flow of production y_{it}. The cumulative production x_{iT} at time T is then

$$(1) \qquad\qquad x_{iT} = \int_0^T y_{it}\, dt.$$

Capacity choice is then equivalent to the choice of x_{iT}.

Each producer has a cost function in terms of cumulated output which incorporates learning effects, fixed cost, and economies of scope. For the purpose of this model, the CES cost function proposed by Baumol, Panzar, and Willig (1982) is chosen. It can incorporate all the desired features. Dropping the time subscripts, the cost of producing $k = 1, \ldots, m$ products for producer i is

$$(2) \qquad C_i(x_i) = F_{ik} + \left(\sum_{k=1}^{m} a_{ik}\, x_{ik}^{\beta_{ik}} \right)^{\theta_i},$$

where F_{ik} is the fixed cost for product k; $a_{ik}, \beta_{ik}, \theta_i > 0$, for all i, k; $x_i = (x_{i1}, \ldots, x_{ik}, \ldots, x_{im})$.

It is assumed that both producers have the same cost function, i.e., that they are equally efficient. Since the incumbent has already realized learning effects he may be on a lower part of his learning curve thus having lower marginal cost. The multiproduct cost function $C_i(x_i)$ has the parameter restriction $0 < \theta_i < 1$, for all i, if there are economies of scope in the production of x. In the one-product case, the cost function reduces to the classic learning curve

$$(3) \qquad \frac{\partial C(x)}{\partial x} = \theta \beta a^{\theta}\, x^{\beta\theta - 1},$$

with learning elasticity

$$(4) \qquad \mu = \beta\theta - 1.$$

5.3.2   Aircraft Demand

All producers face the same expected inverse demand function for aircraft over the time horizon T,

$$(5) \qquad p_k = p_k(x_k, x_{-k}),$$

where

$$x_k = \sum_{i=1}^{n} x_{ik} \text{ and } -k = (1, \ldots, k-1, k+1, \ldots, m).$$

Each firm produces in each market segment an identical product which is subject to cross-price effects from other market segments. For the model simulation, a linear demand representation was chosen:

$$(6) \qquad \sum_{i=1}^{n} x_k = b_k + \sum_{k=1}^{m} d_k p_k,$$

where b_k and d_k are the demand parameters.

5.3.3   Equilibrium

The optimal capacity choice of the two producers, $i = A, B$, is found as the solution of a Cournot-Nash game with cumulated output x_{ik} as the strategic variables. The reaction functions have the familiar form. The optimal strategy of producer i, $(\hat{x}_{i1}, \ldots, \hat{x}_{im})$, is given by the m first-order conditions:

$$(7) \quad p_k \left(\sum_{j \neq i}^{n} x_k + \hat{x}_{ik}, x_{-k} \right) \left(1 + \frac{\hat{x}_{ik}}{\varepsilon_k \sum_{k=1}^{m} \hat{x}_{ik}} \right) = \frac{\partial C_i(\hat{x}_i)}{\partial x_{ik}}, \text{ for all } k = 1, \ldots, m$$

where ε_k is price elasticity of demand for product k. The pair $(\hat{x}_A, \hat{x}_B)$ with $\hat{x}_i = (\hat{x}_{i1}, \ldots, \hat{x}_{im})$, $i = A, B$, is a Nash equilibrium if it satisfies equation (7) for all $i = A, B$, and $k = (1, \ldots, m)$.

5.4   Calibration

The effects of market entry cannot be empirically investigated with historical data since Airbus is only now in the process of becoming a producer of a complete family of aircraft and none of its products have reached the end of a product cycle. The approach taken here relies on the history of Airbus and Boeing production up to 1986 and then uses demand forecasts by the large producers up to the year 2006 as an empirical basis for the calibration of the model. This time period covers a complete product cycle for practically all aircraft types modeled here. The Airbus A330 and A340 are the exceptions, because they will not enter the market before 1992. Therefore demand forecasts for the long-range market will not be an entirely adequate description of the demand over the product cycle for these two aircraft types.

Demand forecasts by Boeing were available for the period 1987–2000 (Boeing Company 1987), by McDonnell Douglas for 1987–2001 (McDonnell Douglas 1987), and by Airbus for 1987–2006 (Airbus Industrie 1987). McDonnell Douglas and Boeing forecast an overall demand for about 5,700 large transport aircraft, which if projected to 2006 would predict demand to be about 8,100 aircraft. The Airbus forecast is more optimistic in predicting a total market for 9,797 airplanes. Although all three producers operate with differently defined market segments, thus making comparisons difficult, the main difference can be attributed to a much larger Airbus prediction for the market for short- to medium-range wide-body aircraft. In light of recent experience with airport congestion, this trend toward larger aircraft seems realistic.

For the calibration of the model, three market segments were defined: a market for short- to medium-range narrow-body aircraft (S), one for short to medium-range wide-body aircraft (M), and one for long-range wide-body aircraft (L). For segment S the more conservative estimate of demand was used, mainly since McDonnell Douglas's MD80s compete in this segment but are not explicitly modeled and because of the recent trend toward larger aircraft. The Airbus estimate of about 3,200 aircraft for segment M was adopted. The 1,750 aircraft estimate adopted for segment L is closer to the projected Boeing estimate than to the Airbus and McDonnell Douglas forecasts. Since the A340 as a competitor for the Boeing 747 in market segment L will not enter service before 1993, this is a conservative estimate if the market over the whole product cycle is the basis for capacity decisions. In summary, the three market segments are calibrated to the following benchmarks:

$$x_S = 3,500, \ x_M = 3,200, \text{ and } x_L = 1,750.$$

Listed market prices do not exist for large transport aircraft. Because different customers get different rebates, varied specifications of airplanes, and different arrangements concerning training, spare parts, and maintenance, price documentation is difficult. The prices used here are average prices derived from listed contracts (*Interavia,* current issues) and interviews. They are modeled in constant prices and calibrated to the following approximate benchmarks:

$$P_S = 27, \ P_M = 62, \text{ and } P_L = 100.$$

Technological characteristics are the launch investment which is taken as a fixed cost. For aircraft launched before 1975 an estimate of $3 billion was taken (U.S. Department of Commerce 1986). Any later aircraft was assumed to have a launch cost of $4 billion (*Economist* 1988). Learning effects are generally believed to be strong. A learning elasticity of 0.2 is widely accepted as the correct benchmark for decreases in marginal cost. In the present model with output in the range of 1,000 to 3,000, one can compute directly the contributions of fixed cost and learning to the economies of scale. It turns out that launch investment accounts for only about 10 percent of the overall economies of scale.

Aircraft producers do not reveal marginal costs and synergy effects among the production of different types of aircraft. Airbus officials, however, claim that Airbus Industrie has reached the same level of efficiency as its American competitors. Since no other verifiable information is available, it is assumed that each producer has the same cost of producing the first airplane.

However marginal cost for different producers may differ widely at some point in time, since their aircraft were launched at different times. Suppose two producers have the same constant production rate and the same cost function but started production at different times. The difference in marginal cost at a particular date is then given by the distance between the two marginal cost curves. This difference becomes smaller the larger cumulative production is. Because of the relatively small number of aircraft produced, this difference is of particular importance in the aircraft industry. For the model calibration, accumulated production of Boeing types 737, 757, 767, and 747 and Airbus types A300 and A310 in each market segment up to 1987 entered the cost function as already acquired learning effects.

Since demand for transport aircraft is derived demand, the shape of the demand curve depends on the elasticity of demand for air transport, which is relatively low due to the absence of substitutes, and on the technology of producing air transport services. The price elasticity of demand for air transport seems to lie somewhere between -1.5 (Kravis, Heston, and Summers 1982) and -2.85 (commercial U.S. domestic passenger air service; Baldwin and Krugman 1988). The Baldwin and Krugman estimate is based on a market with larger cross-price elasticities. Therefore the "true" price elasticity for world air transport will most likely be closer to the Kravis et al. estimate. On the other hand, it is a well-known observation that estimated short-run elasticities are considerably smaller than their long-run counterparts. For large airlines the cost share of aircraft amounts to at most 20 percent of total operating cost, and the elasticity of substitution between aircraft and other inputs is low. Therefore the price elasticity of demand for aircraft in general will be rather small, most likely below one.

This finding does not fit the assumed Cournot-Nash framework of a capacity game, since it requires a much larger elasticity in order to attain an equilibrium. An alternative at this point would be to give up the notion of a capacity game and to look for different models that might more adequately describe competition in the aircraft industry without violating estimated parameters. Krugman and Brainard (1988) have tried alternative approaches but have not yet found a satisfying alternative to the capacity game. The other possibility is to assume the capacity game to be the correct model and to determine demand elasticities in the calibration procedure. This, of course, leads to elasticities that are higher than those derived from empirical estimates.

In this paper, the latter choice was taken, i.e., elasticities are treated as endogenous in this model. Assuming demand elasticities to be endogenous requires us to treat profit rates as exogenous, which follows necessarily from the first-order condition (eq. 7), which states that the price-cost markup is a function of market shares and demand elasticities, i.e., that

$$(8) \qquad \frac{p_k}{MC} = \left(1 - \frac{MS}{|\varepsilon|}\right)^{-1}.$$

Hence one is left with another unobservable variable. The choice of a rate of profit to calibrate the benchmark must therefore remain arbitrary. Several rates of profit (defined as the ratio of profit to revenue) have been tried in order to assess the robustness of the model with respect to this parameter. The lowest number for which an equilibrium could be established was 5.2 percent. The simulations were then run for different rates of profit between 5.2 and 7 percent. The resulting welfare effects remain stable in relative terms, whereas their absolute size changes slightly.[2] The simulations presented here are based on a rate of return of 5.5 percent, which represents the lowest price elasticity compatible with a robust model. The resulting direct price elasticities are larger than -2 and in the long-range market close to -1. Since the model has

---

2. For a listing of sensitivity analyses, see Klepper (1990, tables A.4 and A.5).

a linear demand system, the price elasticities vary slightly with the different simulations.

The parameter value for the degree of economies of scope had to be chosen arbitrarily. Its value of $\theta = .97$ can be interpreted as follows: the introduction of a new generic aircraft, when the firm has already experienced the learning effects of about 1,000 older and different aircraft, reduces marginal cost by some 30 percent compared to the situation where it produces its very first airplane as, e.g., in the case of the A300. For this model, in which both producers supply an aircraft in each size category, the impact of different degrees of economies of scope is marginal since the calibration procedure compensates these different degrees by adjusting the constant term of the learning curve. Economies of scope only become important if one firm produces only two types of aircraft. It would then be unable to compete with a full-scale supplier.

On the demand side, poor data availability would have required us to model demand for each type of aircraft independently by setting cross-price elasticities to zero. This was felt to be unrealistic for two reasons: first, there are obvious opportunities for airlines to substitute aircraft, though at considerable costs; second, without positive cross-price elasticities the price-cost markup for long-range aircraft would be much higher than even European supporters of the Airbus project would claim. The range of elasticities yielding reasonable equilibria was very narrow and confined to values below 0.2. Therefore a zero cross-price elasticity between small- to medium-range narrow-bodied (S) and long-range aircraft (L) was chosen. The elasticity between small- to medium-range narrow-bodied (S) and wide-bodied (M) as well as that between wide-bodied (M) and long-range (L) was set to 0.1.

The calibration proceeded then in the following steps. First, the remaining demand parameters and the cost parameters were derived under the assumption of two producers with identical technology and both on the same points of their learning curves; that is, the production prior to 1987 for each producer was taken to be the average of the Airbus and Boeing production in table 5.1. The benchmarks for total number of aircraft sold over the planning period and for aircraft prices are those given above. The resulting equilibrium has the producers equally sharing the total market. In the second step, the learning effects which each producer has already acquired before 1987 in the production of

Table 5.1   **Production up to 1987**

	Market Segment		
	S	M	L
Airbus	0	288	0
Boeing	1,070	149	609

Source: *Interavia* (current issues).

each aircraft type were used to determine the magnitude of the marginal cost function at the beginning of the planning period. For example, Boeing had already produced 1,070 aircraft in market segment S (see table 5.1); hence the marginal cost of the first aircraft produced in the planning period is derived by computing those costs using the calibrated parameters from the first step and taking the difference between Boeing's actual production and the average of the first step. The allocation derived through this procedure then predicts market shares and cost differences for the two producers; it will be referred to as the base-case calibration.

5.4.1   Base-case Results

The results of the base-case calibration are summarized in table 5.2. Under the assumption of equal technologies for both producers, output in the Nash equilibrium variers due to the cost advantages of previous learning. In market segment S, Boeing's marginal cost advantage is 23 percent, resulting in a market share of 31 percent for Airbus and leaving 69 percent for Boeing. In segment M, where Airbus has a slight advantage through the early launch of the A300, a marginal cost advantage of 6 percent translates into a 53 percent market share. Similarly for segment L, with cost differentials of 15 percent, market shares are 45 percent for Airbus and 55 percent for Boeing.

The expected profitability of the activities of the two producers can be computed either over the complete product cycle of their products, by including the sales prior to the start of the time horizon of the calibration, or for the time horizon of the calibration and the period before, separately. Table 5.3 presents all three computations. For simplicity the prices of aircraft prior to the calibration period are set equal to the calibrated prices. This underestimates the profitability of Boeing in a period where it had a monopoly in the long-range market with its 747 and also sold aircraft which are not counted here such as the 727.

The summary in table 5.3 shows how the late entry of Airbus affects profitability and production well into the next century. Airbus will have almost bro-

Table 5.2   **Market for Large Transport Aircraft:[a] 1987–2006 (base-case calibration)**

| | Market Segment | | | | | |
| | S | | M | | L | |
	Airbus	Boeing	Airbus	Boeing	Airbus	Boeing
Output	1,103	2,430	1,724	1,528	796	967
Market share (%)	31	69	53	47	45	55
Marginal cost	23.7	18.9	51.0	52.3	63.1	54.9
Price	27.7		62.5		101.0	

[a]For parameters, see Klepper (1990, table A1).

Table 5.3   **Revenues, Costs, and Profits**

	Airbus	Boeing
Revenue (billion $)		
Before 1987	18.0	100.5
1987–2006	218.8	260.6
Overall	236.8	361.1
Profits (billion $)		
Before 1987	−14.7	−7.6
1987–2006	11.9	53.0
Overall	−2.8	45.4
Profits/Revenue (%)		
Before 1987	−82.0	−7.6
1987–2006	5.4	20.3
Overall	−1.2	12.6

ken even by the end of our time horizon, but Boeing will have a rate of return of 12.6 percent. For the period 1987–2006 both Airbus and Boeing are profitable, if the start-up investment had high learning cost of the period to 1987 are not counted. These numbers give a rough indication of the cost disadvantage of Airbus in the 30 years after its market entry. At the end of this period, the comparison is not entirely correct, since by that time in market segments S and L Boeing will supply aircraft types which are at the end of their product cycles, whereas Airbus will have aircraft in the S and L segments which are still relatively new. Therefore Boeing will, during the time under investigation, face development costs for a new generation of aircraft.

5.5   Welfare

5.5.1   Effects of Airbus Market Entry

In order to assess the welfare consequences of government-supported market entry, a fictitious market structure without this entry has to be used as a reference allocation. One can imagine two scenarios which could have become reality after 1970. If, on one hand, concentration in the aircraft industry had continued in the 1970s as it had in the decades before and Airbus had not entered the market, Boeing might have eventually become a monopoly. If, on the other hand, the market were large enough for two or more producers and Lockheed or McDonnell Douglas were efficient producers, a duopoly such as the current situation might have emerged. The difference would be that the market would have two established producers instead of one new entrant and one incumbent. Both alternatives are simulated as benchmarks for the effects of alternative market structures.

Monopoly is simulated by leaving all parameters unchanged, except that there is only one producer, Boeing. Accumulated output in the monopoly situation is slightly smaller but not by a large amount, except in the long-range market segment, where the monopoly supplies almost 20 percent fewer aircraft. Prices rise between 3 percent and 16 percent. Profits to the monopolist almost triple so that the rate of profit over the whole product cycle increases from 12.5 percent in the base case to 27 percent in the monopoly case.

The second alternative is a duopoly with established producers of equal efficiency and thus on the same points of their learning curves. Consequently, they will share the market equally. This situation is simulated by assuming that at the beginning of the calibration period the same number of aircraft in each market segment have already been produced as in the base case. But this time the production has been shared equally by both producers. Only in the short-range narrow-body market does the overall output deviate significantly from the base case. This is induced by the large learning effects incorporated in the 1,070 aircraft produced prior to 1987 in the base case. Otherwise there is little deviation in the allocation from the base case.

Whereas the regional distribution of producer surplus is easy to determine, consumer surplus has to be approximated by the distribution of air traffic. Forecasted regional market shares (Airbus Industrie 1987) were used to distribute consumer welfare among Europe, the United States, and the rest of the world.

Table 5.4 summarizes the welfare effects of Airbus market entry when it is compared to a monopoly and when compared to a duopoly. If a monopoly were the alternative market structure, the market entry of Airbus could be considered successful from a consumer's point of view, but the overall welfare impact is negative. A consumer surplus gain of $36.8 billion is dominated by the producer surplus loss of $110.4 billion, most of which is the monopoly profit of Boeing (table 5.4). The regional distribution reveals welfare gains to Europe and the rest of the world, whereas in North America, i.e., the United States, consumers gain and producers lose.

The European producer surplus figures in table 5.4 do not include govern-

Table 5.4   **Distribution of Welfare Effects of Government-supported Market Entry (million 1986 $ U.S.)**

	Producer Surplus	Consumer Surplus	Total
Relative to monopoly			
Europe	−2,826	10,544	7,718
North America	−107,582	12,631	−94,951
Rest of world	0	13,630	13,620
Total	−110,408	36,795	−73,613
Relative to duopoly			
Europe	−2,826	−905	−3,731
North America	11,974	−1,405	10,569
Rest of world	0	−958	−958
Total	9,148	−3,268	5,880

ment subsidies. If indeed the projected $20 billion subsidies were paid by European governments and financed by European taxpayers, there would be a redistribution of consumer and producer surplus. Market entry would cost European consumers roughly $10 billion, but total welfare to Europe would remain unchanged. Taking these subsidies into account, government-supported market entry by Airbus as an antimonopoly policy—as has been claimed by European governments—did indeed help consumers, but only those outside Europe.

If the market entry of Airbus is compared to the hypothetical situation of a duopoly with equal, mature producers, a surprising welfare effect emerges. Overall welfare in the base case is $5.9 billion higher than in the reference situation. Consumers lose in all regions, but these losses are smaller than the gain in producer rents. Boeing has higher profits in the base case than do the two American producers in the hypothetical duopoly. Two forces, scale and scope effects and the competitive effect, can explain this result. Because of increasing returns to scale, the social optimum is one producer with marginal-cost pricing and large output and, consequently, lower average and marginal cost. The simulated duopoly situation forces both producers up their average cost curves.

In the base case, Boeing of course has lower and Airbus higher marginal cost than in the reference situation. But on average both producers together produce at lower average and marginal cost in the base case. This advantage does not show up in prices, it goes to Boeing in the form of profits. Therefore, the market entry of Airbus has forced Boeing into more competitive behavior than was necessary in a Boeing monopoly, but since Airbus is only a small producer, the scale effects of Boeing with its projected market share of around 60 percent are strong enough to compensate for the high-cost production of Airbus.

The simulations and the two alternative welfare comparisons in table 5.4 show that there is a conflict between competition effects—indirectly consumer-welfare and scale effects, i.e., overall welfare effects. Although the market is simulated to sustain two equal producers, welfare is larger in a monopoly situation, and even an inefficient second producer with small market shares is better than the hypothetical duopoly. This suggests that, in the market for large transport aircraft, scale and scope effects are strong enough to outweigh the output-reducing effects of increasing market power and—in the extreme—of a monopoly. If the model represents the replacement of an established American producer by a European entrant, Airbus, the regional distribution of welfare changes looks ironic. Only North America gains from the Airbus market entry.

5.5.2 Production Subsidies

Up to now simulations of industrial policy have focused only on supporting market entry by subsidizing start-up investments. This policy changes the incumbent's pricing policy. Entry-deterring pricing strategies are not rational, if the commitment of European governments is credible as it was in the case of Airbus. These subsidies do not, however, influence the capacity game between the two producers. This game can be influenced only if output decisions are influenced by production or price subsidies. It has been shown by Brander and Spencer (1985) that the optimal export subsidy rate is that which moves the reaction function of the subsidized firm to the point that would have been chosen by the firm if it were in a Stackelberg-leader position. Since in the case of aircraft, production in general is subsidized and there is domestic consumption, the optimal subsidy is higher than a subsidy on exports alone.

In order to determine the optimal subsidy for Airbus, alternative subsidy rates have been simulated. It was assumed that only those aircraft types are subsidized in which Boeing has an advantage in terms of learning effects, i.e., short- to medium-range narrow-body and long-range aircraft. The Cournot-Nash game is played in the same fashion and parameter values are unchanged. Figure 5.2 summarizes the output effects of the increasing subsidization of Airbus. Output is measured in total number of aircraft produced. Total output increases by only 6.6 percent if Airbus is subsidized with a 20 percent subsidy on price. Although only aircraft in two market segments are subsidized, Airbus increases its market share in all three segments: from 31 to 60 percent in the short- to medium-range, from 53 to 61 percent in the medium-range wide-

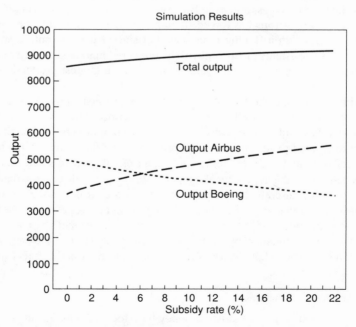

Fig. 5.2   Aircraft production with Airbus subsidies (simulation results)

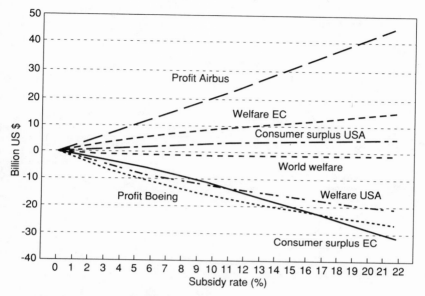

Fig. 5.3 Welfare effects of Airbus subsidies (simulation results)
Note: Consumer surplus EC is net of subsidy payments.

body and from 45 to 53 percent in the long-range market. Figure 5.3 summarizes the welfare effects of increased subsidization. Profits increase faster than subsidies, which does not come as a surprise since Airbus realizes learning effects through larger production, but since Boeing can sell fewer aircraft, prices fall only slightly. Subsidization, in a sense, induces a transfer of learning effects from Boeing to Airbus, leaving consumers relatively unaffected. European consumer surplus net of subsidy payments decreases, e.g., from $33 billion to $5.5 billion in the case of a 20 percent subsidy.

The effect on American and rest-of-the-world consumers and producers is essentially the opposite. There are small gains in consumer surplus due to a slight fall in prices both in the United States and the rest of the world. Boeing's loss in profits is larger than Airbus's profit increases net of subsidy payments. World welfare decreases by less than 1 percent.

Production subsidies have been varied over a large range, but there is no profit- or welfare-maximizing subsidy as in Brander and Spencer (1985). For subsidies higher than 22 percent no equilibrium can be simulated. The reason for this result is essentially the same as for the welfare effects of the market entry of Airbus in the previous section. Airbus profits net of subsidies as a function of subsidy rates are S-shaped, as shown in figure 5.4, with an inflection point around a subsidy rate of 10 percent. This, incidentally, is also the minimum of world welfare (fig. 5.4), and at this subsidy rate Airbus and Boeing have approximately equal market shares. The previous section showed that

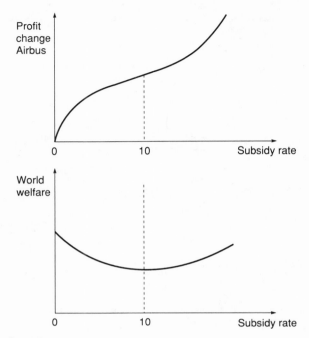

Fig. 5.4   Welfare effects of Airbus subsidies

a monopoly is in overall welfare terms superior to the current situation and even to a duopoly of two identical producers. Welfare effects of production subsidies follow the same logic. Increased subsidization of Airbus first leads to an equalization of market shares and therefore to higher unit cost on average. Hence, world welfare is reduced and the cost advantage of Boeing becomes smaller. Only when subsidization increases beyond 10 percent, does the difference in marginal cost become large enough to ensure that profits increase at a faster rate.

From both a pure profit-transfer perspective and a European welfare perspective, it would be advantageous to subsidize the domestic firm to such a degree that foreign competitors are driven out of the market. This particular simulation result for the aircraft industry depends predominantly on the assumed existence of large economies of scale and barriers to entry. Even though the market is large enough to support two firms—at least in the calibration of this model—a monopoly is superior to a duopoly in terms of world welfare. This result will most likely be true for industries with similar degrees of economies of scale. In that sense, there is a strong incentive to support domestic industry. Although in the present model Airbus is a producer with higher cost, it is advantageous to support the inefficient firm. These arguments, of course,

Table 5.5   **Market Structures with Optimal Production Subsidies**

| European Community/ Airbus | United States/Boeing | |
	Subsidize	Do not subsidize
Subsidize	?	Boeing monopoly
Do not subsidize	Airbus monopoly	duopoly (status quo)

remain valid only as long as retaliation from foreign governments is not considered.

5.5.3   Retaliation

The same logic according to which it is advantageous to subsidize Airbus applies, of course, to subsidizing Boeing, even more so since Boeing has lower unit cost because of learning effects from prior production. Both governments therefore have an incentive to subsidize their respective industries. The interaction of possible outcomes is shown in table 5.5.[3] Whether any government has a dominant strategy depends on the outcome of subsidization with retaliation.

In Brander and Spencer (1985) a Nash equilibrium in export subsidies exists. It is a prisoner's dilemma, since both countries could be better off by jointly reducing subsidy levels but would be worse off by unilaterally reducing subsidies. In the simulation model of this paper, an optimal unilateral subsidy level is not compatible with the existence of two firms. The same is true for retaliation against any subsidy that is low enough to allow both firms to stay in the market. Retaliatory subsidy rates also increase the welfare of the retaliating country up to the point where the foreign firm is driven out of the market. There is no Nash-duopoly equilibrium in government subsidies in this model, so if both governments subsidize, the question is which producer will survive.

Figure 5.5 shows the effects of subsidies on production. The curve labeled "Airbus subsidy effects" shows the different production equilibria traced out for different levels of unilateral production subsidy rates of Airbus by European governments, for a zero production subsidy rate to Boeing. As the European subsidy rate rises from 0 to 20 percent, Boeing output falls from nearly 5,000 to under 4,000, while Airbus output rises from around 3,500 to almost 5,500. The curve labeled "Boeing subsidy effects" shows the effects of varying the Boeing production subsidy rate from 0 to 3 percent, given an Airbus subsidy, which costs $14 billion; a 3 percent subsidy to Boeing, which will cost about $4 billion, will restore Boeing's output to presubsidy levels and therefore restore all of Boeing's learning advantages.

Airbus gains $10 billion of profits in comparison with the no-subsidy equi-

---

3. It is important to note that this comparison excludes all external economic or political costs of such governmental action.

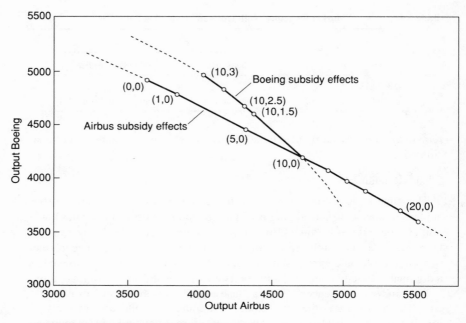

Fig. 5.5 Production effects of subsidies
Note: Numbers in parentheses denote subsidy rates for Airbus and Boeing, respectively.

librium, but the net loss to Europe is $4 billion. Faced with the threat of a Boeing subsidy, Europe does better to close Airbus down. Faced with the possibility of an Airbus production subsidy, the American government can credibly threaten to impose the relatively modest Boeing production subsidy that will make it optimal for Europe not to produce Airbus aircraft.

5.6 Conclusion

In this paper the allocation and welfare effects of industrial policy measures in an industry with strong economies of scale and high entry barriers have been investigated. Production of large transport aircraft has often been considered a prime candidate for the realization, similar to theoretical predictions, of potential welfare gains through industrial and trade policy measures. A stylized simulation model of competition in the aircraft industry is developed, focusing on two distinct industrial policy measures: first, European governmental support of the entry of Airbus Industrie in the market for large transport aircraft and, second, the potential impact of production subsidies, taking into consideration unilateral action as well as possible retaliation.

The welfare effects of government-supported market entry in the aircraft industry are somewhat difficult to interpret, because learning effects and economies of scope are so important that a monopoly would maximize world welfare—not considering distributional aspects. At the same time, the market is large enough to support two producers. It is also ambiguous which hypothetical situation the government-supported market entry of Airbus Industrie should be compared to.

When Airbus's entry is compared to a Boeing monopoly, overall welfare decreases. This is so because monopoly profits disappear, and, while consumers gain in all regions, they do so by less than the profit loss. The reason for this result is that scale and scope effects of producing large transport aircraft are strong enough to outweigh the output-reducing effects of a Boeing monopoly. From the viewpoint of European governments, Airbus's market entry as an "antimonopoly" policy was not successful. Only consumers in the rest of the world will gain. The negative welfare change is due to Airbus's inefficient scale of production relative to Boeing's and due to the high subsidies.

The negative welfare effects of Airbus's entry are even more pronounced when compared to a situation with two established American producers. Airbus's high-cost production yields higher welfare than a duopoly with two identical firms, because the scale effects of the large producer in the unequal situation dominate the competitive effects. Since consumers in all regions lose from Airbus's entry and the American producer, Boeing, gains more than American consumers lose, the market entry of Airbus yields a positive welfare change only in North America.

The basic logic behind these results is not peculiar to the aircraft industry. If economies of scale are large enough, a market structure with a small number of firms can emerge which is, in welfare terms, inferior to a monopoly. Because two or more firms can profitably stay in the market, economies of scale remain unexhausted and—at the same time—are larger than the losses in consumer surplus from monopoly pricing. In asymmetric situations—for example, one large and one small firm—scale effects also come into play. In a symmetric equilibrium, economies of scale are exploited to the least extent. The more asymmetric the equilibrium, the more consumers can gain from the realized economies of scale of the large producers and still have the more competitive output policy. This logic is present in the analysis of production subsidies as well.

Airbus, with a market share of about 30 percent, is the smaller firm. Unilateral subsidization of Airbus will reduce world welfare because of the scale effect just mentioned. The welfare minimum is indeed reached when both producers have approximately equal market shares. Beyond that point, it increases until the other producer leaves the market. Because overall welfare in a monopoly dominates oligopolistic industry structures and because it is usually newcomers and relatively small industries that are supported, the optimal subsidy is one which drives the other firm from the market, i.e., the Stackelberg-leader point is in a region of the other firm's reaction function in which it incurs losses.

With subsidization amounting to a monopolization of the market, retaliation is the natural consequence. The simulations show that the incumbent large firm, through small retaliatory subsidies, can easily be brought into a position where support by the foreign government can be neutralized. The ability and willingness to retaliate should therefore effectively threaten any desire to improve the market position of a small firm by subsidizing it.

This simulation study had to be based on extremely few observable parameters so that a number of educated guesses were necessary in order to attain the necessary degrees of freedom for calibration. The most crucial point is the demand elasticity which—compared to empirical predictions—must be higher for securing the existence of a Cournot-Nash equilibrium. If one takes this restriction as given, the sensitivity analysis of alternative values showed that there is only a very narrow range of elasticities for which equilibria exist and for which reasonable results of the calibration come out. Within this range, the welfare results of the simulation study remain robust, if not in their absolute value then in their distributional consequences. Within this Cournot-Nash capacity game framework, one can hardly come up with different welfare results. It remains to be explored, however, whether one can find a theoretical model which represents a reasonable capacity game and at the same time fits beliefs about demand elasticities for large transport aircraft.

Appendix

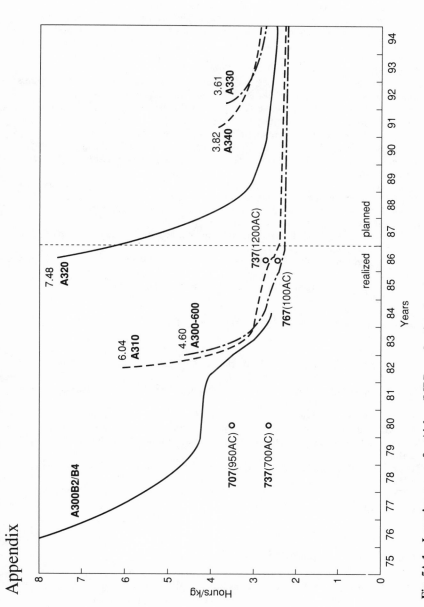

Fig. 5A.1 Learning curves for Airbus (MBB production share)
Source: Supplied by MBB, Germany.

References

Airbus Industrie. 1987. Global market forecast: 1987–2006. Blagnac.
Baldwin, Richard, and Harry Flam. 1989. Strategic trade policies in the market for 30–40 seat commuter aircraft. *Weltwirtschaflitches Archiv* 125 (3): 484–500.
Baldwin, Richard, and Paul R. Krugman. 1988. Industrial policy and international competition in wide-bodied jet aircraft. In *Trade policy issues and empirical analysis,* ed. R. E. Baldwin. Chicago: University of Chicago Press.
Baumol, William J., John C. Panzar, and Robert D. Willig. 1982. *Contestable markets and the theory of industry structure.* New York: Harcourt Brace Jovanovich.
Berg, Hartmut, and Notburga Tielke-Hosemann. 1987. Branchenstudie Luftfahrtindustrie: Der Markt für Großraumflugzeuge des zivilen Luftverkehrs. Dortmunder Diskussionsbeiträge zur Wirtschaftspolitik, no. 24. Universität Dortmund.
———. 1988. Vom Glanz und Elend staatlicher Technologieförderung: Das Projekt "Airbus." Dortmunder Diskussionsbeiträge zur Wirtschaftspolitik, no. 27. Universität Dortmund.
Boeing Company. 1987. Current market outlook world travel market perspective and airplane equipment requirements. Seattle.
Brander, James A., and Barbara J. Spencer. 1983. International R&D rivalry and industrial strategy. *Review of Economic Studies* 50:707–22.
———. 1985. Export subsidies and international market share rivalry. *Journal of International Economics* 18:83–100.
Coopers & Lybrand. 1988. The Airbus enterprise—A review of the public record. Manuscript.
Economist. 1985. The big six—A survey of the world's aircraft industry. June 1.
———. 1988. All shapes and sizes—A survey of the civil aerospace industry. September 3.
Hofton, Andy. 1987. Commercial aircraft of the world. *Flight International,* October 10, 36–80.
Interavia. current issues.
Klepper, Gernot. 1990. Entry into the market for large transport aircraft. *European Economic Review* 34:775–803.
Kravis, Irving, Alan Heston, and Robert Summers. 1982. *World Product and Income.* Baltimore: Johns Hopkins University Press.
Krugman, Paul R., and Lael Brainard. 1988. Problems in modelling competition in the aircraft industry. CEPR-NBER Conference on Strategic Trade Policy, Sussex.
McDonnell Douglas. 1987. Outlook for commercial aircraft 1987–2001. Long Beach, Calif.
Spence, Michael. 1981. The learning curve and competition. *Bell Journal of Economics* 12, 1:49–70.
U.S. Department of Commerce. 1986. *A Competitive Assessment of the U.S. Civil Aircraft Industry.* Boulder: Westview.

Comment   Heather A. Hazard

The commercial aircraft industry presents a highly seductive case study in strategic trade policy. As one of the most concentrated industries in the world it is

Heather A. Hazard is associate professor of business at the Institute of International Economics and Management, Copenhagen School of Business.

a clear example of a market shaped by "small numbers of large strategically self-conscious agents (firms and governments), [rather than] by large numbers of small agents competing at arm's length" (Richardson 1989, 1.1). In addition, the cast of characters has been stable (only one firm has exited and one firm has entered in the last 30 years), production is geographically concentrated, and product cycles are long. Despite these characteristics, researcher after researcher has been frustrated in his or her modeling attempts.

Formal modeling efforts have stalled and left us with a paucity of specific advice to offer policymakers. Policymakers, however, must move with the course of events and have had to deal with flare-ups in the GATT over Airbus subsidies, potential joint ventures between U.S. and European firms, and, intriguingly, a new partnership between Boeing and a Japanese consortium of Fuji, Kawasaki, and Mitsubishi. What roadblocks did the researchers run into? What questions might be tackled to assist policymakers?

Dixit and Kyle (1985) began the work on aircraft by setting up a dynamic oligopoly model with both firms and governments as players. They did not attempt to inject any empirical data into their modeling effort, however, and more insight was gained into potential welfare effects than how competition would actually ensue. Baldwin and Krugman (1988) followed with a Spence (1981) type learning curve model (modified to include fixed costs) but deprived the firms of the ability to act strategically (by having them assume the other firm's whole stream of output as given). Through this work they developed insights into the importance of consumer surplus in determining optimal policy and of dynamic economies of scale. They also discovered that they had limited the model unintentionally by neglecting a key aspect of the product: commercial aircraft are extremely durable capital goods. Krugman and Brainard (1988) attempted to overcome this and other problems of modeling demand (such as expectations regarding future products, implicit contracting, and oligopsonistic demand) by turning to a variant of Baumol, Panzar, and Willig's (1982) contestable markets approach. Rejecting the familiar models of competition, they were unable to run the standard simulations. The Krugman and Brainard approach appears to hold further potential to be exploited despite the remaining technical difficulties.

In the paper Klepper has presented here, he turns back to a track of Spence-style modeling he began in 1988. He focuses on economies of scale (both static and dynamic) and economies of scope as the key industry characteristics. Despite his effort to set up a sophisticated framework in which the long-run quantity game serves as a restriction on the short-run price game, his results are unsatisfying. He finds that if demand turns out to be larger than expected, firms will produce at their capacity limit and choose prices which maximize profits. This does not seem to be a good description of the behavior observed in 1989 when the three big producers held orders totaling an estimated $133 billion and yet margins in the industry were still thin.

We clearly need to push our models further, but in what directions? If researchers want to go on and enrich their models in ways that would increase their utility to policymakers, they might want to try and answer a number of questions, including:

1. How should the objective function of government be represented? Should it be restricted to maximizing consumer plus producer surplus and partial equilibrium, or expanded to include (i) technological spillovers from R&D, including learning of engineers about production, (ii) human resource development to encourage workers to invest in learning and to handle upswings in demand, (iii) national prestige (advertisement for technological capability), and (iv) national security?

2. How do we model governments? Should they be modeled as monolithic actors? Or should the United States be modeled as the executive branch and the Congress, for example, and the European Community as member governments and the Commission?

3. What is a subsidy? Is it building military planes first to create economies of scope for commercial aircraft? Building planes without contracts in hand and absorbing inventory costs? Covering exchange rate risk? Cross-subsidization from the military? Accumulated learning from earlier generations?

4. How do we model the buyers, the unions, or the engine suppliers? Do we give them market power or not? (I would argue that we should.)

5. How do we deal with the aging stock problem? We know we see old planes substituting for new planes when (i) fuel prices fall, (ii) capacity constraints combined with strong demand drive prices up, (iii) manufacturers start quoting long delivery lags, or (iv) demand profiles change (for size and length of haul).

6. What are the defects of the GATT Civil Aircraft Agreement? Does it need to be amended? How should it be amended? The heat of this long-standing international trade dispute varies by the state of industry.

7. Can we model the potential of Japanese entry?

This has been a long list of modeling questions but our modeling efforts to date have proved how difficult the competition in even a simple industry can be to penetrate. Fortunately, we have several modeling paths available to us as we continue.

References

Baldwin, R. E., and P. R. Krugman. 1988. Industrial policy and international competition in wide-bodied jet aircraft. In *Trade policy issues and empirical analysis,* ed. R. E. Baldwin, 45–78. Chicago: University of Chicago Press.

Baumol, W. J., J. C. Panzar, and R. D. Willig. 1982. Contestable markets and the theory of industry structure. New York: Harcourt Brace Jovanovich.

Dixit, A., and A. Kyle. 1985. The use of protection and subsidies for entry promotion and deterrence. *American Economic Review* 75:139–52.

Krugman, P. R., and L. Brainard. 1988. Problems in modelling competition in the aircraft industry. CEPR-NBER conference on Strategic Trade Policy, Surrey. Mimeograph.

Richardson, J. D. 1989. Empirical research on trade liberalization with imperfect competition: A survey. Cambridge, Mass.: National Bureau of Economic Research.

Spence, A. M. 1981. The learning curve and competition. *Bell Journal of Economics* 12(1):49–70.

6   Trade and Industrial Policy for a "Declining" Industry: The Case of the U.S. Steel Industry

Richard G. Harris

6.1 Introduction

The economics of the U.S. steel industry is not simple. Much maligned and much studied, the U.S. steel industry illustrates the problems of considering an industry in apparent decline. The loss of market in the 1970s and 1980s by the large integrated producers has been characterized by the joint presence of a growth in import pressures, and consequent protection, and the growth of a new lower-cost domestic source of supply based on minimill technology. Observers have characterized this industry as a classic example of Schumpeter's creative destruction in market economies, with the new replacing the old. At the same time, others have been more concerned about lost jobs and output due to the dramatic decline of the traditional part of the industry, and steel is often listed as one of the key strategic industries any major world economic and military power must preserve.

The simultaneous presence of an old and a new technology within the same industry and the importance of international competition in the U.S. steel market suggest that explicitly modeling the industry along the lines presented in the newer theories of international trade might be fruitful. While there are numerous sources of conventional microeconomic analysis of the U.S. steel industry, there is little in the way of analysis based on the newer trade theories.[1]

This paper describes a calibrated imperfect-competition model of the U.S. steel industry in the partial equilibrium tradition of Baldwin and Krugman

Richard Harris is the B.C. Telephone Professor of Economics at Simon Fraser University.

The author appreciates the comments of Jim Markusen and the participants at the NBER conference. All remaining errors are the author's own responsibility. Research support of a Killam Research Fellowship and the hospitality of the Department of Economics at the University of Colorado, Boulder, are gratefully acknowledged.

1. Examples of microeconomic analysis of the U.S. steel industry include Tarr and Morkre (1984), which uses the competitive industry model as the basic framework.

(1988) and Dixit (1988). The model in this paper is distinguished in a number of ways, however, from those papers. First, the essential problem is one of dealing with the cost heterogeneity of firms within the steel industry due to the presence of old and new technologies. Second, the modeling of intertemporal competition is complicated by the small size and competitiveness of the U.S. minimill sector. The particular model used to address the nature of intertemporal competition will undoubtedly affect the results. The model used in this paper is one which might be summarized as mixed price-quantity competition during the "declining phase" of the industry, with a contestable-markets view of the longer term over which the industry may or may not be reborn as a high technology/high productivity industry.

The model used in this paper is highly stylized. It considers a hypothetical 10-year period in the industry, which could be imagined to be 1990–99. The period is characterized by constant (nongrowing) demand, constant real factor prices, and constant foreign supply prices. Furthermore it is assumed that the 1985 quotas, or voluntary export restraints (VERs), are in place over the entire 10-year period. The five-year period of 1990–94 is assumed to be one of competition between the minimills and the remaining integrated producers on their old plants. At the end of this period, it is assumed that existing integrated producers will exit the market completely, if they have not already done so. The period 1995–99 is characterized as a period of industry rebirth in which minimills in the United States are the least-cost source of domestic supply; however their success in that period will depend upon the nature of competition and the degree to which they were able to get costs down during the first five years.

The paper focuses on a basic descriptive model of the steel industry calibrated to a 1985 data set, and then a number of alternative trade and industrial policy experiments are carried out. These include (a) relaxed VERs on steel imports into the U.S. market, (b) increased protection of the U.S. market, (c) subsidies to integrated producers, (d) subsidies on operating costs during set-up periods to minimills, (e) cartelization of the market by forced mergers of integrated producers and minimills resulting in forced technical efficiency within the industry, (f) rationalization cartels with the additional constraint of price controls, and finally for reference (g) a type of second-best optimum taking the level of imports into the U.S. market as given. All of these represent elements of industry policy proposals that have come forward at one time or another for dealing with the peculiar problems of steel.

The basic result of the simulations is rather striking. The cost of the current VER protection is quite large, compared to either free trade or to a second-best optimum. For example in present-value terms the cost of protection over a 10-year period *relative to a second-best optimum* is approximately 6.85 percent of the present value of the base consumption stream, or about $4.6 billion (1985 dollars). The welfare gains to complete elimination of protection on steel are substantially larger. However, *partial trade reform* in the sense of a small change in the level of quota protection is actually welfare reducing. The particular nature of these results is explored in some detail. It is surprising how sensitive to different policies the market shares of integrated and minimill producers are, and furthermore how sensitive cost inefficiencies within the industry are, both to policies and to the degree of protection. Furthermore, the quantitative results are somewhat more significant than other calibrated strategic trade policy exercises, suggesting that the scope for strategic trade policy may be greater than heretofore imagined.[2]

The rest of the paper proceeds as follows. Section 6.2 provides the details of the basic industry model used. Section 6.3 provides a brief summary of some salient features of the U.S. steel industry and details of the calibrations. Section 6.4 outlines the results of a variety of policy alternatives and the impact of partial trade reforms taking existing market structure as given. Section 6.5 examines some sensitivity analyses by considering issues of labor rents in base-cost calculations, alternative calibration procedures, and the sensitivity to demand elasticities. Section 6.6 concludes with some comments on the interpretation of the results and difficulties with this particular model of the steel industry.

6.2   An Industry Model

Many economists might think it is natural to use a competitive model to look at the U.S. steel industry. There are 14 large integrated steel producers using open-hearth furnaces and basic oxygen furnaces (BOFs), with many having moved to continous casting. As of 1986 there were about 55 minimill plants using electric furnaces and continuous casting, with scrap metal as the basic raw material input. Minimills are about one-sixth the size of an large integrated firm and typically produce a narrower product line. Minimill technology has been changing, however, with what can be regarded as classic industry- and firm-specific learning effects occuring within the industry. A typical start-up time is about two years for a minimill, and unit costs decline dramatically during this period. Integrated producers are operating plants well in excess of 20 years old, and modernization of these processes is technologically infeasible without complete scrapping. Minimills have a 30 to 60 percent operating cost advantage over the integrated firms. New integrated plants have been built abroad, principally in Brazil, Germany, Korea, and Japan. Crandall (1981) concluded that to build a new integrated plant in the United States was simply not economic at 1982 wages and exchange rates.

---

2. This is a disturbing conclusion for economists, who are prone to take noninterventionist positions. In this respect the "small numbers" that have come out of most of the quantitative strategic trade policy literature thus far are rather comforting; while theory predicts that the scope for intervention is there, quantitatively the gains do not seem to be that great. This particular resolution of the tension in the strategic trade policy literature may be temporary, as this paper suggests. For further discussion of this issue, see Harris (1989).

Thus competition within the U.S. market is between existing integrated producers, existing and new minimills coming on stream, and imports. Virtually all imports were under VER arrangements after 1983, and for most of the period 1983–88 the VERs were binding. For the purposes at hand it is assumed the import sector can be modeled simply as producing up to the level of the VER.

In constructing a model of the U.S. steel industry there are at least three reasons why imperfect competition may be a more appropriate paradigm than the static competitive model traditionally used.

1. There is a long history of price-setting practices by the integrated producers, resulting in numerous instances of policy confrontation in the industry. Oligopolistic pricing practices may be facilitated by the presence of a heavily unionized labor force within the industry.[3]

2. Minimills, while small relative to the integrated producers, have technologies which are characterized by the presence of significant sunk and fixed costs to building a plant, as well as the presence of a short but steep learning curve within a given plant life. Accounting for either of these important technological characteristics of the industry within a competitive framework is close to impossible.

3. Given the presence of the large competitors and the nature of their technology, minimills must make strategic pricing decisions in light of present and future competition. At the same time, entry into the industry by a new minimill usually means a period of losses, followed by a period of profitability. Modeling future industry output and price is an important determinant of minimill behavior within a framework in which equilibrium depends on producers' expectations of the future.

6.2.1   Model Details

The industry life consists of two periods, each equal to five years, with a common private and social discount factor δ connecting the two periods. Two important characteristics of demand are relevant in the case of steel: no real growth in domestic demand and a fairly low price elasticity of demand (clearly less than one). It is also reasonable to assume that intertemporal substitution effects in the demand for steel are small. The demand structure in each of the two periods is therefore a linear inverse demand curve:

(1) $P_i = \alpha - \beta Q_i, \quad i = 1, 2,$

where P_i is the market price in period i, and Q_i is total quantity sold. The advantage of linear demand over iso-elastic demand curves in this case is obvious, as it prevents industry revenues from becoming unbounded as output falls and provides a determinate solution to the monopoly problem.[4]

---

3. See Crandall (1981, 31–32) for a discussion of oligopolistic pricing in the U.S. steel industry.
4. An advantage of the linear demand structure over the iso-elastic is that we can consider the impact of monopolization on price and output, while calibrating the model to a base with a (absolute) price elasticity less than one.

Integrated producers, minimills, and importers produce perfect substitutes all selling at a common price in the domestic market. The level of imports under an assumed binding VER is M in both periods. Integrated producers are assumed to be operating plants which collapse at the end of the first period. They have excess capacity throughout the first period and operate with constant unit operating costs (marginal variable costs) of v dollars per unit output. Integrated producers' collective output in period 1 is denoted by x. If price is below v, integrated producers will shut down. Accounting profits, including charges against fixed capital, are typically negative for these firms, but this will play no role in the analysis.

Minimill producers have an aggregated industry technology characterized by a fixed number of plants with fixed set-up cost, F. Costs in period 1 given an output y in period 1 are

(2) $$c_1(y) = wy + F, \text{ if } y > 0; \text{ otherwise } c_1 = 0.$$

Costs in period 2 given an output level z in period 2 are

(3) $$c_2(y,z) = ay^{-\varepsilon}z.$$

The unit operating costs in period 2 are given by an iso-elastic learning function $m = ay^{-\varepsilon}$, with a learning curve elasticity of $\varepsilon > 0$, so unit costs in period 2 decline as output in period 1 increases. While the learning curve interpretation is popular, the elasticity can be nonzero for a number of reasons summarized simply as the value of experience. It will be assumed that the number of minimills is fixed; this implies that all have the same cost curves, and interpreting z and y as aggregate minimill output implies that the number of firms is buried implicitly in the constant term a in the aggregate cost function.[5]

6.2.2   Period-1 Equilibrium

In period 1 integrated producers and minimills take the supply of imports as given by the VER. They face a residual demand curve determining the quantity over which they compete. This quantity competition is treated as a duopoly between the two sectors with exogenous conjectural variations on the part of minimills and integrated producers. At this point it must be admitted that this is a clear case of heroic aggregation across two classes of firms, ignoring competition between firms of each group in the first period. A weak but not com-

---

5. Suppose there are n identical minimills, each producing $\gamma = y/n$ in the first period, and δ in the second period. Each minimill has a second-period cost function $\hat{c}(\delta) = b\gamma^{-\varepsilon}\delta$. Total costs to producing $z = n\delta$ are

$$c = n\hat{c}\,\delta = nb\left(\frac{y}{n}\right)^{-\varepsilon}\left(\frac{z}{n}\right) = \left(\frac{b}{n-\varepsilon}\right)y^{-\varepsilon}z,$$

which is the functional form used in equation (3).

As y is aggregate minimill output, ε could capture learning effects which spill over between firms within the minimill sector. However, the interpretation of the first-order conditions strictly requires that learning effects be firm specific.

pletely satisfactory answer to this objection is that the number of firms are implicitly buried in the exogenous conjectural variation coefficient. Another unsatisfactory defense, but one commonly used, is that there is within-group collusion but not across-group collusion.

Let ψ^I denote the conjecture of the integrated producers as to $\partial Q_1/\partial x$, and ψ^M denote the minimill conjecture $\partial Q_1/\partial y$. The first-order condition describing the integrated producers' reaction function is given by

$$(4) \qquad\qquad P_1 - \beta x \psi^I = v.$$

In the case of the minimills one must take account of how current output affects future profits. Let z^* denote equilibrium output levels in period 2. By the envelope result, assuming the firm has chosen z^* such as to equate marginal revenue and marginal cost in period 2, period-1 output y must satisfy

$$(5) \qquad\qquad P_1 - \beta y \psi^M + \delta \varepsilon a y^{-\varepsilon-1} z^* = w.$$

The term $\varepsilon a y^{-\varepsilon-1}$ represents the operating-cost savings per unit of period-2 output due to an additional unit of period-1 output.

The market share in the period-1 equilibrium is critical in determining future minimill costs. Any policy or external shock which lowers the market share of integrated producers raises the future competitiveness of minimills. As such, therefore, the determination of output between the two types of producers is of considerable private and social importance.

A second characteristic of this equilibrium is that we assume that $w > v$; that is, that first-period operating costs of the minimill are higher than the variable costs of the old plants in the integrated sector. This simply reflects the start-up costs of a new technology. At the same time it is expected that future operating costs in minimills, m, will be less than both v and w.

The heterogeneity of costs across firm types means that, in general, the equilibrium of this industry will not be "technically efficient"; that is, marginal costs of different firms will differ and total costs will not be minimized. In a simple static sense this is true, as w is not equal to v. In an intertemporal model, though, the definition of technical efficiency is complicated, as one must account for the cost of producing future output. A standard definition of technical efficiency would be an allocation of outputs across plants which minimized the present-value cost of producing a given aggregate output *stream*. Solving this problem yields the cost efficiency condition

$$(6) \qquad\qquad v = w - \delta \varepsilon a y^{-\varepsilon-1} z^*.$$

This simply says that allocation of output between new and old plants must account for the future cost savings as a result of allocating additional output to new plants. Outcomes other than planning or monopoly solutions will not generally be technically efficient. A measure of technical inefficiency reported in the simulations is the percentage difference in true cost between old and new plants, expressed as a percentage of old plant operating costs, v. Hence we define

$$(7) \qquad \text{efficiency gap} = 100 \frac{[v - (w - \delta\varepsilon a y^{-\varepsilon-1} z^*)]}{v}.$$

An approximate interpretation of the efficiency gap would be the percentage cost savings on a unit of output shifted from the integrated sector to the minimill sector.[6]

It is generally acknowledged that the minimill sector is quite competitive. A central problem in this model is allowing for the presence of competitive pressures on price and entry in some appropriate way. It would seem desirable to enforce a zero present-value condition on minimills, which by assumption are assumed to start production at the beginning of period 1 and operate through the end of period 2. The traditional way of enforcing the zero-profit condition is by changing the number of firms, but with firms ignoring the effect of their pricing behavior on the number of firms in the industry. An extreme alternative is a type of contestable-markets model, where the number of firms is taken as fixed and pricing is such as to enforce zero profits. For a variety of reasons having to do with the availability of data, it seemed desirable to avoid the issue of how many minimills the U.S. market might accommodate. To do so requires detailed information about the cost curve at all levels of output. For this reason the contestable-markets view of future price competition was adopted. The basic idea is that price is set in period 2, conditional on output and price in period 1. The price is set such that second-period profits just cover first-period losses in present-value terms. Thus equilibrium in the minimill segment of the market is characterized by a zero present-value constraint. As in the static contestable-markets theory, it is price that changes so as to ensure zero profits, not the number of firms. At the same time the price in the period-1 market game is set based on the calibrated conjectural variations.

As another way of thinking about this equilibrium, imagine a minimill forecasting future sales in the first period. One reasonable conjecture would be that output in any equilibrium would be sufficient to yield operating profits so that, over the course of a plant's life, a normal rate of return would be earned. The major problem with this equilibrium concept is that it suffers from problems of the usual ex post sort when open loop equilibria are used. When period 2 is reached, the price forecast may not be sustainable against some deviations in behavior by some fraction of the minimill sector. Price competition in particular would be ruinous, forcing operating profits to zero and losses on the plants in the industry.

One reasonable way out of this predicament is to assume that z corresponds to a long-run capacity level chosen in period 1, when the plant is set up. In the case of minimills this is not an unreasonable assumption, given that these plants are designed with a particular level of output in mind. The period-2 price is therefore stable against price cutting in the second period, as all firms

6. This interpretation is only approximate in this model however, as period-2 output, z^*, might change in response to this experiment. In a simple static model with homogeneous output and constant marginal costs in both plants, however, this interpretation would be exact.

are capacity constrained. It must be assumed however that firms do not attempt
to cut capacity in period 1 in an attempt to raise price. The contestable-markets
story is that firms assume, were this to happen, that new minimills would enter,
lowering price in both periods, and making the initial decision unprofitable.

Without further justification we simply assume that output is set in period 2
such as to force the present value of the profit stream on a minimill to zero.
Letting Π_i denote period-i profits in a minimill, equilibrium implies that (x,y,z)
satisfies the constraint that

(8) $$\Pi_1 + \delta\,\Pi_2 = 0.$$

Equation (8) provides the link connecting periods 1 and 2. Any change resulting in an increase in period-1 operating losses—say, due to an increase in
fixed plant costs, F—will result in a corresponding increase in Π_2, meaning
usually lower period-2 output and higher period-2 prices. Note the structure of
the model: an increase in F has *no* effect on period-1 prices. There are a number of other interesting linkages induced by the zero present-value condition.
For example, a relaxation of the VERs will reduce the profitability of both the
minimill and integrated sector in period-1 competition. Holding second-period
imports constant, this will result in higher prices in the second period as minimills attempt to recoup their higher losses in the second period. Policy instruments therefore result in an intertemporal shifting of consumer and producer
surplus through the profitability constraint on the minimill sector.

6.2.3   The Second-Best Problem

We report the solution to the second-best problem of maximizing consumer
surplus plus domestic producer surplus, taking the level of the quota as given.
This asks how a planner would organize the industry in the aggregate
efficiency-maximizing way, taking as the second-best constraint the level of
imports into the market. Because quota rents are assumed to accrue to foreigners, a feature of the second-best solution is that domestic output is used as
a tool to lower prices and thus transfer surplus from foreigners to domestic
consumers. For example, consider the simple problem in a constant-cost industry, with domestic cost c and foreign costs c^*. If the inverse demand curve is
$D(Q)$, the exogenous quota level is q^+, and domestic production is x, the
second-best problem is

(9) $$\max_{x \geq 0} W \equiv S(q^+ + x) - cx - D(q^+ + x)q^+,$$

where $S(Q)$ is the gross domestic surplus function. Letting P denote the consumer price in the solution to this problem, generally P will be below $c,$ and
in fact P satisfies the first-order condition

(10) $$\frac{c - P}{P} = \frac{m}{\eta},$$

where m is the import share and η is the absolute price elasticity of demand. Implicitly, $c - P$ can be thought of as a production subsidy. With $\eta = 1.0$ and $m = 0.25$, the subsidy is 25 percent of selling price. The solution must satisfy the constraint that $p \geq c^*$, otherwise foreigners would not supply q^+ to the domestic market. It is possible that a corner solution, $P = c^*$, is optimal, with an implicit production subsidy of $s = c - c^*$.

The quota-revenue function $R(q^+, x) \equiv D(q^+ + x)q^+$ is globally decreasing in x. Note however that holding x constant,

$$\frac{\partial R}{\partial q^+} \gtrless 0 \text{ as } \frac{m}{\eta} \gtrless 1.$$

From the perspective of piecemeal reform of the quota levels, it is possible that increasing the allowable imports (increasing q^+) is locally welfare decreasing if $\partial R / \partial q^+ > 0$ or $m/\eta < 1$. If x is chosen optimally in (9) then, by the envelope theorem, $\partial W / \partial q^+ = -D'(q^+ + x)q^+ > 0$, so in this case the effect on welfare is unambiguous, with an increase in the quota leading to an increase in welfare. However in the model used here, x set in a market equilibrium will not be a solution to (9).

6.4   Calibration

The model was chosen with the U.S. steel industry in mind, over a hypothetical 10-year period using 1985 data on costs, growth, and the like, as the benchmark. For the sake of concreteness the 10-year period is referred to as the decade of the 1990s. It was desirable to break this decade into two periods: a period of competition between minimills and existing integrated producers and a period in which integrated producers retire their plants and competition is between minimills and imports. Taking 10 years as a horizon beginning in 1990, we chose the period 1990–94 as the period of integrated/minimill competition. The period 1995–99 is taken as the period in which domestic minimills are the sole U.S. source of steel. Rather than building a model with 10 separate periods, a drastic simplification was adopted whereby "period 1" is thought of as a sequence of five years of identical price, output, and the like, and "period 2" is a sequence of five years of identical price and output. Aggregation across time is done simply by weighting each year appropriately given an interest rate. Thus the model's period-2 "weight" reflects a ratio of summed discount factors over years allocated to periods 1 and 2 respectively. Using a real interest rate of 8 percent the weight on period 2 is 0.68. Interpreted properly this means a $1 cash flow each year from 1995 to 1999 is worth 0.68 of a sequence of $1 cash receipts in each of the years 1990 to 1994 valued in 1990 dollars. While clearly simplifying the dynamics of the problem, the two-period model captures much of the essence of the problem and allows calibration of the model to otherwise "static" data.

Price elasticities of demand for steel are notoriously low. The estimated elasticity in this paper from Crandall (1981) is taken at −0.90. The low price elasticities reflect the presence of few good short-term substitutes, plus a demand curve which has been shrinking to the left. The inelasticity of demand means that efforts to increase output result in large price decreases, giving additional reasons for efforts by the industry to restrict output, or at least avoid output increases.

The rest of the parameters for the model are taken from the books by Crandall (1981), Barnett and Schorsch (1983), and Barnett and Crandall (1986). While there are no formal models in these books, they each take a fairly similar view of demand, costs, and future technology from the perspective of the first half of the 1980s. As of 1989 the major factor not accounted for in these books was the fall in the value of the U.S. dollar from 1985 to 1988. This has led to foreign supply prices in terms of U.S. dollars which are higher than those used in this paper. It should be emphasized that the purpose of this paper is not to offer realistic "forecasts" of the steel industry but rather to highlight the problems of a declining, internationally noncompetitive industry within a partial-equilibrium framework. High domestic costs could be due to a variety of reasons including an overvalued exchange rate.

The facts on the state of the industry in the mid-1980s are fairly indisputable, although engineering estimates of costs are always subject to some disagreement. As of the mid-1980s the U.S. market for carbon steel products was about 94 million tons per year. Barnett and Crandall (1986, 96–98) suggested that at current rates of economic growth, this demand would remain about constant over the 1990s. In 1985 dollars the current price was in the range of $430 to $440 per ton. Imports accounted for about 25 percent of the U.S. market, with most of those imports covered by a VER agreement. The supply price of foreign imports depended on the country supplying, the method of production, and of course the exchange rate. The lowest cost source of imports was probably Korea, coming in at about $270 per ton using a 1985 exchange rate. These may obviously have changed but for the moment we will assume these costs remained constant. Given that the trade policy instrument of choice has been VERs, we will assume that all quota rents accrued to non–U.S. residents. Note that because of this, from a social point of view policies which indirectly shift quota rents may be nationally beneficial.

Integrated U.S. producers (about 14 firms) had mid-1980s unit operating costs of about $403 per ton (1985 dollars). All of the sources cited above agree that new greenfield integrated plants, with a minimum efficient scale (MES) of around 4 million tons per year, were not competitive in the United States at existing prices. As far as the integrated sector goes, therefore, the central question is when it will be displaced, and, until then, how large a market it might get in the absence of draconian government intervention.

Minimills constitute the new competitive and growing sector of the U.S. steel industry. Thus far they have operated on a much smaller scale than the integrated plants, at about 500,000 tons per year. The minimill sector has been growing rapidly from about 15 percent of the U.S. market in the early 1980s to a projected 27 percent in 1989. This sector remains very dynamic, with technology changing both in terms of increased productivity and changing scale. Some observers feel that efficient scale is growing within the minimill sector, and some consolidation is likely to take place. Engineering studies provide two important numbers on minimill technology: best-practice operating costs (at around $311 per ton) and the fixed costs of building a minimill plant.[7] Some of these studies also argue that the plant life of a minimill, in the range of 10 years, is significantly shorter than that of an integrated facility. This provides some justification for focusing on a 10-year horizon in the model.

The literature is not as helpful at providing information on the intertemporal structure of costs in the minimill sector, which are an important point in this exercise. First, an estimate of the operating costs in the early life of the representative plant is necessary, including start-up costs. While there are numerous qualitative stories about these costs, I have not found any precise estimates. Using the well-known "10 percent" rule, therefore, it is assumed that operating costs in new minimills, inclusive of start-up costs, are 10 percent above the operating cost found in existing integrated facilities. From the static perspective of near-term supply, this means that the existing integrated facilities are the least-cost source of domestic supply.

The second important parameter describing minimill technology is the "learning elasticity," ε. While the general literature on learning gives ranges for this parameter from 0.10 to 0.40, they differ by product and length of product cycle. It seems that a modest estimate for this parameter value is 0.15, meaning a one percent increase in output over the first five years of the plant reduces future operating costs by 0.15 percent. The cost function parameter, a (the constant in the learning curve), is then calibrated such that at the observed level of minimill output the best-practice operating cost of $311 per ton is reached after five years of plant operation.

This calibration is summarized in table 6.1. The observed price-cost margins and market shares are used to calibrate the reaction coefficients ψ^I and ψ^M. In the case of minimills one must also infer the zero present-value output level in period 2; this turns out to be about 72 million tons. It is interesting that the value for both reaction coefficients are fairly close to zero, implying that pricing is a long way from Cournot duopoly, reflecting competition both with and between the integrated and minimill sectors of the market. The calibrated values of the reaction coefficients suggest the minimill sector is the least aggressive, and the integrated sector the most aggressive, in terms of price cutting. This is partially consistent with the evidence of substantial excess capacity in the integrated sector, forcing integrated producers to price close to marginal variable cost as a means of maintaining output. At the same time the minimill sector is also fairly competitive, but it still suffers significant losses in the first

---

7. The engineering literature is surveyed by Barnett and Crandall (1986, chap. 5).

Table 6.1   Parameters and Data for Calibrated Intertemporal Model of U.S. Steel Market, 1990–95

Parameter	Data
Average annual U.S. consumption	94 million tons
Base price (1985 $)	$435 per ton
Price elasticity of demand	$\eta = -0.90$
Import share of market under VER's (%)	25
Integrated producer share of market (%)	48
Minimill share of market (%)	27
Integrated average annual operating cost	$403 per ton
Foreign least-cost supply (Korea) price	$270 per ton
Minimill fixed costs (hundred million $)	22.08
Minimill intertemporal cost elasticity	$\varepsilon = 0.15$
Minimill five-year target operating cost at existing output rates	$311 per ton
Discount factor on 1995–99 period	0.68 (or 8% real interest rate)

Calibrated reaction coefficients for period-1 market structure:
  Integrated producer $\quad \partial Q_o/\partial x \equiv \psi^1 = 0.006553$
  Minimills $\quad \partial Q_o/\partial y \equiv 0.04508$

five years as prices are not sufficient to cover operating and fixed costs. The low operating costs in the second half-life of the plant, however, provide profits sufficient to ensure the present-value constraint is satisfied. It should be noted that in both periods the domestic price is sufficiently above the foreign supply price to ensure the VERs are binding and are giving rise to positive quota rents in equilibrium.

6.5   Simulation Results

In this section a number of alternative simulations are presented, which are designed to shed light on the current state of the industry and policies which have been recommended from time to time to deal with the steel industry. A summary of these results are presented in table 6.2. Eight different simulations are reported and discussed below.

6.5.1   The Second-Best maximum

For a point of reference it was decided to calculate a second-best optimum, maximizing consumer surplus plus producer surplus subject to the constraint that the quota, or level of imports, be taken as given and prices are bounded from below by foreign supply prices. What is interesting about the solution to this second-best problem is that prices are close to the foreign supply prices, quota rents are negligible, and the minimill market share is quite large relative to all other equilibria, with one exception. The fact that prices are driven below domestic production costs in both sectors reflects the second-best nature of the

Table 6.2   Alternative Policy Simulations for U.S. Steel Industry, 1990–99 (CV calibration method; high demand elasticity)

	Status Quo	VERs Relaxed	VERs Tightened	Monopoly	Rationalization Cartel	Integrated Subsidies	Minimill Subsidies	Second-Best Maximum
Price 1 (hundred $ per ton)	4.35	4.25	4.42	6.01	4.27	3.69	4.28	2.83
Price 2 (hundred $ per ton)	3.52	3.93	3.38	5.46	4.35	4.33	2.85	2.71
Minimill output 1 (million tons, per annum)	25.42	19.27	28.48	36.71	51.57	18.04	38.21	70.08
Integrated output 1 (million tons per annum)	45.08	29.83	54.78	1.65	20.50	65.34	33.83	30.15
Minimill output 2 (million tons per annum)	86.67	55.26	103.57	48.95	70.45	71.07	99.85	102.43
Quota level (million tons per annum)	23.50	47.00	9.40	23.50	23.50	23.50	23.50	23.50
Minimill unit cost 2 (hundred $ per ton)	3.11	3.24	3.06	2.94	2.79	3.27	2.92	2.67
Welfare 1 (billion 1985 $)	2.1739	2.1798	2.1956	1.3722	2.0861	2.3576	2.1459	2.2223
Welfare 2 (billion 1985 $)	3.4744	3.0658	3.6097	2.5807	3.3651	3.1966	3.8271	4.1159
Welfare cost[a] (%)	32.88	36.71	31.27	52.77	36.45	32.95	29.89	26.03
Efficiency gap[b] (%)	16.90	13.59	18.20	0.00	−0.26	22.70	9.41	0.00
Integrated producer surplus (billion 1985 $)	.1462	.0646	.2154	.0326	.0500	.3060	.0830	−.3629
Quota rents[c] (billion 1985 $)	.5203	1.1199	.2054	1.2184	.6346	.4929	.3935	.0318

Note: "Price 1" refers to annual price in period 1 (years 1–5), "price 2" refers to annual price in period 2 (years 6–10), etc.

[a] Welfare cost is measured as

$$100 \times \frac{\text{present value of free-trade welfare} - \text{present value of actual welfare}}{\text{present value of benchmark consumption}}$$

[b] Efficiency gap is eq. (7) expressed as a percentage.

[c] Quota rents are the present value of quota rents over both periods.

problem, with quota revenues being distributed abroad as discussed in section 6.3. Clearly in period 1 of the second-best optimum, given a price of $271 per ton, steel producers are receiving a substantial subsidy. Domestic output becomes an instrument whereby the quota rents on imports are reduced, resulting in welfare gains to the domestic economy in the absence of other instruments to reduce the quota rent transfer. The justification for using this particular second-best optimum as a reference point is motivated by the observation that free trade in steel is probably irrelevant as a domestic policy objective; the best that can be hoped for is to maximize efficiency within the domestic industry taking as given the level of imports, and in this case the policy that ensures that level of imports is met—the VER. Obviously tariffs are welfare-superior to VERs, but they are presumed to be unavailable as a policy tool.

Another characteristic of the second-best optimum is that the technical efficiency gap, as defined in equation (7), is zero, meaning the present-value costs of total domestic production are being minimized, or equivalently that the output allocation in the solution is technically efficient.

Welfare cost is measured relative to a free-trade equilibrium in which the equilibrium price is $270 per ton in both periods and imports have 100 percent of the U.S. market. Thus the welfare loss of the second-best maximum expressed as a percentage of the present value of consumption in the status quo, or benchmark, is 26 percent. From a pure efficiency point of view, free trade is vastly superior to any of the alternative equilibria considered.

6.5.2 The Status Quo

The status quo is basically the benchmark data set with slight changes.[8] There are at least two important observations about this equilibrium. First, in the status quo there are much higher prices and positive profits on integrated producer capacity, while in the second-best equilibrium the integrated producers actually operate at a loss. In a true first-best equilibrium the latter would never occur, but in this framework the presence of transfers to foreigners means that domestic output is used as a device to lower prices and hence the transfers.

Second, it is noteworthy that the allocation of output across sectors is quite different than in the second-best optimum. The share of minimill output in total domestic output is considerably greater in the second-best optimum than in the status quo. Indeed market shares are almost exactly reversed across the two equilibria. The cost efficiency gap in the status quo is a reflection of this difference; at 16.9 percent the efficiency gap indicates too much period-1 output is allocated to old plants in the integrated sector. Interpreting the welfare results requires some caution. The welfare cost number is the welfare loss relative to free trade expressed as a percentage of the present value of the status

---

8. The benchmark consists of an average of data over the first half of the 1980s expressed as a "typical" year. The model has two periods which differ. The calibration process is such that second-period price and output may differ from the benchmark first-period price and output.

quo consumption stream. This number can be quite sensitive to the assumed foreign supply price. In any case the welfare cost of any of these simulations as compared to free trade is substantial. At a welfare cost of 32.88 percent, the existing structure of protection and industry organization results in very large welfare costs. However, as remarked earlier, free trade may not be the relevant basis for comparison. Compared to the second-best outcome, which takes the level of imports and protection in the form of quotas as given, the status quo situation is only 6.85 percent worse than the second-best. This number might be interpreted as the impact of inefficiently allocated market resources, given the existence of an institutionally constrained level of protection. We shall return to this point later. It is also noteworthy that the second-best allocation relative to the market allocation shifts welfare intertemporally toward the second period. This suggests that the status quo market allocation, which is "biased" against the minimill sector's output, tends to result in an intertemporal distortion as well, shifting consumer surplus toward the current period at the expense of the future period.

6.5.3   Partial Trade Liberalization

A natural question is to ask what marginal value the VERs might have in maintaining domestic output, and what welfare benefits or costs they induce. The simulation "VERs relaxed" looks at the effect of doubling the level of allowable imports in *both* periods on the equilibrium of the model. This has the effect on consumers of reducing period-1 price and raising period-2 price, reflecting the significantly reduced output of the minimill sector in period 1 and thus reduced period-1 profitability. Relative to the status quo, integrated firms' output falls by about 33 percent and minimill output by about 24 percent. Also, not surprisingly, integrated producer surplus falls sharply with the output reduction and import expansion. What is a little surprising is that quota rents actually rise as a result of the increase in allowable imports. The quota-revenue function is actually increasing in the level of imports around the observed equilibrium. Relaxing the VERs actually reduces welfare both because period-2 prices are forced up and because quota rents more than double. The increase in welfare cost to doubling the allowable imports is about 4.8 percent (as a percentage of the base stream of consumption). Quantitatively this is fairly significant and at the same time suggests that a *movement* toward free trade can be nationally welfare decreasing. This conclusion is explored further below.

6.5.4   Increased Protection

If trade liberalization will not work, what about enhanced protection? The "VERs tightened" column in table 6.2 reports the effect of reducing the level of imports under a VER tightened to ten percent of the total market (base). In this case the domestic price rises in period 1, but falls in period 2, although not by a great amount. Consumers on balance are worse off, not surprisingly.

Protection does little for the minimill sector; most of the output gains due to the increased size of the domestic market accrue to the integrated producers in period 1, although the minimill sector obviously expands output in period 2 and produces at a lower cost relative to the benchmark equilibrium. There are some small welfare gains from this policy, about 1.6 percent, but hardly large enough to suggest that protection is the cure-all for the industry. From a technical efficiency perspective, increased protection actually reduces the cost efficiency of the industry, by shifting output toward the integrated sector.

6.5.5   Monopolization

In the course of the steel industry's history it has occasionally been suggested that, by cartelizing the industry, the efficient rationalization of existing resources in the industry and restructuring might be promoted. The Japanese model of a recessionary cartel is often cited. Given that a multiplant monopolist would act as a true joint-profit maximizer, this certainly makes sense. However, the consequences for consumer welfare of this policy are bound to be detrimental, and in the presence of VERs might be extremely harmful from a national efficiency perspective. The "monopoly" column in table 6.2 bears this out. Welfare costs are an astounding 53 percent, explainable in large part by the low initial price elasticity of demand. A significant fraction of these losses are caused by transferring surplus to foreigners through the quota rents generated by higher prices. The dramatic price increases experienced under this policy obviously make it politically unacceptable as an industrial policy. Note that, as theory predicts, monopoly results in a cost-efficient industry with an efficiency gap of zero percent.

6.5.6   Rationalization Cartels

The stories about rationalization cartels one reads in the industrial policy literature seem to imply that a monopolist could rationalize and restructure the industry, but at the same time, some other policy tool would be used to keep prices low. It is not clear what model of industry one has in mind here. A public steel monopoly maximizing aggregate welfare subject to a budget constraint might be one model. A more practical model, however, might simply be a monopolist maximizing profits subject to price constraints. Such a policy simulation is reported in the "rationalization cartel" column. Prices are constrained in this equilibrium not to exceed 4.36, reflecting the use of the status quo equilibrium price as a reference point. The results are quite interesting. The rationalization process involves an expansion of minimill sector output and a contraction in integrated sector output relative to the status quo. Unit costs in period 2 in the minimill sector are 10 percent lower under this policy than in the status quo. This result, together with the second-best results clearly suggest that in the status quo equilibrium minimill output is being crowded out by integrated sector output relative to the "efficient" policy. Under the rationalization cartel policy, first-period minimill sector output more than doubles, going up by 202 percent.

Whatever the technical efficiency gains from a rationalization cartel is does not rank high in terms of total welfare. There are fairly significant welfare losses under this model. The cartel attempts to make profits on the minimill sector, exploiting the relatively generous price constraint available in the second period. To do this it cuts back on the integrated sector output in the first period; this is welfare reducing because price exceeds marginal cost of production in integrated plants. In period 2 there is a transfer from consumers to the cartel.

6.5.7   Subsidies to Integrated Producers

A policy often suggested is to subsidize the costs of declining industries presumably with the objective of preserving output and jobs. In this case we focus on subsidies equal to 20 percent of operating costs, best thought of as a wage subsidy. The policy more or less produces the intended results; integrated sector output with a 20 percent operating subsidy expands by about 20 million tons relative to the status quo and price is reduced in period 1. The intertemporal linkage through the zero present-value condition shows up clearly. In the second period price rises by about 12 percent, reversing the pattern of declining prices over time evident in the status quo. The net welfare effect is positive relative to the status quo, although very small. The benefit seems to come largely from the fact that price is closer to the marginal cost of integrated producers in period 1. Intertemporally the policy shifts welfare from period-2 to period-1 consumer and producer surplus.

6.5.8   Subsidies to Minimills

The infant industry argument might suggest that because the minimill sector is "too small" relative to the second-best optimum it should be subsidized. As it turns out, a 20 percent operating subsidy to minimills results in about a 50 percent increase in output in this sector, with the major benefit in form of reduced prices in the second period. The subsidy which is offered during the industry's first five years has the effect of also reducing integrated sector output by about 25 percent and produces net welfare gains of about 2.9 percent. While not insignificant, the quantitative gains might be reduced if one were to attach a deadweight loss to the additional tax revenue required by subsidies.

6.5.9   Trade Reforms Again

The results on trade reform do not at this point seem clear. In particular the large welfare costs in the status quo–free trade comparison do not seem to reconcile with the welfare decrease of more generous VERs against steel imports. In figures 6.1–6.3 we present the results of varying the quota level from 0 to 48 million tons into the market in both periods. Results are presented so as to set the welfare gain equal to zero in the status quo situation of a VER of 23.5 million tons.

Figure 6.1 presents the apparently "paradoxical" results that as the quota is

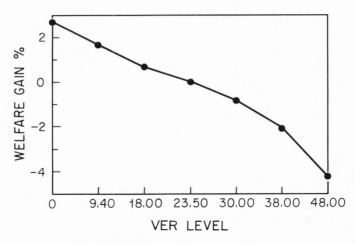

Fig. 6.1   Protection and welfare: U.S. steel industry

reduced the welfare *gain* is positive, rising to a high of 2.8 percent when all imports are excluded from the market, while there is a welfare loss of 4.2 percent when imports are about half the domestic market. The apparent conclusion is that, on a partial reform basis, over a fairly wide range of import penetration levels, the optimal trade policy is to restrict imports of steel.

This would be an erroneous conclusion, however. The real problem has to do with the use of an inefficient instrument, the VER; in this case the policy choice is driven by the issue of shifting the implicit terms of trade between U.S. and foreign steel suppliers because rents accrue to non–U.S. residents. Suppose an instrument were available such as a tariff or quota auctions such that all quota rents accrued to the U.S. economy in lump-sum fashion. The estimated impact on welfare is dramatically different as illustrated in figure 6.2. Using a quota-rent-inclusive measure of welfare we see that the conclusions about protection are actually reversed. Prohibiting imports results in a welfare loss of about 5 percent,[9] while progressive liberalization of the market by allowing increased imports increases welfare continuously. Neither welfare gains nor welfare costs to significant trade reform are trivial. They are all substantially in excess of the usual 1 percent gains in much of the partial-equilibrium strategic trade literature. Figure 6.3 illustrates the perverse effect protection has on industry cost efficiency. Restricted levels of quota protection raises the efficiency gap between integrated and minimill producers, contributing to the usual welfare losses imposed by protection.

It is important to emphasize that the paradoxical results on partial trade re-

9. Note that the base is redefined in this situation to be one in which the rents on the 23.5 million tons of imports accrue to U.S. residents.

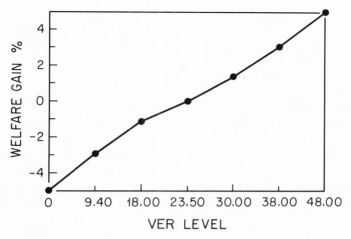

Fig. 6.2   Quota-rent-inclusive welfare change: U.S. steel market

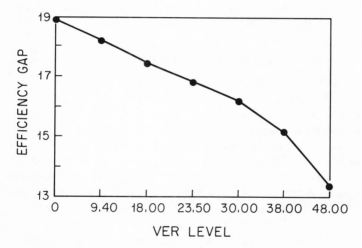

Fig. 6.3   Protection and technical inefficiency: U.S. steel industry

form are closely linked to the assumption of imperfect competition. In a perfect-competition model increasing the level of allowable imports, given a constant foreign supply price which is less than the domestic price, is always welfare nondecreasing. With imperfect competition there are a number of complications: (i) Price exceeds marginal cost in domestic production. By increasing imports and reducing domestic production the cost of this distortion is enhanced. (ii) In the competitive model, relaxing the VER would reduce price, increase total output, and leave costs unchanged. In the imperfect-competition model of this paper, the learning-cost effect in the minimill sector implies that a relaxed VER reduces current minimill output and thus raises future minimill cost and hence price. Therefore it is the interaction between the joint assumptions of a rent-transferring voluntary restraint agreement (VRA) and an imperfect market structure which leads to the possibility that tighter quotas could be welfare increasing.

What can we conclude from this exercise? There are three points to make:

1. In the presence of VERs on which foreigners are collecting rents, partial trade reforms involving changes in the level of quotas must be carefully considered. Partial liberalization may well be nationally harmful.

2. Industrial subsidy policies targeted to particular subsectors can have a substantial effect on the allocation of output between the subsectors. In general, subsidies to the new technology in this framework are appropriate, although the welfare gains would be enhanced were other instruments available to solve the quota-rent transfer problem.

3. Trying to correct the technical efficiency losses by rationalizing integrated capacity and shifting output toward the new technology part of the industry is of dubious quantitative significance within this model, at least over the range of parameter values considered. Given the possible cartelizing side effects of such policies one would want to proceed very carefully.

6.6   Alternative Specifications and Procedures

Tables 6.3–6.5 report some alternatives to the exercise reported in the last section. In many calibration exercises the empirical aspect of the procedures adopted are never clear-cut.[10] In the steel industry the cost figures in the integrated sector are particularly suspect because of a rather high wage differential of about 20 percent between it and average manufacturing in the United States. If this wage differential reflects rents to labor, and not differences in the opportunity cost of labor in alternative sectors, the results could be seriously misspecified. In table 6.3 we report the same policy exercises assuming such a distortion in labor markets. Standard theory suggests that the integrated sector may be too small due to the presence of the wage premium to employment in the integrated steel sector. Assuming that these rents exist implies that the integrated sector would have a much greater output in the second-best equilibrium than in the status quo, reversing the "no-rent" simulation result. The aggregate welfare cost of the status quo measured against the second-best is 7.8 percent—about 1 percent more than in the calibration without labor rents. The other notable distinguishing feature of these simulations is that the efficiency gap is much less than in the simulations without labor rents. In this instance the issue of output allocation across plants within the steel sector is less serious than in the previous case, as integrated producers are actually lower cost than

---

10. See the discussion of this issue in Harris (1988, chap. 4).

Table 6.3   Alternative Policy Simulations for U.S. Steel Industry, 1990–99 (CV calibration method; labor rents = 20% of wage bill in integrated sector; high demand elasticity)

	Status Quo	VERs Relaxed	VERs Tightened	Monopoly	Rationalization Cartel	Integrated Subsidies	Minimill Subsidies	Second-Best Maximum
Price 1 (hundred $ per ton)	4.35	4.25	4.42	5.83	4.28	3.69	4.28	2.70
Price 2 (hundred $ per ton)	3.52	3.93	3.38	5.60	4.35	3.94	2.85	2.69
Minimill output 1 (million tons per annum)	25.41	19.27	28.49	19.98	30.20	18.04	38.21	41.03
Integrated output 1 (million tons per annum)	45.08	29.83	54.78	21.37	41.71	65.34	33.83	61.64
Minimill output 2 (million tons per annum)	86.67	55.26	103.57	46.21	70.57	78.51	99.85	102.83
Quota level (million tons per annum)	23.50	47.00	9.40	23.50	23.50	23.50	23.50	23.50
Minimill unit cost 2 (hundred $ per ton)	3.11	3.24	3.05	3.22	3.02	3.27	2.92	2.89
Welfare 1 (billion 1985 $)	2.3362	2.2872	2.3928	1.6261	1.1790	2.5929	2.2676	2.5589
Welfare 2 (billion 1985 $)	3.4744	3.0657	3.6096	2.3472	3.2034	3.1965	3.8271	3.8912
Welfare cost[a] (%)	32.21	37.07	30.01	54.17	52.16	31.21	29.67	24.69
Efficiency gap[b] (%)	8.76	5.12	10.17	0.01	−1.04	18.87	0.53	−0.56
Integrated producer surplus (billion 1985 $)	.1465	.0646	.2153	.3930	.1051	.3060	.0830	−.8193
Quota rents[c] (billion 1985 $)	.5205	1.1199	.2054	1.1987	.6356	.4318	.3935	−.010

Note: See note to table 6.2.

[a] Welfare cost is measured as

$$100 \times \frac{\text{present value of free-trade welfare} - \text{present value of actual welfare}}{\text{present value of benchmark consumption}}$$

[b] Efficiency gap is eq. (7) expressed as a percentage.

[c] Quota rents are the present value of quota rents over both periods.

they appear to be in the market allocation, which is biased against the minimills.

One of the key problems in the calibration of the model is the use of the conjectural variations as the "free parameter." Numerous commentators have remarked as to the possible misspecifications this may impose on the model. An alternative in the case of minimills is to assume the sector as a whole acts as a Bertrand-pricing oligopolist. Given the fairly large number of minimills relative to integrated producers, this may be appropriate. In table 6.4 the results are based on the model in which the period-1 operating costs, w, of minimills are calibrated assuming Bertrand pricing by minimills. In this model that calibration produces a cost estimate for w of 5.12, which is greater than the 4.43 estimate used in the previous case. This change in calibration procedure now means both (a) that operating costs are higher in the minimill sector than the first set of simulations reported and (b) that pricing by the minimill producers is more competitive. This tends to put the integrated producers at a disadvantage in that their rivals are pursuing a more aggressive output strategy, but also at an advantage given the now-higher minimill costs.

The results of the Bertrand minimill pricing are that the welfare losses are about 8.7 percent relative to the second-best—certainly larger than in the first set of simulations. As in the last case however the conclusions about the relative share of the two sectors in an efficient allocation is reversed. In the second-best equilibrium the minimill sector is much smaller than in the first set of simulations. Indeed you will note that the efficiency gap has actually changed sign. As a result, subsidization of the minimills results in quite significant welfare losses relative to the status quo.

One parameter value which seems of some dispute in the case of steel is the demand elasticity. Some estimates come in much lower than -0.90. Jondrow (1978), for example, estimates it to be in the range of -0.45—half the assumed value. Low demand elasticities are an important part of the problems plaguing declining industries, so it was thought to be a useful exercise to see how conclusions changed if a much lower demand elasticity was assumed. These results are reported in table 6.5, again employing the conjectural variations calibration method. Obviously with lower demand elasticities prices are much more sensitive to output changes around the benchmark. This shows up dramatically in the "monopoly" column of table 6.5 with a period-1 monopoly price of 43! Clearly the linear demand specification is suspect at this point. The welfare costs of trade restrictions are of course dramatic given the steep demand curve and the redistributive implication of a VER. The status quo is characterized by a welfare loss of 99 percent relative to free trade; however relative to the second-best equilibrium the welfare loss is only about 8.5 percent. The other qualitative conclusions do not change much.

Table 6.4   Alternative Policy Simulations for U.S. Steel Industry, 1990–99 (cost calibration method; Bertrand minimill pricing)

	Status Quo	VERs Relaxed	VERs Tightened	Monopoly	Rationalization Cartel	Integrated Subsidies	Minimill Subsidies	Second-Best Maximum
Price 1 (hundred $ per ton)	4.35	4.31	4.40	5.83	4.30	3.71	3.95	2.71
Price 2 (hundred $ per ton)	4.00	5.52	3.80	5.79	4.35	4.33	3.39	2.71
Minimill output 1 (million tons per annum)	25.50	8.96	31.94	9.51	16.09	15.15	78.39	20.32
Integrated output 1 (million tons per annum)	45.01	38.88	51.74	32.35	55.53	67.88	0.00	82.16
Minimill output 2 (million tons per annum)	77.43	24.34	95.38	42.53	70.50	71.07	89.30	102.53
Quota level (million tons per annum)	23.50	47.00	9.40	23.50	23.50	23.50	23.50	23.50
Minimill unit cost 2 (hundred $ per ton)	3.11	3.63	3.00	3.60	3.33	3.36	2.62	3.21
Welfare 1 (billion 1985 $)	2.1109	1.6805	2.1464	1.6218	1.1353	2.3321	1.3751	2.5365
Welfare 2 (billion 1985 $)	3.3042	1.7655	3.5765	2.0504	2.9899	2.9812	3.9467	3.5586
Welfare cost[a] (%)	36.69	58.30	33.46	56.33	54.10	36.67	41.07	27.93
Efficiency gap[b] (%)	−18.52	−17.30	−19.81	0.03	−4.19	−0.94	−36.43	0.34
Integrated producer surplus (billion 1985 $)	.1459	.1093	.1923	.5812	.1483	.3301	0.00	−1.0840
Quota rents[c] (billion 1985 $)	.5962	1.6583	.2303	1.2288	.6397	.4971	.4034	.038

Note: See note to table 6.2.

[a]Welfare cost is measured as

$$100 \times \frac{\text{present value of free-trade welfare} - \text{present value of actual welfare}}{\text{present value of benchmark consumption}}$$

[b]Efficiency gap is eq. (7) expressed as a percentage.

[c]Quota rents are the present value of quota rents over both periods.

Table 6.5   Alternative Policy Simulations for U.S. Steel Industry, 1990–99 (CV calibration; low demand elasticity)

	Status quo	VERs Relaxed	VERs Tightened	Monopoly	Rationalization Cartel	Integrated Subsidies	Minimill Subsidies	Second-Best Maximum
Price 1 (hundred $ per ton)	4.39	4.26	4.46	42.73	4.36	3.63	4.32	2.71
Price 2 (hundred $ per ton)	3.67	4.10	3.50	42.25	4.36	4.06	2.99	2.70
Minimill output 1 (million tons per annum)	21.39	16.48	24.07	28.06	50.54	15.55	30.71	51.49
Integrated output 1 (million tons per annum)	49.79	31.32	61.14	7.69	20.67	56.33	40.53	21.24
Minimill output 2 (million tons per annum)	71.84	47.95	86.10	36.20	71.21	71.48	72.47	72.74
Quota level (million tons per annum)	23.50	47.40	9.00	23.50	23.50	23.50	23.50	23.50
Minimill unit cost 2 (hundred $ per ton)	3.19	3.31	3.13	3.06	2.80	3.34	3.02	2.79
Welfare 1 (billion 1985 $)	48.4590	48.4577	48.4902	19.4739	44.3387	48.6609	48.4371	48.7260
Welfare 2 (billion 1985 $)	49.5378	49.1644	49.6690	33.4732	49.6472	49.3318	49.8203	50.0519
Welfare cost[a] (%)	99.12	103.07	97.26	716.12	161.67	98.17	96.49	89.59
Efficiency gap[b] (%)	17.19	14.50	18.45	0.07	0.07	29.00	8.12	0.07
Integrated producer surplus (billion 1985 $)	.1782	.0714	.2658	2.9775	.0673	.2288	.1187	−.2803
Quota rents[c] (billion 1985$)	.5522	1.1783	.2170	15.7265	.6535	.4364	.4280	.0023

Note: See note to table 6.2.

[a] Welfare cost is measured as

$$100 \times \frac{\text{present value of free-trade welfare} - \text{present value of actual welfare}}{\text{present value of benchmark consumption}}.$$

[b] Efficiency gap is eq. (7) expressed as a percentage.

[c] Quota rents are the present value of quota rents over both periods.

6.7 Conclusion

Policies to favor new industries over old are at the crux of the debate on industrial policy in many countries. The steel industry provides an interesting case study of an industry that can be thought of as containing both declining and expanding subsectors, both of which compete in the short term with imports for the same market. What this paper suggests is that the answer to the question of in which direction the industry should be pushed depends on market structure, costs, and demand conditions. In the case of the U.S. steel industry, taking the level of imports as the relevant constraint, the existing industry structure is inefficient, but cost estimates are crucial to deciding in which direction the industry should be pushed. Taking the existing industry structure as given, small changes in trade and industrial policy can affect welfare, but the conclusions are very sensitive to the disposition of the rents created under the VER programs. It is quite possible that restricting imports is welfare increasing, given the imperfectly competitive nature of the steel industry.

These results must be qualified by the relatively simple structure of the model used and the crude nature of the data used in calibration. Perhaps more fundamental, however, is the structure of the model itself. A particular worry is the fact that integrated plants are assumed to exit after five years of operation. Clearly with some expenditures it is possible to keep these plants operating over a period longer than the next five years. Endogenizing this decision is the next logical step to take in model construction.

References

Baldwin, R., and P. Krugman. 1988a. Market access and international competition: A simulation study." In *Empirical methods in international trade,* ed. R. Feenstra. Cambridge: MIT Press.

———. 1988b. Industrial policy and international competition in wide-bodied jet aircraft. In *Trade policy issues and empirical analysis,* ed. R. E. Baldwin. Chicago: University of Chicago Press.

Barnett, D., and R. W. Crandall, 1986. *Up from the ashes: The rise of the steel minimill in the United States.* Washington, D.C.: Brookings Institution.

Barnett, D., and L. Schorsch. 1983. *Steel: Upheaval in basic industry.* Cambridge, Mass.: Ballinger.

Crandall, R. W. 1981. *The U.S. steel industry in recurrent crisis.* Washington, D.C.: Brookings Institution.

Dixit, A. K. 1988. Optimal trade and industrial policies for the U.S. automobile industry. In *Empirical methods for international trade,* ed. R. Feenstra. Cambridge: MIT Press.

Harris, R. G. 1988. A guide to the GET model. Department of Finance, Government of Canada, Ottawa.

———. 1989. The new protectionism revisited. *Canadian Journal of Economics* 22 (4):751–78.

Jones, K. 1986. *Politics vs economics in world steel trade.* London: Allen & Unwin.

Jondrow, J. 1978. Effects of trade restrictions on imports of steels. In *The impact of international trade and investment on employment,* U.S. Department of Labor, Bureau of International Labor Affairs. Washington, D.C.: Government Printing Office.

Keeling, B. 1982. *The world steel industry: Structure and prospects in the 1980s.* Economist Intelligence Unit Special Report, no. 128. London.

Tarr, D., and M. Morkre. 1984. *Aggregate costs to the United States of tariffs and quotas on imports.* Washington, D.C.: Federal Trade Commission.

7 Strategic Manpower Policy and International Trade

David Ulph and L. Alan Winters

In many countries growing concern is being expressed about the position of skilled manpower—particularly of scientists and engineers. In some cases the complaint is about skill shortages, and in others about "brain drains"—the flow of highly trained manpower to other countries. While these are sometimes coupled as different facets of the same problem, the first phenomenon arises because of a "failure" of supply, while the second reflects a "failure" of demand.

Many arguments (not all very convincing) have been used to suggest that these phenomena are undesirable and that governments should develop policies to produce more skilled labor or better retain that which they already have. We focus on the argument that this skilled manpower is of strategic importance to an economy because it is essential to the performance of its "high-tech" sector. We will show that the recent work on strategic trade and industrial policy using models of international trade with imperfect competition and economies of scale provides a useful framework in which arguments about the scope and desirability of such manpower policies can be assessed and quantified. When calibrated, our model shows that manpower policies are potentially extremely powerful and important.

However, the focus of the paper is not really manpower policies, for we hope our analysis will demonstrate the crucial importance of understanding these

David Ulph is professor of economics at University College, London. L. Alan Winters is professor of economics at the University of Birmingham and codirector of the International Trade Programme at the Centre for Economic Policy Research.

The authors are grateful for the financial support received from the Ford Foundation through the NBER/CEPR program Empirical Studies of Strategic Trade Policy. They are also grateful to Larry Katz, participants at the conference, and anonymous referees for comments on an earlier version.

manpower issues when formulating trade and industrial policies aimed at supporting a country's high-tech sector.

In section 7.1 we develop a model of an open economy with a high-tech sector in which skilled manpower is used in R&D to produce improved lower-cost techniques of production. There are three further crucial features of the high-tech sector. The market for the output of this sector is the world market, of which the particular economy is only a very small part. Because of the fixed costs of R&D there are only a few major international firms competing in this market, so it is inherently imperfectly competitive. However, because in R&D success breeds success, entry cannot prevent these major firms from enjoying supernormal profits or rents even after deduction of the costs of R&D. The simplest way of capturing this in our model is to operate with a fixed number of firms. Cantwell (1989a) provides the most recent evidence and a good discussion of this persistence phenomenon. Taken together these assumptions mean that the model is essentially one in which countries are in competition with one another through their manpower and industrial policies to get as large a share of these rents from the international market as they can.

This framework is essentially that used by Brander and Spencer (1983) in their argument for support of R&D. As is well known, there are a number of objections to the Brander and Spencer analysis. Dixit and Grossman (1986) show that it depends crucially on the assumption that scientific manpower is essentially in perfectly elastic supply to the high-tech sector. They show that if it is completely inelastic and immobile, then support to the high-tech sector has to be very carefully targeted to have a beneficial effect. While concerns over skill shortages are captured by the inelastic supply assumption, the "brain drain" phenomenon suggests that the immobility assumption is unrealistic. We show that if scientific manpower is mobile then, while support to any arbitrary high-tech industry could be damaging, a policy giving more general support to the high-tech sector as a whole will be beneficial. We extend this to consider the arguments for policy when it is science that is mobile, with companies setting up their R&D labs at centers where scientific manpower is concentrated.

These arguments for support of high-tech industries are tested by allowing for the possibility of international spillovers (in which case it may pay to free-ride on the R&D of other countries), and by having research undertaken by internationally mobile scientists while development is performed by immobile engineers. The final part of section 7.1 considers the nature of R&D policies and shows that if scientists are indeed mobile, then policies should be aimed at encouraging greater demand for them, and a policy of encouraging supply is positively harmful.

The model in section 7.1 is what is known in the R&D literature as a *non-tournament* model, in which each firm can pursue its own independent line of R&D. Even if one firm makes its discovery first and patents it, the lines of research are sufficiently different that this does not prevent other firms from successfully developing, patenting, and using their own discoveries. In section 7.2 we briefly consider what happens when R&D takes the form of a *tournament,* in which firms race to be the first to patent their discovery, because the patent prevents any other firms from exploiting its R&D. We show that many of the arguments of the nontournament model are reversed.

In section 7.3 we calibrate the model of mobile scientists developed in section 7.1 and show that R&D policy can be powerful. Thus a given amount of resources transferred as a subsidy to R&D can increase GNP by two-and-a-half times the amount transferred—an extremely high rate of return. Finally, in section 7.4 we present the evidence that is available on mobility and on spillovers. Unfortunately, none of this is in a form that would enable us to calculate an elasticity. Nevertheless, it does seem to suggest a fair degree of mobility and so, within our framework, definite scope for beneficial policy support of the high-tech sector.

7.1   Nontournament Models

7.1.1   The Basic Model

There are two countries, each having two sectors. In the first sector a homogeneous product is produced under constant returns to scale and perfectly competitive conditions using labor alone. Output is measured in such a way that one unit of output requires one unit of labor to produce it. Thus taking the output of this sector as numeraire, the wage rate of labor will be one.

In the second sector there are n imperfectly competitive industries. In each industry production takes place under constant returns to scale using labor alone. For each industry there is a single firm in each of the two countries undertaking production in that industry. For country 1, a_j represents the amount of labor required per unit of output; for country 2 the labor requirement is denoted by b_j. Given our previous assumptions, a_j and b_j also represent unit production costs in each of the two firms in industry j.

Given these unit production costs, the profits/rents accruing to country 1 in a Cournot equilibrium in industry j are denoted by $r_j(a_j, b_j)$. Introducing the notation

$$r_{ja} \equiv \partial r_j / \partial a_j, \text{ etc.,}$$

then standard models of imperfect competition suggest that the functions $r_j(\cdot,\cdot)$ will satisfy the following properties:

(1) $$r_{ja} < 0, r_{jaa} > 0, r_{jb} > 0, r_{jab} < 0.$$

Thus an increase in the unit labor requirements of country 1 reduces its profits, but at a diminishing rate as these requirements get larger: if country 1's labor requirements are already large, then its market share will be small, and so further increases in its labor requirements will be less damaging than if its labor requirements had initially been smaller and market share consequently larger. An increase in country 2's unit production costs increases country 1's profits, while finally, the larger country 2's labor requirements are, the greater country 1's market share is, and so, again, the more it will be damaged by further increases in its own labor requirements.

We now assume that each firm's unit production costs/labor requirements depend on the amount of R&D it undertakes, while this in turn depends on the number of scientists/engineers it employs. Thus if we let x_j be the number of scientists employed by the firm in the jth industry in country 1 and y_j the number in country 2, then we assume that

$$a_j = a_j^0 - \phi_j(x_j), \text{ and}$$
$$b_j = b_j^0 - \psi_j(y_j),$$

where

(i) $\qquad\qquad \phi_j(0) = \psi_j(0) = 0;$

(ii) $\qquad\qquad \phi_j'(x_j) > 0, \psi_j'(y_j) > 0;$

(iii) $\qquad\qquad \phi_j''(x_j) < 0, \psi_j''(y_j) < 0;$

(iv) $\qquad\qquad \phi_j(x_j) < a_j^0 \text{ for all } x_j, 0_j(y_j) < b_j^0 \text{ for all } y_j.$

If we let c_j be the effective wage rate of a scientist/engineer faced by the firm in industry j in country 1, then, taking the unit production cost in the firm in country 2 as given, x_j is chosen to be

$$\max_{x \geq 0} r_j \left[a_j^0 - \phi_j(x_j), b_j \right] - c_j x_j.$$

Assuming that $\phi_j(\cdot)$ is sufficiently concave that the overall maximand is concave in x_j and that we always have interior solutions then, the unique solution to the above maximization problem is characterized by the first-order condition (f.o.c.)

(2) $\qquad\qquad -r_{ja} \cdot \phi' = c_j.$

If d_j denotes the effective wage rate of scientists in the jth industry in country 2, then the Nash equilibrium inputs of scientists in industry j in the two countries will be functions of the effective wage rates of scientists in these two countries: c_j and d_j. Write these as

(3) $\qquad\qquad x_j = \xi_j(c_j, d_j), \text{ and}$

(4) $\qquad\qquad y_j = \eta_j(c_j, d_j).$

Standard conditions suggest that for a wide class of cases

(5) $\qquad\qquad \xi_{jc} < 0, \eta_{jd} < 0,$

so an increase in each firm's costs of hiring scientists lowers its equilibrium input of scientists. In addition, we assume

(6) $$- \eta_{jd} > \xi_{jd} > 0, - \xi_{jc} > \eta_{jc} > 0,$$

so that an increase in a firm's costs of hiring scientists increases the demand for scientists by the other firm but by less in absolute magnitude then it reduces the firm's own demand, thus leading to a net fall in the demand for scientists.

In a similar vein we assume

(7) $$- \xi_{jc} > \xi_{jd} > 0, - \eta_{jd} > \eta_{jc} > 0,$$

so that if the costs of hiring scientists in both countries increase, then the cross-price effect of this is less than the own-price effect, leading to an overall reduction in demand.

Thus the fundamental determinants of the rents/profits earned by each country in any industry are the effective wage rates of scientists faced by that industry in each of the two countries. For through (3) and (4) these determine the number of scientists employed in that industry in each of the two countries: these determine the unit production costs a_j and b_j, which in turn determine the rents.

Having set out the basic model we can now turn to a variety of policy issues. Throughout our analysis we will equate welfare with national income. This involves, among other things, following Brander and Spencer in assuming that all high-tech goods are exported. Thus we can ignore consumption distortions and terms of trade effects on consumers. We start with the standard Brander and Spencer result.

7.1.2   The Brander and Spencer Result

Suppose country 1 introduces an R&D subsidy in industry k, which we take to be a subsidy, s_k to the costs of hiring scientists in industry k, $k \in \{1, \dots, n\}$. What effect does this have on its welfare?

Implicit in the Brander and Spencer analysis is the assumption that the subsidy does not affect the (gross) prices at which industries in the high-tech sector can hire resources from the competitive sector. In our model this is equivalent to the assumption that labor and scientists are perfect substitutes.

Welfare in country 1 is given by income, which is labor income plus profits (rents minus costs of hiring scientists). Given the above assumption this can be written

$$W = L + \sum_j \{r_j[a_j^0 - \phi_j(x_j), b_j^0 - \psi_j(y_j)] - x_j\},$$

where L is the total amount of labor, and we note that the profits of industry k are the social profits—that is scientists are priced at their true cost (unity) since the subsidy is a pure transfer within the economy.

The x_j and y_j terms that appear in W are determined by

(8) $$x_j = \xi_j(1, 1), j \neq k; x_k = \xi_k(1 - s_k, 1), \text{ and}$$

(9) $$y_j = \eta_j(1, 1), j \neq k; y_k = \eta_k(1 - s_k, 1).$$

So to determine the effect on welfare of an increase in s_k evaluated at the point where $s_k = 0$, we differentiate W totally w.r.t. s_k, using (8) and (9) to take account of how s_k affects x_k and y_k. Doing this, and recalling the f.o.c. (2), we get

(10) $$dW/ds_k = r_{kb} \cdot \psi_k' \cdot \eta_{kc},$$

which, from (1) and (6), is strictly positive.

The intuition behind the result is straightforward. The subsidy to the industry increases the amount of R&D the firm in industry k in country 1 does and lowers the amount done in country 2. However, with s_k initially zero, the firm in country 1 was doing the socially optimal amount of R&D, so increasing the amount it does has no first-order effect on welfare. But lowering the amount done in country 2 increases its costs, contracts its output, and so raises the price at which country 1 can sell its output, and this brings a first-order increase to the rents earned by country 1. Thus Brander and Spencer conclude that introducing an (R&D) subsidy into any imperfectly competitive high-tech industry is always beneficial.

7.1.3 The Dixit and Grossman Results

Dixit and Grossman argue that what makes these industries high-tech industries are essential inputs of "scientists" or "technologists," which are not used at all in sector 1, but are essential inputs to industries in sector 2. The critical feature which this introduces is that an industry in sector 2 cannot expand just by drawing in additional labor from the non-rent-generating sector 1, but now, assuming a fixed supply of scientists, will have to absorb additional scientists from other high-tech sectors, thus impairing their rent-generating capability.

To capture these ideas, Dixit and Grossman assume that labor and "scientists" are combined in fixed proportions in each high-tech industry. However, we have modeled the role of scientists more explicitly, and in terms of our model the essence of the Dixit-Grossman model is that scientists are no longer perfect substitutes for labor and have a separate endogenously determined gross wage rate. If we let w be the wage of scientists in country 1 and v their wage rate in country 2, then social welfare in country 1 can be written

(11) $$W = L + \sum_j r_j[a_j^0 - \phi_j(x_j), b_j^0 - \psi_j(y_j)],$$

where now, once we add the income of scientists to the profits of the high-tech industries, national income is just labor income plus rents, the question of who gets the rents being a distributional one of no direct relevance to total welfare.

Assuming once again that a subsidy s_j is introduced into industry j, the number of scientists in each industry is given by

(12) $$x_j = \xi_j(w - s_j, v), \text{ and}$$

(13) $$y_j = \eta_j(w - s_j, v),$$

while the wage of scientists in country 1 is determined by the condition

(14) $$\sum_j \xi_j(w - s_j, v) = S.$$

Following Dixit and Grossman, we assume the wage of scientists in country 2, v, is fixed.

Now when we want to examine the effects of a subsidy on, say, industry k alone we have to differentiate (11) totally w.r.t. s_k, taking account of how all the x_j, y_j, and w vary through (12)–(14). Using the f.o.c. (2) we get

(15) $$dW/ds_k = (dw/ds_k)\left[\sum_{j=1}^{n}(w \cdot \xi_{jc} - r_{jb} \cdot \psi_j' \cdot \eta_{jc})\right] + \left(-w \cdot \xi_{kc} + r_{kb} \cdot \psi_k' \cdot \eta_{kc}\right),$$

while from (14),

(16) $$dw/ds_k = \xi_{kc} \Big/ \left(\sum_j \xi_{jc}\right) > 0.$$

The intuition behind (15) is as follows. The second term, in parentheses, on the right-hand side tells us that the subsidy has two direct effects. The first, represented by the last term, is just the Brander and Spencer effect already discussed. The second is that it expands the number of scientists in industry k earning the rent w. However, because the number of scientists is fixed, the subsidy has the indirect effect of raising the wage rate of scientists, which will act like a tax on every high-tech industry, having precisely the reverse of these two effects on every industry. This is what the first term on the right-hand side of (15) shows.

The most important point to notice here is that, if we sum (16) over all k we get

(17) $$\sum_{k=1}^{n}(dw/ds_k) = 1,$$

and so, on substituting (16) into (15) and summing over all k we get

(18) $$\sum_{k=1}^{n}(dW/ds_k) = 0,$$

so that introducing a subsidy into all industries simultaneously just drives up the scientists' wage rate to exactly offset the effect of the subsidy, and so has no effect on any industry, or on welfare. But then, looking at subsidies on individual industries, there must be some industries for which a subsidy has positive welfare effects and others for which it is harmful. Thus while a carefully targeted subsidy can be beneficial, an arbitrarily chosen one may not be—the essential Dixit-Grossman conclusion.

7.1.4   Mobile Scientists

A key feature of the Dixit-Grossman model is the fact that scientists are internationally immobile, and so a country's expansion of one industry can only take place at the expense of another in that country. The frequently voiced concerns about "brain drains" suggests that this feature of the model may be crucially unrealistic, so it is interesting to explore the policy implications of allowing scientists to be internationally mobile.

We therefore adopt the alternative extreme assumption that scientists are perfectly mobile internationally. This has two immediate effects on our previous model:

1. In (12) and (13) $v = w$, as there is now a single international wage for scientists.

2. The scientists' resource constraint (14) now has to be written

$$(19) \qquad \sum_{j=1}^{n}\left[\xi_j(w - s_j, w) + \eta_j(w - s_j, w)\right] = S,$$

where now S is the total supply of scientists in the world.

The formulation of the welfare function now needs some consideration. If we assume that the income of scientists accrues to the country in which they work, then the welfare function is once again given by (11). This assumption clearly reflects deeper underlying assumptions about both the behavior of scientists (not remitting their income home) and of the tax authorities (they cannot or do not tax the income of people working abroad, but can and do tax all the income of people working within their country). This latter statement is made in the context of our earlier assumption, in which we just equated welfare with GNP. When we move beyond that framework, we also have to confront more fundamental issues concerning what set of citizens is to be included in a nationalistic welfare criterion. An alternative assumption about where the income of scientists accrues will be considered in the next section.

Suppose then country 1 imposes a subsidy on industry k. What is the effect on welfare? Differentiating (11) totally w.r.t. s_k gives

$$(20) \qquad dW/ds_k = (dw/ds_k)\left\{\sum_{j=1}^{n}\left[w(\xi_{jc} + \xi_{jd}) - r_{jb} \cdot \psi_j' \cdot (\eta_{jc} + \eta_{jd})\right]\right\} +$$

$$(-w \cdot \xi_{kc} + r_{kb} \cdot \psi_k' \cdot \eta_{kc}),$$

while, from (19),

$$(21) \qquad (dw/ds_k) \sum_{j}[\xi_{jc} + \xi_{jd} + \eta_{jc} + \eta_{jd}] = \xi_{kc} + \eta_{kc}.$$

The intuition behind (20) is precisely the same as for (15), the only difference being that the increase in the wage rate affects the equilibrium outputs by raising costs in both country 1 and country 2.

From (5), (6) and (21) it follows that

$$0 < dw/ds_k < 1,$$

and indeed that, if we define

$$\theta = \sum_{k=1}^{n} (dw/ds_k),$$

then $0 < \theta < 1$.

Moreover, summing over (20), we get,

$$(22) \qquad \sum_{j=1}^{n}(dW/ds_j) = \theta \sum_{j=1}^{n} (w \cdot \xi_{jd} - r_{jb} \cdot \psi'_j \cdot \eta_{jd}) + $$
$$(1 - \theta) \sum_{j=1}^{n} (-w \cdot \xi_{jc} + r_{jb} \cdot \psi'_j \cdot \eta_{jc}),$$

which, given our sign conventions in (1), (5) and (6), is strictly positive.

The intuition is that blanket subsidies to all high-tech industries in country 1 cause them to attract scientists from other parts of the world by increasing the wage rate. But, because there are scientists elsewhere, their wage does not have to rise by as much as the subsidy. This means that overall costs in country 1 do fall, which benefits the country. However, there is a second effect, which is that the rise in the international wage of scientists increases costs of production elsewhere, which is again to the benefit of country 1. Now, as in Dixit and Grossman, there is no guarantee that a subsidy to any given industry increases welfare, but, in contrast to their model, a general subsidy to the high-tech sector is warranted.

An important point about the results in this section is that although we have assumed that scientists are perfectly mobile internationally, in fact, any degree of mobility will be sufficient to generate the two effects of a blanket subsidy discussed above: that the wage of domestic scientists does not rise by as much as the subsidy and that there is an increase in the wage of overseas scientists. Hence any degree of mobility will suffice for a policy of blanket support to be beneficial.

Notice also that, as Dixit and Grossman themselves recognize, if there were some degree of internal supply elasticity of scientists, a policy of blanket subsidies could have positive welfare effects. However, the magnitude of the response could be different, because of the different effects of the subsidy on the wages of scientists in the overseas country. Also, as we show in section 7.8, the interpretation of policy can be very different when there is international mobility rather than internal supply elasticity.

7.1.5   Immobile Scientists, Mobile Science

An alternative possibility is that scientists are internationally immobile but that science is not—that is, that firms can buy scientific research from scientists located in other parts of the world. Given problems of confidentiality, this may entail locating an R&D lab in that other country—which appears to be what multinational corporations (MNCs) do (see section 7.4.2, below). Formally this is equivalent to the outcome that arises when scientists are mobile but either they remit their earnings home or else their "home" country can tax away their earnings. What are the policy implications of the possibility of mobile science?

We assume that science is perfectly mobile in the sense that it is perfectly homogeneous so that companies always buy their science at the lowest price, so once again the wage of scientists will be the same in both countries. If S once again stands for the total number of scientists in both countries, while S^1 stands for those in country 1, then the overall scientist resource constraint is once again given by (19), while the equilibrium outputs of the various industries are once again given by (12) and (13), with $w = v$.

The main difference is that since country 1 is not confined to buying its science at home and its scientists are not confined to working for home industries, the welfare function becomes

$$W = L + \sum_j \{r_j[a_j^o - \phi_j(x_j), b_j^o - \psi_j(y_j)] - w \cdot x_j\} + w \cdot S^1.$$

We then find that

$$(23) \qquad dW/ds_k = (dw/ds_k) \cdot \left\{ S^1 - \sum_j x_j - \sum_j [r_{jb} \cdot \psi_j' \cdot (\eta_{jc} + \eta_{jd}] \right\}$$
$$+ r_{kb} \cdot \psi_k' \cdot \eta_{kc},$$

where dw/ds_k is once again given by (21) and so is positive. The last term on the right-hand side of (23) is the Brander and Spencer effect.

From (7) the last term in the braces is positive, reflecting the fact that all industries in country 1 gain because the increase in the wage induced by the subsidy forces all industries in country 2 to contract. Finally if $S^1 \geq \sum_j x_j$, meaning that the country is not a net importer of science, then driving the price of science up is not harmful.

We thus reach the conclusion that if the country is not a net importer of science, then a subsidy to any arbitrary high-tech industry is positively beneficial—which is the Brander and Spencer conclusion. However, if the country is a net importer of science, then even a uniform subsidy may not be desirable. A major determinant of whether or not a country is a net importer or exporter of science will be the number of scientists it has. In this case, to justify what is here a policy of encouraging the demand for scientists may only be appropriate if the supply has also been increased.

7.1.6   Distinguishing between Research and Development

In most of the economics literature, research and development are treated as a single process labeled R&D. However, in a number of contexts it is now being recognized that it is important to distinguish carefully between research and development as two distinct though interrelated features of the process of generating new products/technologies. This distinction could be particularly important in the context of the models discussed in the preceding two sections, for it might be that while the "scientists" who work on research are fairly mobile, the "engineers" who work on development are not. Equally, while it may be possible for companies to locate research labs abroad where the scientists are, development work must take place where production is to be carried out.

To explore the implications of this distinction we will now assume that research requires inputs of scientists, while development requires inputs of engineers, and that, in country 1 (resp., country 2), for every scientist employed in industry j, α_j (resp., β_j) engineers have to be employed. Thus there are fixed proportions in research and development, capturing the idea that the two are distinct and necessary phases of investment, and one cannot be substituted for the other.

Even though on the demand side, scientists and engineers may not be substitutable, it is always possible that they are perfect substitutes on the supply side—that essentially there is a pool of people who become either scientists or engineers, depending on which pays most. In this case nothing in our model would be affected. The more interesting case, then, is where scientists and engineers are imperfect substitutes on the supply side as well. We will assume that there is a fixed supply of scientists and a fixed supply of engineers.

Without working through the analysis formally, it is fairly clear from our earlier work that if both factors are internationally immobile then we will once again obtain the Dixit-Grossman results implying that subsidies are unlikely to be beneficial. On the other hand if both factors are perfectly mobile internationally we will replicate the results of section 7.1.4, and a general sector-wide subsidy to R&D will be beneficial.

Suppose then that scientists are internationally mobile, with world wage w, while engineers are internationally immobile, with a wage v in country 1 and v' in country 2. Since the income of engineers nets out from the profits of the firms, social welfare is once again given by (11). If we think of the government introducing a subsidy which either lowers the wage of scientists (in all industries) by an amount s, or the wage of engineers by an amount σ, then the resource constraints become

$$\sum_{j=1}^{n}\left\{ \xi_j[w - s + \alpha_j(v - \sigma), w + \beta_j v'] + \right.$$

$$\left. \eta_j[w - s + \alpha_j(v - \sigma), w + \beta_j v'] \right\} = S,$$

and

$$\sum_{j=1}^{n} \alpha_j \cdot \xi_j[w - s + \alpha_j(v - \sigma), w + \beta_j v'] = E,$$

where S is the world supply of scientists, and E is the supply of engineers in country 1.

If we just differentiate these two equations, it is easily seen that $dw/d\sigma = 0$ and $dv/d\sigma = 1$, so an attempt to subsidize the demand for engineers just drives up their wages to exactly offset the subsidy and has no welfare gain at all. Thus we get the Dixit-Grossman result again.

A subsidy to the use of scientists has more complex effects. However, one special case is where $a_j = a$ for all j. In this case $dw/ds = 0$ and $dv/ds = 1/\alpha$, so the wage of engineers rises to exactly offset the subsidy to scientists, and we once again get the Dixit-Grossman results. The intuition is clear. The mobility of scientists is irrelevant when faced with completely immobile engineers who are required in a fixed ratio to scientists.

When the a_j are not uniform there will be some cases where a general subsidy to scientists is beneficial and some where it is not, but the information required to determine when these cases arise will be difficult to obtain. The general conclusion then is that policies of subsidy are not a good idea when there is some irremovable fixity of supply, however much flexibility there might be elsewhere.

7.1.7   Spillovers

In the literature on spillovers it is generally argued that the presence of spillovers is a reason why the private rate of return to R&D is less than the social rate of return, so there is a justification for policy intervention to encourage firms to undertake R&D. However, strictly speaking, this only applies to a closed economy. In terms of our model this could be interpreted as the case where the spillovers occur purely within each country, and, given that there is only one firm in each industry, these would then be pure interindustry spillovers. Since this case is familiar we will not analyze it formally here.

An alternative case that we *will* consider here is where the spillovers are purely intraindustry, but cut across national boundaries. As is intuitively obvious, and as we will show, such spillovers could provide a reason for *not* undertaking a policy of supporting domestic R&D, essentially because the country could free-ride on R&D being undertaken elsewhere. These two cases by no means exhaust all the possibilities, but it is clear that in general how far spillovers provide a rationale for supporting R&D is going to depend on the balance between internal and external spillovers.

We can capture the presence of intraindustry cross-national spillovers by assuming that now

(25) $a_j = a_j^0 - \phi_j(x_j + \beta_j \cdot y_j)$ and $b_j = b_j^0 - \psi_j(y_j + \beta_j \cdot x_j)$,

where $\beta_j, 0 \le \beta_j \le 1$, is the degree of spillover in industry j.

We assume that spillovers are recognized by firms in each country, so that, for example, the first-order condition for choice of x_j is now

$$(26) \qquad - (r_{ja} \cdot \phi'_j + \beta_j \cdot r_{jb} \cdot \psi'_j) = c_j,$$

with an analogous condition for the firm in country 2.

We assume that the cross-effects of the spillovers are not sufficiently strong to offset the direct effects, so that once again there are interior solutions for x_j and y_j and all the properties of the scientists' demand functions, $\xi_j(\cdot,\cdot)$ and $\eta_j(\cdot,\cdot)$, continue to hold.

Then it is easily seen that in the Brander and Spencer case the effect of introducing a subsidy to the kth industry in country 1 is given by

$$(27) \qquad dW/ds_k = (\beta_k \cdot r_{ka} \cdot \psi'_k + r_{kb} \cdot \psi'_k) \cdot \eta_{kc}.$$

Given our assumptions that own-effects dominate cross-effects then it is possible that for sufficiently large values of β_k the term in parentheses in (27) could be zero or negative, thus negating even the basic Brander and Spencer argument for subsidies.

7.1.8   The Nature of Policies

So far we have talked rather vaguely about the government adopting a policy of subsidizing R&D in either one or all high-tech industries without its being very clear what the nature of this subsidy is. Formally we have treated it as something which just lowers the effective cost of scientists. It might be thought that this could encompass a number of different policies, such as allowing companies a more generous provision to write off R&D expenditures for tax purposes, explicit cooperative ventures with government, R&D expenditures by government that generates significant spillovers to the private high-tech sector, or a policy of generous grants to students to become scientists, thus lowering the costs of scientists to private industry. The point we wish to make here is that, while in a closed economy it probably does not matter very much which of these policies are adopted, in an open economy with mobile labor it matters a great deal. The essential point is that the fundamental market failure that generates the rationale for policy in all of these models is that, due to its imperfectly competitive nature, the private sector does not sufficiently expand its production. Consequently, it insufficiently expands its use of R&D and hence its demand for scientists. Fundamentally it is this lack of demand that has to be tackled.

While in a closed economy this lack of demand can be cured by reducing the cost of training scientists and hence encouraging firms to use more of them, in an open economy with mobile scientists this policy is disastrous because it simply lowers the cost of scientists to the rival country conferring to it all the benefit.

To demonstrate this more formally we need to extend our analysis to model more explicitly the decision to undergo training to become a scientist. Suppose then we have a pool of labor L. A worker in this pool can either remain an unskilled worker getting a wage of 1, or else become a scientist. To do this she has to spend a proportion π of her working life in training, during which she earns nothing and incurs recurrent costs c, but then earns w for the remaining proportion of her working life. Clearly this will be worthwhile only if $(1 - \pi)w - \pi c > 1$, that is, if $\pi < (w - 1)/(w + c)$.

We assume that people differ in their ability to become scientists, which we capture by their having different values of π, which we assume to be distributed in the population according to the density function $F(\cdot)$. Given w, the critical value of π at which an individual is indifferent between becoming and not becoming a scientist is

(28) $$\hat{\pi}(w) = (w - 1)/(w + c).$$

With these changes, then, assuming once again that scientists are perfectly mobile, social welfare becomes

$$W = L[1 - F(\hat{\pi})] - Lc\int_0^{\hat{\pi}} \pi dF + \sum_{j=1}^{n} r_j[a_j^0 - \phi_j(x_j), b_j^0 - \psi_j(y_j)].$$

If we consider first the case where there is a uniform subsidy s to the *demand* for scientists, then the international wage of scientists is determined by the resource constraint

(29) $$\sum_{j=1}^{n}[\xi_j(w - s, w) + \eta_j(w - s, w)] = L\int_0^{\hat{\pi}} (1 - \pi)dF + S_2(w),$$

where $S_2(w)$ is the supply of scientific manpower from country 2, and we assume $dS_2/dw \geq 0$.

Proceeding as before in section 7.1.4 we find that

$$dW/ds = \theta w dS_2/dw + (1 - \theta)\sum_{j=1}^{n}(r_{jb} \cdot \psi' + w)\eta_{jc} - \theta\sum_{j=1}^{n}(r_{jb} \cdot \psi' + w)\eta_{jd}.$$

If we compare this with (23) we see that the only difference from our previous analysis is that there is now an additional potential gain to country 1 from its subsidy policy, because the higher wage of scientists could induce additional supply from country 2. Although this also induces more supply from country 1, since the individuals who are affected were initially indifferent between becoming a scientist and not, this additional supply confers no welfare gain.

An alternative policy could be to subsidize the *supply* of scientists which we could interpret as a reduction in c. Thus, now

(30) $$\hat{\pi} = (w - 1)/(w + c - s).$$

With an appropriate adjustment to the resource constraint (29) to take account of the fact that there is no longer a demand subsidy, we find

(31) $$dW/ds = dw/ds\left[w \cdot dS_2/dw - \sum_{j=1}^{n}(r_{jb} \cdot \psi' + w)(\eta_{jc} + \eta_{jd})\right].$$

Given our sign conventions the term in square brackets is unambiguously positive, but it is easy to see that $dw/ds < 0$, since encouraging supply lowers the wage, so the policy of subsidizing the supply of scientists is unambiguously harmful. It both reduces the supply of scientists from country 2 and lowers the cost of R&D for all the rival industries. Thus if scientists are internationally mobile, policies should be targeted at increasing demand for them, not their supply.

7.2 Tournament Models

7.2.1 The Basic Model

Here we just sketch the outlines of the model. The details are given in Beath, Katsoulacos, and Ulph (1989). Since the issues we wish to discuss in this section arise even if there is a single industry, we will confine attention to the case of a single industry and drop all subscripts. Thus the two firms in countries 1 and 2 (which we will call firms 1 and 2) have initial unit costs a and b, respectively. They compete to discover a new technology with unit costs $c < \min(a, b)$. Whichever firm discovers this first obtains an infinitely lived and effective patent on this new technology, so there is a single prize to be won, which is what gives this model its tournament structure.

To discovery this new technology firms commit resources to R&D (hire scientists). Conditional on no one having discovered by t, the probability that a firm will discover in the time interval $(t, t + dt)$ depends on the flow rate of resources it devotes to R&D (number of scientists hired) at t—so there is no learning by doing. Thus the problem is stationary in that if one firm chooses to commit a constant flow rate of resources to R&D, the optimal response of the other is to also commit a constant flow rate. The constant flow rate of scientists hired by firm 1 will be denoted by x, that by firm 2 by y. For simplicity we will assume that the hazard rate corresponding to x (y) is just $\sqrt{x}$ ($\sqrt{y}$), so there are diminishing returns to R&D.

There are two factors which completely determine the nature of firm 1's reaction function—optimal choice of x for any given choice of y. The first is the *profit incentive*. This is the optimal choice of x if y is zero. Denote this by x_0. Since, if y is zero, the only consideration affecting the choice of x is balancing off the increased gain from bringing forward the likely date of discovery of the new technology against the increased costs, in terms of scientists, of doing so, the major factor determining the size of the profit incentive is the difference between profits from successfully obtaining the new technology and those currently being earned: $r(c,b) - r(a,b)$.

The second factor determining the nature of the reaction function is the amount of R&D firm 1 would do as $y \to \infty$. Denote this by $\bar{x}$. This factor we call the *competitive threat* since, as $y \to \infty$, firm 2 will almost surely innovate immediately. Given the inherently random nature of discovery, if firm 1 commits some resources to R&D there is still a chance that, even with $y \to \infty$, it could win the race. Balancing off the costs and benefits, it is clear that the major factor determining the amount of resources to spend on R&D is the difference between firm 1's rents if it successfully innovates first and those it would earn if firm 2 innovates first: $r(c, b) - r(a, c)$.

It turns out that in the absence of imitation or spillovers the competitive threat is typically greater than the profit incentive, giving rise to a reaction function for firm 1 like that shown in figure 7.1. There are two points to notice about this reaction function. The first is that x is increasing in y, for if stopping firm 2 from winning is a more important objective than bringing forward the likely date of innovation, then clearly firm 1 will respond to an increase in firm 2's R&D spending by increasing its own. The second is that as we move along the reaction function, the expected present value of firm 1's profits are falling as y (and hence x) increases. The amount x_0 effectively represents the profit-maximizing value of x arrived at by balancing off the gains from having the new technology by a particular date against the costs of doing so. Thus moving along the reaction function from x_0 to $\bar{x}$ is to move further and further from the profit-maximizing position.

7.2.2   Brander and Spencer Revisited

To see the effects of introducing a subsidy to R&D costs in country 1, we first need to consider the reaction of country 2. Once again, in the absence of

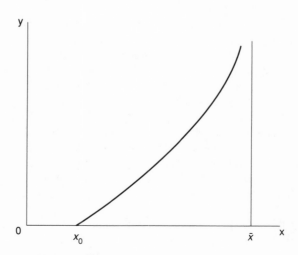

Fig. 7.1   Reaction function of country 1

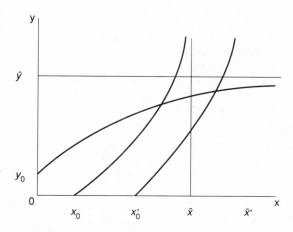

Fig. 7.2   Effect of R&D subsidy in country 1

imitation and spillovers, it is likely to have a greater competitive threat than profit incentive, and so to have a reaction function like that shown in figure 7.2.

Now a subsidy to R&D will shift country 1's reaction function out as shown in figure 7.2, leading to higher equilibrium values for x and y, though, since the ratio of x to y has increased, firm 1 is relatively more likely to innovate first. However, since this subsidy is a pure internal transfer, the gain to the country from introducing it has to be evaluated using the iso-profit functions relevant to generating the initial reaction function for firm 1. Since the original choice of x was profit-maximizing given the original equilibrium value of y, then, just as in Brander and Spencer, to first order the increase in the equilibrium value of x has no welfare gain. The only effect of the subsidy comes from the induced impact on y, and since y increases, and since we know profits fall as y increases, the subsidy definitely harms country 1.

Essentially both countries are indulging in wasteful overinvestment in R&D in a bid to stop the other from innovating first, and all the subsidy does is intensify this wasteful competition. Thus in a wide class of cases even the standard Brander and Spencer result fails to go through. Since, as we saw, this effect enters the formulae in all the cases where the availability of scientists is an issue, the case for R&D subsidies is likely to be problematic in those cases, too, whenever innovation takes the tournament form of a race to be first.

7.2.3   Spillovers in a Tournament Model

The above results were based on a tournament model where there were no spillovers, and consequently competitive threats were likely to exceed profit incentives for both firms. When there are spillovers then the competitive threats and profit incentives facing firm 1 become:

> competitive threat: $(1 - \beta)[r(c, b) - r(a, c)]$, and
> profit incentive: $\{[r(c, b) + \beta \cdot (a, c)]/(1 + \beta)\} - r(a, b)$.

The intuition is as follows. Consider what happens as $\beta \to 1$. The fact that $y \to \infty$ is now likely to benefit firm 1 almost as much as firm 2, while any R&D undertaken by firm 1 will add effectively the same (infinitesimal) amount to the likely success of both firms. Firm 1 is therefore just as likely to innovate almost surely now as firm 2, whatever R&D it does, and therefore faces effectively no competitive threat and consequently finds it not worthwhile to do any R&D.

On the other hand, if $y = 0$, then, as $\beta \to 1$, any R&D done by firm 1 will not just bring forward the expected date of innovation, but is as likely to make firm 2 the winner as firm 1. Thus the likely gain it gets from bringing forward the date of innovation is the difference between the average of the profits it gets if it wins and if it loses and its current profits.

Thus profit incentives and competitive threats are affected in an asymmetric fashion by the presence of spillovers. To see the implications of this, consider the case where firm 1 is currently very far behind firm 2, and there is a new innovation which gives a moderate advantage over the technology currently employed by firm 2. Indeed assume that firm 1 is so far behind that its current profits and those it gets if it loses are zero. However, if it wins it will face reasonably intense competition from firm 2, but will still make positive profits. Essentially then the profits that enter the determination of its competitive threat are $(1 - \beta) \cdot r(c, b)$, while those that affect its profit incentive are $[r(c, b)/(1 + \beta)]$. As long as β is large enough, its profit incentive exceeds its competitive threat, while, as long as $\beta < 1$, both are positive. Its reaction function is now as shown in figure 7.3.

The important points to notice about this are: (i) now the larger y is, the smaller the amount of R&D firm 1 does, since it can use the spillovers to free-ride on firm 2's R&D effort, and (ii) now the expected present value of profits made by firm 1 are increasing in y as we move along the reaction function from x_0 to $\bar{x}$—again because it can substitute firm 2's R&D spending for its own while keeping the likely date of innovation more or less constant.

Consider firm 2. It too will have a positive competitive threat since it stands to lose its monopoly position if firm 1 innovates ahead of it. However, since the innovation is fairly moderate, its profits from winning may not greatly exceed its current profits, while given the large amount of competition it will face if firm 1 innovates ahead of it, its profits if it loses may be considerably less than its current profits. Thus if β is large enough, the profits that enter the calculation of its profit incentive could be very small, if not zero or negative. In any event, it is likely to have a competitive threat that exceeds its profit incentive, as is illustrated in figure 7.3. But now an R&D subsidy to firm 1 is beneficial, for it once again expands the equilibrium values of x and y, and, while the expansion in x has, to first order, no effect on country 1's welfare, the expansion in y is, as we have seen, now positively beneficial, since it allows country 1 to free-ride on country 2's R&D effort. Thus with tournament models, and with initially very asymmetric firms, large spillovers can actually be a

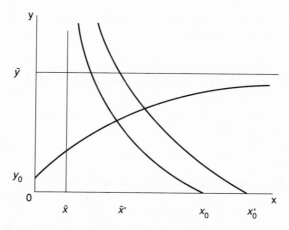

Fig. 7.3   Effect of R&D subsidy in country 1 with spillovers

reason for R&D subsidies. Thus arguments about the desirability of R&D subsidies depend rather crucially on the kind of innovation that takes place in any given industry.

Note that while the analysis in this section bears some resemblance to the contrast in policy conclusions one obtains when policy is conducted in the context of a Cournot model (with downward-sloping reaction functions) as against a Bertrand model (upward-sloping reaction functions), what this analysis shows is that policy depends on more than just knowing whether reaction curves are upward-sloping or downward-sloping. We also need to know how profits move along the relevant curves. Thus here subsidies are harmful whenever reaction curves have the *same* slope—whatever that is.

7.3   Measuring the Gains to R&D Policy

In this section we show how the model proposed in section 7.1 can be used to quantify the gains to R&D policy. We concentrate on the case where scientists are completely mobile and the government introduces a uniform R&D subsidy. As we saw there, the effects of such a subsidy are obtained by summing the effects on each industry, so there is no loss of generality if, to simplify the discussion, we concentrate on the case where the high-tech sector comprises a single representative or average industry.

However, for reasons that will become apparent, it is important that we generalize the model in section 7.1 to allow the possibility that there are n different countries or firms competing in this industry. We also focus throughout on the case where initially the industry is in a symmetric equilibrium, and one government introduces a subsidy. This is because all the elasticities we need become far more complex in asymmetric equilibria, and, although we could probably perform all the calculations using numerical methods, we simply do not have enough data to calculate them.

7.3.1   The Model

Suppose we have a single industry where demand is given by

$$(32) \qquad p = A \cdot Q^{-\varepsilon},$$

where

$$(33) \qquad Q = \sum_{i=1}^{n} q_i.$$

Here $A > 0$ is a parameter measuring the size of the market, q_i is the output of firm i, and $\varepsilon > 0$ is the inverse elasticity of demand. For the moment we will assume that since this is an imperfectly competitive industry $\varepsilon < 1$.

Although the initial equilibrium is symmetric we need to explore the consequences of having an asymmetry introduced via government policy pursued in country 1 which could give the firm there an R&D and hence a production cost advantage. Let us assume therefore that unit costs are a in firm 1 and b in firms 2 to n. For an interior solution we have the following first-order conditions for profit maximization:

$$(34) \qquad A \cdot Q^{-\varepsilon} - A \cdot \varepsilon \cdot q_1 \cdot Q^{-(1+\varepsilon)} - a = 0,$$

and

$$(35) \qquad A \cdot Q^{-\varepsilon} - A \cdot \varepsilon \cdot q_i \cdot Q^{-(1+\varepsilon)} - b = 0, \, i = 2, \ldots, n.$$

Adding gives

$$(36) \qquad (n - \varepsilon)A \cdot Q^{-\varepsilon} = a + (n - 1) \cdot b.$$

Now the profits of firm 1, r, are

$$r = (A \cdot Q^{-\varepsilon} - a) \cdot q_1.$$

So, from (36), the profits to sale ratio,

$$(37) \; r/(p \cdot q_1) = (p - a)/p = [(n - 1) \cdot (b - a) + a\varepsilon]/[a + (n - 1)b],$$

which, in a symmetric equilibrium, gives

$$(38) \qquad r/(p \cdot q_1) = \varepsilon/n.$$

If we now introduce the notation

$$(39) \qquad B = (1/\varepsilon) \cdot A^{1/\varepsilon} \cdot (n - \varepsilon)^{(1/\varepsilon) - 1},$$

then it is easy to show that the profits of firm 1, r, are given by

$$(40) \; r = B \cdot [(n - 1) \cdot b - (n - 1 - \varepsilon) \cdot a]^2 \cdot [a + (n - 1) \cdot b]^{-(1+\varepsilon)/\varepsilon}.$$

From this we get

$$\frac{\partial ra}{\partial ar} = -a\Big\{[2(n-1-\varepsilon)]/[(n-1)b - (n-1-\varepsilon)a] +$$

(41)
$$(1+\varepsilon)/\{\varepsilon[a + (n-1)b]\}\Big\} < 0,$$

$$= -\{[2(n-1)n + 1] - (2n-1)\varepsilon\}/n\varepsilon, \text{ when } a = b,$$

and

$$\frac{\partial rb}{\partial br} = b \cdot \Big\{2/[(n-1)b - (n-1-\varepsilon)a] -$$

(42)
$$(1+\varepsilon)/\{\varepsilon[a + (n-1)b]\}\Big\}$$

$$= [2n-1-\varepsilon]/n\varepsilon, \text{ when } a = b.$$

Here the interpretation of $\partial r/\partial b$ is the increase in firm 1's profits if the unit costs of *one* of the remaining $n-1$ firms were to increase. If they all increased then we would simply multiply the above formulae by $n-1$.

For later purposes it is also worth reporting that, when $a = b$, then

(43) $a \cdot r_{ad}/r_a = -(1/\varepsilon) \cdot \Big\{(n-1-\varepsilon) + [(1+2\varepsilon)/n] +$

$$[(n-1-\varepsilon)(1-\varepsilon)]/[2(n-1)(n-\varepsilon) + (1-\varepsilon)]\Big\},$$

and

(44) $b \cdot r_{bd}/r_a = (1/\varepsilon) \cdot \Big\{1 - [(1+2\varepsilon)/n] + [1 + \varepsilon(2n-1)$

$$- 2\varepsilon^2]/[2(n-\varepsilon)(n-1) + (1-\varepsilon)]\Big\}.$$

Note that, from (43), $r_{aa} > 0$, so that, at least in the neighborhood of a symmetric equilibrium, r is convex in a. Of course it has to be convex at some point in its range, since profits decrease to zero at a finite value of a. But this means that the more that is spent on R&D to lower costs, the more worthwhile it becomes to further lower them. Nor is this a peculiarity of the particular model we have employed, but must be true of any model where firm 1's profits go to zero if its costs get too far out of line with those of the other firms. This implies that to get a well-defined story of R&D spending we are going to have to make the R&D costs of lowering production costs rise very fast. So let us assume

(45)
$$a = a^0 \cdot x^{-\gamma},$$

where x is the amount of R&D done by firm 1. This functional form is used in much of the empirical literature on estimating the effects of R&D on output and productivity. Later we will call on this literature for an estimate of γ. If the price of R&D for firm 1 is c, then the cost of achieving unit production costs a is

(46) $$C(a) = c \cdot (a^0/a)^{1/\gamma}.$$

If we now think of firm 1 taking b as given and choosing a to maximize

$$r(a,b) - C(a)$$

then this produces the first-order condition

(47) $$-\partial r/\partial a = (c/\gamma) \cdot (a^0)^{1/\gamma} \cdot a^{-(1+1/\gamma)}.$$

It is easy to check that in order to have the second-order conditions for a maximum satisfied we need

(48) $$\alpha \equiv 1 + (1/\gamma) + (a \cdot r_{aa}/r_a) > 0.$$

From (43) it follows that this will not be true for any arbitrary positive value of γ and that we will need γ to be suitably small, as we would have expected from the previous discussion.

It is easy to check that if (48) holds then

(49) $$\partial a/\partial b < 0, \text{ and}$$

(50) $$\partial a/\partial c > 0,$$

so that, from (49) an increase in R&D by one of the other firms, which lowers its unit costs, causes firm 1 to cut back on its R&D, giving it higher unit costs, while, from (50), an increase in the price firm 1 has to pay for its science causes it to do less R&D and so have higher unit costs.

We assume now that firms 2 to n have the same R&D cost function, the same initial costs a^0, and all face the same price, d, for science. Initially we will start with $c = d$, so that we will indeed have a symmetric equilibrium, and we will examine the effects of policies that lower c.

To examine the effects of such a policy let us introduce the notation

(51) $$\beta = b \cdot r_{bd}/r_a,$$

and

(52) $$\Delta = (n - 2)\alpha\beta + \alpha^2 - (n - 1)\beta^2.$$

It is easily checked that a sufficient condition for the reaction functions to intersect in the right way and produce a stable (symmetric) equilibrium is that

(53) $$\Delta > 0, \text{ or, equivalently, } \alpha > \beta.$$

It is also easily verified that

(54) $$\frac{\partial a}{\partial c}\frac{c}{a} = [(n - 2)\beta + \alpha]/\Delta > 0,$$

and

(55)
$$\frac{\partial b}{\partial c}\frac{c}{b} = -\beta/\Delta < 0.$$

Thus in the full Nash equilibrium it is still the case that a rise in the price of firm 1's science causes it to do less R&D and so have higher unit costs, while it causes firms 2 to n to do more R&D and so have lower unit costs. By symmetry the effect of an increase in d on b is the same as the effect of c on a, while the effect of an increase in d on a is the same as the effect of c on b.

7.3.2   Calibrating the Effects of Policy

The policy effects we want to calibrate are those arising from the mobile-scientists case, assuming that there is just one industry, but allowing now for n firms in the industry.

We know that when there are just two firms the effect of introducing a small subsidy is given by

$$\frac{dW}{ds} = -(1-\theta)\left(\frac{\partial r}{\partial a}\cdot\frac{\partial a}{\partial c} + \frac{\partial r}{\partial b}\cdot\frac{\partial b}{\partial c}\right) + \theta\left(\frac{\partial r}{\partial a}\cdot\frac{\partial a}{\partial d} + \frac{\partial r}{\partial b}\cdot\frac{\partial b}{\partial d}\right),$$

where $\theta = dw/ds$. More generally we have

$$\frac{dW}{ds} = -(1-\theta)\left[\frac{\partial r}{\partial a}\cdot\frac{\partial a}{\partial c} + (n-1)\frac{\partial r}{\partial b}\cdot\frac{\partial b}{\partial c}\right] +$$
$$\theta\left\{(n-1)\frac{\partial r}{\partial a}\cdot\frac{\partial a}{\partial d} + (n-1)\frac{\partial r}{\partial b}\cdot\left[(n-2)\frac{\partial b}{\partial c} + \frac{\partial b}{\partial d}\right]\right\}.$$

Now it is easy to check that, given symmetry, $\theta = 1/n$. We also exploit symmetry to write $\partial a/\partial c = \partial b/\partial d$, $\partial b/\partial c = \partial a/\partial d$, and to evaluate everything at a symmetric equilibrium where $a = b$ and $c = d = w$, the wage of scientists. We then get, after some rearranging

(56) $$w\cdot\frac{dW}{ds}\cdot\frac{1}{W} = \frac{r}{W}\cdot\frac{(n-1)}{n}\cdot\left(\frac{\partial r}{\partial b}\frac{b}{r} - \frac{\partial r}{\partial a}\frac{a}{r}\right)\cdot\left(\frac{\partial a}{\partial c}\cdot\frac{c}{a} - \frac{\partial b}{\partial c}\cdot\frac{c}{b}\right).$$

If, instead of a uniform absolute subsidy s, we had thought of a proportional subsidy, $\tilde{\sigma}$, where $s = \tilde{\sigma}\cdot w$, then the left-hand side of (56) is just the percentage change in GNP brought about by a unit increase in $\tilde{\sigma}$, i.e., from introducing a 100 percent subsidy to the cost of R&D. The term (r/W) on the right-hand side of (56) is just the share of profits from the high-tech sector in GNP. We can write

(57) $$r/W = (r/pq)\cdot(pq/W) = (\varepsilon/n)\cdot\Sigma,$$

where $\Sigma \equiv (pq/W)$ is the share of the output of the high-tech sector in GNP.

From (56) and (57) it is clear that the effects of R&D subsidies on GNP will be proportional to the size of the high-tech sector. However if we want to measure the power of the policy of subsidizing R&D it makes sense to measure the effects of policy relative to the size of the sector to which they are applied. Thus we should divide (56) by Σ.

Finally, if we wish to know the effectiveness of a 1 percent subsidy to R&D costs we have to divide (56) by 100. Thus if we let $\tilde{\sigma} = 100 \cdot \sigma$ then $dW/d\sigma \cdot 1/W$ will measure (relative to the initial size of the high-tech sector) the percentage effect on GNP of a 1 percent R&D subsidy. From our above discussion, we can rewrite (56) to obtain

$$
(58) \qquad \frac{dW}{d\sigma} \cdot \frac{1}{W} = \frac{\varepsilon}{n} \cdot \frac{(n-1)}{n} \cdot \left[\frac{\partial r}{\partial b} \cdot \frac{b}{r} + \left(\frac{-\partial r}{\partial a} \cdot \frac{a}{r} \right) \right] \cdot \left[\frac{\partial a}{\partial c} \cdot \frac{c}{a} + \left(\frac{-\partial b}{\partial c} \cdot \frac{c}{b} \right) \right] / 100.
$$

Estimates of this measure of the effectiveness of R&D subsidies will be presented in tables 7.1 and 7.2 below.

One problem with this measure is that how powerful a 1 percent subsidy is depends in part on what percentage of a firm's expenditure is represented by R&D. Thus, if R&D represents a relatively small part of a firm's expenditure, a 1 percent subsidy might not have as much impact as, say, a 1 percent production subsidy, but on the other hand the amount of money given by way of the subsidy will also be smaller. This suggests an alternative measure of the effectiveness of an R&D subsidy which is the increases in GNP it induces relative to the amount of the subsidy. We will refer to this as the "policy multiplier." This will be a particularly useful measure to employ when comparing the effectiveness of different kinds of policy.

Now the expenditure involved in implementing the subsidy is

$$
E = s\xi(w - s, w),
$$

so, evaluated at the initial zero-subsidy position, we have

$$
(59) \qquad w \cdot \frac{dE}{ds} = w \cdot \xi.
$$

Hence if we divide (56) by (59) we get

$$
(60) \qquad \frac{dW}{dE} = \frac{r}{w\xi} \cdot \frac{(n-1)}{n} \cdot \left(\frac{\partial r}{\partial b} \cdot \frac{b}{r} - \frac{\partial r}{\partial a} \cdot \frac{a}{r} \right) \cdot \left(\frac{\partial a}{\partial c} \cdot \frac{c}{a} - \frac{\partial b}{\partial c} \cdot \frac{c}{b} \right),
$$

where dW/dE is the increase in GNP brought about per unit amount of resources transferred as a subsidy to R&D—i.e., the policy multiplier. Note that this measure is independent of the size of the sector.

It is easily checked from (47) that the ratio of r to the costs of doing R&D is

$$
(61) \qquad \frac{r}{w\xi} = \frac{r}{C(a)} = 1 / \left[g \cdot \left(\frac{-\partial r}{\partial a} \cdot \frac{a}{r} \right) \right].
$$

We can therefore rewrite (60) as

(62) $\dfrac{dW}{dE} = \left\{ 1 / \left[\gamma \cdot \left(\dfrac{-\partial r}{\partial a} \cdot \dfrac{a}{r} \right) \right] \right\} \cdot \dfrac{(n-1)}{n} \cdot \left(\dfrac{\partial r}{\partial b} \cdot \dfrac{b}{r} - \dfrac{\partial r}{\partial a} \cdot \dfrac{a}{r} \right) \cdot$
$\left(\dfrac{\partial a}{\partial c} \cdot \dfrac{c}{a} - \dfrac{\partial b}{\partial c} \cdot \dfrac{c}{b} \right).$

Estimates of this measure of the effectiveness of R&D subsidies will be presented in tables 7.3 and 7.4 below.

We have estimates of γ from empirical studies. So given values for n and ε, we can perform all the necessary calculations of both measures. The next subsection sets out the details and the results.

7.3.3   The Results

Estimates of γ vary both across different studies and, within studies, across different industries. Thus early studies using U.S. data by Mansfield (1968), Terleckyj (1974), Miniasian (1969), and Griliches (1980) found estimates of γ in the range 0.1–0.12. Griliches and Mairesse (1984) and Cuneo and Mairesse (1984) look further at the relationship of firms' R&D spending to productivity performance for the United States and France, respectively. They find estimates of γ in the range 0.08–0.15, with higher values for science-based firms—confirming a similar finding by Griliches (1980) that R&D-intensive industries have higher values of γ. There is therefore some consensus that γ lies in the range 0.1–0.15, with the more technologically advanced industries having higher values. Accordingly we have undertaken calculations with three different values of γ: 0.1, 0.125, and 0.15. We have also allowed n to take the three values 2, 3, and 4.

The most problematic parameter to obtain estimates for was ε. Baldwin and Krugman (1988a) suggest the price elasticity for wide-bodied jets lies in the range 1.57–2.57 ($\varepsilon = 0.39$–0.64). Baldwin and Krugman (1988b) report a price elasticity for 16K chips of 1.8 ($\varepsilon = 0.56$). Based on this evidence we performed two separate exercises. The first was to simply calculate the welfare gains using values of ε ranging from 0.35 to 0.75. This encompasses all of the values for various high-tech sectors reported above. In table 7.1 we report the results of this exercise when the measure of welfare gain is the percentage increase in GNP (relative to the size of the high-tech sector) brought about by a 1 percent R&D subsidy. In table 7.3 we report the results using as our measure dW/dE—the size of the gain relative to the resources transferred as a subsidy.

An implication of this exercise is that, from (38), the price/cost margin (or, equivalently, the markup of price over cost) will vary quite sharply with the number of firms. Accordingly in our second exercise we fixed the price/cost markup, m, where

(63) $m/(1 + m) = (p - c)/p = \varepsilon/n,$

and then used (63) to determine ε. The values of m we chose were 0.15, 0.2, and 0.25. Empirical evidence suggests that markups of this order are fairly typical. The results of this exercise are reported in table 7.2, using as a measure of the gains the increase in GNP (relative to the size of the high-tech sector) from a 1 percent subsidy, and in table 7.4 where we use as our measure the increase in GNP relative to the amount of resources transferred by way of a subsidy.

Incidentally, if we take $n = 3$, then the implied value of ε from a markup of 20 percent is approximately 0.55. In what follows we will therefore take 0.55 as our central estimate of ε, and 0.2 as our central estimate of m.

Let us turn then to look at the results in the tables. From table 7.1 a number of points emerge. The first is that while the figures are fairly sensitive to the underlying parameters, the majority of parameter values produce percentage gains of less than 1 percent, and values greater than 1 percent only seem to arise for extreme parameter values.

The second feature is that while, as expected, the effects of subsidies are greater the larger γ is, they are also greater the more competitive the market is—the larger n is and the smaller ε. The reason is that the gains from policy arise from expansion of the home firms and more particularly from contraction of the overseas opposition. These are greater, the more elastic demand and the larger the number of other firms that will be affected by policy.

Table 7.2 presents essentially similar results for the magnitude of effects. Once again policies are more effective the more competitive the market is, as reflected by a smaller value of m. However the effects of variations in n are less clear-cut, because now there are associated variations in ε as well.

While the relatively small size of the effects of policy shown in tables 7.1 and 7.2 are in line with others' findings on the magnitudes of the effects of strategic trade policy, there are some crucial differences in the nature of the policies and in the underlying models which make a straight comparison rather difficult. The first is that trade policy affects both consumer surplus and producer surplus (rents), and in some calculations more than half the gain comes from consumer surplus. We have ignored this on the assumption that most of the gains from price reductions accrue outside the country.

Table 7.1   **Percentage Increase in GNP from 1% Subsidy to R&D Costs**

	$\gamma=0.1$			$\gamma=0.125$			$\gamma=0.15$		
ε	$n=2$	$n=3$	$n=4$	$n=2$	$n=3$	$n=4$	$n=2$	$n=3$	$n=4$
0.35	0.18	0.47	—	0.31	2.26	—	0.62	—	—
0.45	0.13	0.25	0.51	0.19	0.44	2.27	0.27	0.92	—
0.55	0.10	0.19	0.30	0.14	0.28	0.57	0.19	0.43	1.38
0.65	0.09	0.15	0.23	0.12	0.22	0.37	0.15	0.30	0.60
0.75	0.08	0.13	0.19	0.10	0.18	0.28	0.13	0.24	0.41

Note: Cells without entries indicate that for these parameter values the model has no stable solution.

Table 7.2   **Percentage Increase in GNP from 1% Subsidy to R&D Costs**

	$\gamma=0.1$			$\gamma=0.125$			$\gamma=0.15$		
m	$n=2$	$n=3$	$n=4$	$n=2$	$n=3$	$n=4$	$n=2$	$n=3$	$n=4$
0.15	0.37	0.33	0.34	2.56	0.78	0.70	—	7.24	2.49
0.20	0.19	0.21	0.22	0.36	0.34	0.35	0.83	0.57	0.55
0.25	0.14	0.17	0.18	0.23	0.24	0.26	0.36	0.35	0.36

Note: See note to table 7.1.

Table 7.3   **Policy Multiplier**

	$\gamma=0.1$			$\gamma=0.125$			$\gamma=0.15$		
ε	$n=2$	$n=3$	$n=4$	$n=2$	$n=3$	$n=4$	$n=2$	$n=3$	$n=4$
0.35	1.79	3.74	—	2.50	14.50	—	4.15	—	—
0.45	1.37	2.08	3.77	1.62	2.95	13.27	1.98	5.12	—
0.55	1.21	1.63	2.29	1.35	1.98	3.45	1.51	2.51	6.98
0.65	1.14	1.42	1.81	1.22	1.62	2.29	1.32	1.87	3.12
0.75	1.10	1.31	1.57	1.16	1.43	1.84	1.23	1.58	2.23

Note: See note to table 7.1.

The second difference is that strategic trade policy considers policies such as export or production subsidies which are potentially very powerful, because they represent subsidies to a large part of a firm's activities. Since, even in the high-tech sector R&D accounts for a small fraction of all costs, a 1 percent R&D subsidy may not represent a very significant subsidy. For this reason it is worth looking at our second measure of the effectiveness of R&D policy—the increase in GNP relative to the amount given as a subsidy. Figures for this are given in tables 7.3 and 7.4.

Thus if we take as our central case the values $\gamma = 0.15$ (the "high-tech" end of the spectrum), $\varepsilon = 0.55$, and $n = 3$, we see that the gain in GNP relative to the size of the subsidy is 2.5. Thus if the government raises £1 billion in taxes and then gives this in the form of an R&D subsidy to firms in the high-tech sector, then GNP would rise by £2.5 billion. Therefore while a 1 percent subsidy to R&D may not have much of an impact on GNP, because it is a rather weak stimulus, in terms of pounds spent, it offers a potentially very high rate of return.

Of course, in a fuller and more careful evaluation of policy, account would have to be taken of any deadweight loss the transfer would impose. Also it must be recalled that we have considered the most favorable case, where scientists are fully mobile, and these results would have to be scaled down to reflect the degree of immobility that exists in practice. However, offsetting this is the fact that we have also ignored any beneficial spillover effects within the economy.

Table 7.4   **Policy Multiplier**

	$\gamma=0.1$			$\gamma=0.125$			$\gamma=0.15$		
m	$n=2$	$n=3$	$n=4$	$n=2$	$n=3$	$n=4$	$n=2$	$n=3$	$n=4$
0.15	3.52	2.70	2.53	19.39	5.06	4.21	—	39.34	12.42
0.20	1.92	1.80	1.76	2.86	2.32	2.19	5.56	3.25	2.91
0.25	1.52	1.51	1.49	1.91	1.76	1.71	2.56	2.11	2.00

Note: See note to table 7.1.

In addition, account would also have to be taken of the effects of policy on terms of trade, on consumer surplus, and on the policy choices of rival governments. While these are all important issues, a serious treatment lies well beyond the scope of this paper. Nevertheless the conclusion seems to emerge that giving R&D support to the high-tech sector is potentially an extremely powerful and important policy.

7.4   Empirical Evidence

The preceding sections identified four issues critical to the application of strategic trade policy: (i) the mobility of scientists, (ii) the mobility of science, (iii) the existence of spillovers, and (iv) tournament versus nontournament R&D environments.

Although recent theoretical work on R&D races has focused rather heavily on tournament models, the requirements an R&D environment must satisfy to be of a tournament kind are very restrictive. Effectively, the requirements are a single product or process that firms are competing to introduce, and just one central idea or technique lying behind the product or process so that whoever develops and successfully patents this technique first can prevent rivals from using the new technology. No formal tests exist of what proportions of R&D activity may reasonably be classified as tournament and nontournament. Clearly even within a given industry some R&D activity may fall in one category and some in the other. Impressionistically, however, pharmaceuticals is an industry where some of its R&D exhibits many of the features of tournament models, while aerospace is more representative of the nontournament case. Our view is that the nontournament model describes a sufficiently large part of R&D activity to make the policy implications of sections 7.1 and 7.3 worth taking seriously. Since these depend crucially on the degree of mobility and the extent of spillovers, the rest of this section will examine the evidence on these issues.

7.4.1   The Mobility of Scientists

Any degree of international mobility of scientists is sufficient to undermine the Dixit and Grossman result, and there is obviously some such mobility. For policy purposes, however, the important issue is to measure it, because the scope for improving welfare by general or arbitrary R&D subsidies must be balanced against factors such as the probabilities of retaliation, the costs of financing subsidies, and the dangers of a subsidy policy being captured by interest groups. All of these trade-offs require quantification. This subsection therefore surveys the evidence on the extent of migration by scientists and engineers. It concludes that migration does occur in response to economic factors in the long run and finds that, for the United States, the principal conduit is the higher education system. The effects of migration are felt throughout the economy, however, because, within specialisms, there is a fairly free flow of scientists between sectors.

The evidence on migration is based on three principal sources: the National Science Foundation (NSF 1986, 1973), the Office of Scientific and Engineering Personnel (OSEP 1988), both from the United States, and the Science and Engineering Policy Studies Unit (SEPSU 1987) from the United Kingdom. All three sources rely on survey data, although the NSF also makes use of immigration authority information. The NSF considers all scientists and engineers (referred to as S/Es below) while OSEP refers mainly to trained engineers working as engineers (Es). SEPSU deals with just five disciplines—biochemistry, chemistry, earth sciences, physics, and electronic engineering—and is cautious about extrapolation to the population of all scientists and engineers.

The principal conclusion from these studies is that there is an international market for S/Es, but that it is far from perfect. International flows are small relative to total stocks of S/Es: SEPSU, for example, finds that U.K. annual immigration and emigration are both about 2 percent of total S/Es over 1976–85. Stocks of nonnational scientists, on the other hand, can be significant: NSF (1986) reports that, in 1982, while only 3.5 percent of S/Es in the United States were noncitizens, a further 13.5 percent were of foreign origin but had taken U.S. citizenship. Migration is more significant among better-qualified S/Es. The OSEP shows that over one-third of doctorate-level engineers in the United States are of non-U.S. origin (OSEP 1988, table A-2) and that in 1982 over one-third of labor force entrants holding Ph.D.s were noncitizens (OSEP 1988, table D-2).

The most obvious institutional feature of the international market for scientists is immigration control; virtually every industrial nation now controls immigration to try to ensure that available jobs go to suitably qualified local residents. In the United States, for example, overall immigration quotas are imposed, and the secretary of labor has to certify that each act of permanent immigration "will not adversely affect the wages or working conditions of similarly employed labor" (NSF 1986). Places are granted to would-be immigrants on the basis of shortages of skills, and OSEP reports that, across broad subject areas, Ph.D.-level immigration is positively correlated with reported skill shortages (OSEP 1988, 95). The connection is less clear within the S/E group, however, although foreign-born S/Es account for relatively high proportions of researchers in fields that were previously unfashionable in the United States but are now of high commercial significance (OSEP 1988, 3). Thus it appears that immigration does serve to alleviate crucial skill shortages, especially at high levels.

Two exceptions make it relatively straightforward for S/Es to immigrate even if, at the time of entry, they are not highly qualified or experienced. First, temporary work visas of one year's duration are granted liberally to S/Es and without quota limits (NSF 1986). Moreover, these visas are renewable and in many cases can be translated into permanent visas and eventually into naturalization without great difficulty. Temporary visas are automatically granted to foreign engineering students on graduation in order that they may obtain practical training in the United States. The temporary visa system brings several benefits to the functioning of U.S. skilled labor markets. First, it permits short-run adjustment to shortages; for example, in 1978, the latest year recorded, 30 percent of foreign S/Es admitted were on temporary visas (NSF 1986). Second, the temporary visa system offers an effective screening mechanism of candidates' ability, motivation, and the like; permanent immigration will be possible only if they find a sponsor/employer and so will require some minimal standard of performance. Such screening clearly enhances immigration as a means of increasing and improving the labor force.

The second fast track through immigration formalities is the education system—especially at the second-degree level. Foreigners on temporary visas accounted for 40 percent of engineering enrollments in U.S. doctorate-giving institutions and 41 percent of Ph.D.s awarded by U.S. engineering schools in 1985; in 1982, 62 percent of foreign S/E Ph.D. recipients stayed in the United States. Two-thirds of engineering postdoctorates were foreign (noncitizen) in 1985, rising to four-fifths in metallurgy/materials engineering, and half of all engineering assistant professors under 35 years of age were foreign. Around 80 percent of non–U.S. origin S/Es employed in the United States in 1982 had received U.S. training and 80 percent had entered the United States after the age of 15, presumably for the express purpose of work or training. Most of the growth of employment of S/Es of foreign-origin since 1972 has been among naturalized citizens, not aliens. Thus it would hardly be an exaggeration to say that a principal function of the U.S. higher education system has been to supply the U.S. economy with S/Es from abroad on a fairly permanent basis.

Although there are few discernible patterns in the specialisms of U.S. foreign S/Es, there are patterns in their occupations. Foreign-origin S/Es are underrepresented in the defense and government sectors relative to industry as a whole and relatively overrepresented in education and the hospital/nonprofit sectors (NSF 1986). They are concentrated in research and development/design tasks and are underrepresented in general management (though not the management of R&D). This research concentration also explains the high proportion of foreign-origin staff in education—they are not overrepresented in teaching. The OSEP suggests that foreign and foreign-born engineers earn the same wages as indigenous engineers once allowance is made for qualifications, age, field, experience, and so forth. This suggests that within skill and subject groups, foreign and domestic S/Es are good substitutes. U.K. evidence also suggests fairly high mobility between sectors (university, industry, government), so that overall we may conclude that for each specialism there is a single fairly well functioning market for S/Es.

Two sources present direct evidence on the motives for migration among S/Es. The NSF (1973) found that economic and job factors were the most significant considerations for U.S. immigrants from industrial countries, while SEPSU found that for U.K. emigrants relative career opportunities at home and abroad predominated, followed by rates of pay, research facilities, and the desire for experience. Higher pay was particularly important to emigrants from the university sector. While both sources listed many other motives for migration, they both leave an overwhelming impression that the economic resources devoted to science matter most of all: S/Es do seem to be attracted to areas of high net rewards.

The evidence presented in this section is open to at least one coherent interpretation that has profound policy implications, not least in the area of strategic trade policy. The international migration of S/Es is a long-run phenomenon but is, nonetheless, subject to market forces. It takes time for market signals to build up and be acted upon, but migration, once undertaken, tends to be permanent. A principal medium for migration is the university system, in which there are relatively few cultural barriers to international movement. Most liberal is the system of educating foreign students. At least for migrants to the United States, S/E doctoral studies are more often than not the first step on an American S/E career. Obviously this is not universally true, and it is particularly difficult to identify how many foreign S/Es return home after several years' employment in the United States, but the evidence suggests that the education system is a primary route through which U.S. industry recruits foreign talent. The universities and research foundations also provide a good medium for postdoctoral migration, attracting, for example, about half of U.K. S/E emigrants and providing work for a relatively high proportion of the foreign S/Es in the United States.

That a high proportion of migration occurs via universities does not mean, however, that its principal effects lie in that sector. As students graduate, they mostly pass out into noneducation sectors. Moreover, mobility between university faculties and other employers of S/Es means that the ability of universities to recruit immigrants for teaching and research releases manpower for other sectors. It is true that foreign-origin S/Es are strongly represented in industrial research and development activities, but again, the ability of U.S. industry to have R&D done by foreign S/Es releases indigenous S/Es for management posts. Thus even if foreign-origin S/Es are not well represented in the commanding heights of U.S. industry, their availability somewhere in the system makes a fundamental contribution to the U.S. economy.

The policy implications in the context of strategic trade policy is as follows. In the short run, a country's stock of S/Es is probably fairly rigid. This gravitates away from activist trade policies for the reasons set out by Dixit and Grossman (1986). On the other hand, a long-term commitment to the employment of and provision for S/Es may reap benefits in terms of increased net immigration. However, given the intersectoral mobility of S/Es, the requirement is more for general scientific facilities than for industry or project-specific subsidies.

The evidence above suggests a close connection between U.S. training for S/Es and U.S. employment, but it did not identify the direction of causation. Given the strong economic motives among qualified scientists and the high stay-on intentions expressed by U.S. S/E students (NSF 1986), we suspect that students seek U.S. education as an entry ticket to U.S. employment rather than seek U.S. employment as a result of obtaining a U.S. education. In other words, it is likely that stimulating the demand for scientists is more effective than stimulating the supply.

In terms of the model considered in section 7.1 and calibrated in section 7.3 there seems to be a significant amount of mobility, which could help justify policies of support for the high-tech sector. Moreover the degree of mobility among engineers seems to be as high as among scientists, so it is possible that the problems alluded to in section 7.1.6 would not arise. However this depends on our ad hoc designation of the key workers in the development process as engineers, and it is possible that there are yet other strategically important but immobile factors that we have ignored.

7.4.2   The Mobility of Science

If scientists are immobile, it may still be possible to import their services by subcontracting R&D abroad. As we saw above, "mobile science" is, broadly speaking, a substitute for mobile scientists, although its implications for policy are rather different. It is easy to conceive of research problems being contracted out to foreign researchers—indeed, this paper is an example—so again the important issue is quantitative rather than qualitative.

The most detailed data and analyses of offshore R&D refer to multinational corporations (MNCs). Crude data suggest that around 70 percent of technological royalties and fees paid by residents of industrial countries represent transfers between related organizations—see, for example, Ledic and Silberston (1984). Although these data may exaggerate the proportion of "affiliated" transfers—for example, royalties offer more scope for transfer pricing than do goods flows (Hirschey and Caves 1981), and nonaffiliated transactions are more likely to include other means of payment for technology, such as tie-in sales, purchases of inputs, and the like (Bond 1981)—the importance of the

MNCs in technology transfer is undeniable. The difficulty of interpreting these data for our purposes is that they include both R&D that is a substitute for local, home-country, effort and R&D that must necessarily be conducted abroad because it is complementary to foreign sales or production. The former is "footloose" and a legitimate component of mobile science: the latter is not.

Three sets of studies suggest the importance of production and sales activities in determining the location of the R&D that MNCs do locate abroad. First, foreign-based R&D is biased toward development and adaptation rather than basic or applied research—Creamer et al. (1976), Hood and Young (1976), and Mansfield et al. (1979). The last found that around three-quarters of U.S. MNCs restricted their overseas R&D activities to improvements or modifications of products or processes rather than allowing them to work on entirely new cases. The proportion of domestic laboratories so limited was much smaller. Firms also reported that some third of overseas R&D expenditure contributed nothing to their U.S. operations, and fewer than one-half of firms attempted to integrate all their laboratories into a single worldwide research program.

The second set of evidence comes from Teece (1976). He offers direct evidence that foreign technology cannot be imported and applied costlessly, but rather that it requires significant inputs of both local and foreign skilled labor and scientists to exploit it. Although generalization is difficult, Teece notes a number of common features of technology transfer. First, transfer costs are lower the larger, more experienced in production, and more R&D intensive is the transferee organization. Second, transfer costs are lower the more times the technology has been transferred previously and the greater the production experience with the technology. Except in a small subset of his 26 instances, Teece found that transfer prior to any production experience was very expensive. This last result bodes ill for transferring fundamental research.

The third body of evidence is based on statistical models of the share of R&D undertaken abroad; see, for example, Mansfield et al. (1979), Lall (1979), Hirschey and Caves (1981), and Pearce (1988). All of these authors find that sales by foreign subsidiaries are positively related to the proportion of R&D undertaken abroad. Hirschey and Caves also find that overseas R&D increases with the need to adapt products to local market conditions and with the level of host country R&D.

All of these results suggest that a substantial proportion of MNC overseas R&D activity is determined by overseas production and sales requirements. However, the degrees of explanation that these studies attain are generally quite low; thus there still remains scope for further explanations, including that firms locate some footloose R&D in a cost-minimizing fashion. Only Mansfield et al. (1979) offer direct evidence on this. Based on admittedly very small samples, they suggest that laboratories devoted to minor adaptation could be efficient at a considerably smaller scale than those devoted to genuine research or development, which in turn could be smaller than research *and* development laboratories. Thus it is possible that the development activities noted by the various studies will form the basis of future research laboratories, or indeed, given the date of Mansfield et al.'s work, that they have already done so.

Mansfield et al. also found that Canada, Europe, and Japan had been considerably cheaper locations for R&D than the United States in 1965 (by 30 percent, 40 percent, and 20 percent, respectively) and in 1970, but that by 1975 the differentials had largely disappeared. Their respondents also suggested that over the decade 1965–75 the share of R&D done overseas had expanded rapidly, but that in the late-1970s it was expected to do so only slowly. This confirms evidence from Pearce (1986) that the proportion of R&D expenditures undertaken by U.S.-owned foreign affiliates in the total R&D spending of the corporate group rose from 6.6 percent in 1966 to 8.8 percent in 1982. This is at least consistent with firms responding to economic pressures to locate footloose R&D efficiently.

There is one further aspect of the MNC literature relevant to our hypothesis. Reddaway (1968) noted that U.K. foreign direct investment abroad generated significant back-flows of information from certain host countries—mainly the United States and West Germany. In part this was due to R&D undertaken by the foreign subsidiaries and is akin to the R&D that Mansfield et al. identified as being of relevance to the parent company. Reddaway, however, also writes of "informal know-how" and of the United States as a "source of general expertise" (1968, 322). This appears to entail U.K. firms benefiting by learning by doing abroad, and the implication seems to be that such knowledge is transferable back home. Further evidence of learning by doing abroad is quoted by Caves, who notes its role in certain Japanese companies' foreign investment (1982, 198).

Taken as a whole these results suggest that at least some footloose R&D can be located abroad, and thus that to some extent science can be brought in to overcome a local shortage of scientists. The results are not strong, however, and none of the studies really tackles the question of what proportion of foreign science was undertaken by home-country scientists. If this were high, it would reduce the role of offshore R&D in supplementing home efforts.

There are also direct but less comprehensive indicators of the existence of offshore R&D. For example, Porsche is reported to fund nearly 40 percent of its R&D laboratories' turnover with projects undertaken for other companies, including a complete car design for the Soviet firm Lada. Indeed it is suggested that most car producers in the world make some use of the Porsche laboratories (Note 324/88, Science and Technology Section, British Embassy, Bonn). In 1987, 3.1 percent of total German-funded R&D was conducted abroad, and 1.1 percent of German-conducted research was funded from abroad. While small, these figures were both the fastest growing elements of their respective aggregates (Federal Republic of Germany 1988). In the United Kingdom, some 13 percent of R&D performed by U.K. companies was funded from overseas, although how much of this was MNC developmental work is unknown.

On the output side of R&D, Cantwell (1989a, 1989b) and Pearce (1986) have analyzed data on patents taken out in the United States. This data has the advantage that it records both the nationality of the parent company and the location where the R&D leading to the patent was actually undertaken. Comparing the period 1963–70 with 1978–84, they find evidence that the link between the locus of production and the locus of R&D was weakening. Also, while the degree of concentration of research activity was much the same over the period, the pattern was actually different, suggesting that concentration of research activity was being driven by considerations other than the locus of production or the head office of the parent company.

The interpretation of these various snippets of information must be that it *is* possible to undertake R&D offshore and to a greater and growing level of sophistication than merely adapting home-country technology to local conditions. However, while such activity is growing rapidly, it still accounts for only a small share of R&D activity. Thus overall we suggest that offshore sourcing is not yet a practical means of significantly relaxing a domestic "science constraint." However, as this international mobility of science becomes increasingly important, so too do the conclusions of section 7.1.5. It will be recalled that while there was again support for policies that increased the demand for scientists, this was only unambiguously desirable for countries which had a sufficiently large stock as to make them net exporters, suggesting that supply policies could also be desirable.

7.4.3   Spillovers

There are now a number of studies that have investigated R&D spillovers and have calculated private and social rates of return to R&D, where the social rate of return takes into account the effect of spillovers. Griliches (1964) and Evenson and Kislev (1973) investigated the effects of R&D spillovers on U.S. agricultural production. They estimated the social rates of return on agricultural R&D projects were 150 to 300 percent greater than private rates of return. Mansfield et al. (1977) compared private to social rates of return on 17 innovations introduced in the United States. The variation in the private rates of return was from 214 percent to less than 0 percent with a median 25 percent rate of return. The social rates were calculated to range from 209 percent to less than 0 percent with a median rate of return of 56 percent.

Jaffe (1986) attempts to gauge the broad importance of spillovers by looking at the average effect that other firms' R&D has on the productivity of a firm's own R&D. He finds that firms whose research is in areas where there is much research by other firms have, on average, more patents per dollar of R&D and a higher return to R&D in terms of accounting profits or market value, though firms with very low own R&D suffer *lower* profits and market values if their neighbors are R&D-intensive. All of these effects remain after controlling for the possibility that the technological areas themselves are associated with variations in the productivity of R&D.

Levin and Reiss (1984) also dealt with a cross-section of U.S. firms and estimated that a 1 percent increase in R&D spillover caused average costs to decline by 0.05 percent. Bernstein and Nadiri (1989) estimated the effects of intraindustry spillovers for four U.S. industries. A firm's R&D spillover was defined as the sum of the R&D capital stocks of the firm's rivals. It was estimated that a 1 percent increase in the spillover decreased average cost in the long run by between 0.1 and 0.2 percent. It was also estimated that the social rate of return was up to twice the private rate. If we recall that, in section 7.3, a 1 percent increase in a firm's own R&D spending was estimated to reduce costs by 0.15 percent, these results by Bernstein and Nadiri seem to imply very large spillover effects. However, their methodology is very different from those used in the studies reported in section 7.3 to estimate the effects of R&D spending on costs, so the elasticities are not strictly comparable.

In all these studies the R&D spillover is defined as a single aggregate with individual industries not treated as separate spillover sources. Bernstein and Nadiri (1988) developed and estimated a model for five U.S. high-tech industries which allowed each one to be a distinct spillover source. The paper by Bernstein (1989) uses a variant of this framework and applies it to nine Canadian industries. The production cost of each industry is affected separately by the R&D capital of each of the other industries. He finds that, for each receiving industry, cost effects depend on the particular source of R&D spillover. Six industries were affected by multiple spillover sources. All nine industries were influenced by R&D spillovers, and the cost reductions attributable to these ranged from 0.005 percent for chemical products to 1.082 percent for electrical products. Private rates of return to R&D ranged from 24 to 47 percent, approximately 2 and one-half times the returns on physical capital. Social rates of return ranged from four times the private rate (for nonelectrical machinery) to twice the rate. Unfortunately, none of these studies deal with international R&D spillovers, so while there clearly is considerable knowledge diffusion between Europe, Japan, and the United States, we have no feel for its quantitative impact on technology and costs.

7.5 Conclusion

In this paper we have argued that the recent literature on strategic trade policy provides a natural framework in which to discuss some issues of manpower policy, while conversely, arguments about trade and industrial policies toward the high-tech sector depend critically on certain manpower issues. In particular we have shown that the view one takes of policy depends critically on whether it is scientific manpower or science itself which is mobile. We have also shown that, in an international context, spillovers can undermine rather than support the case for policy intervention as they are taken to do in a closed economy.

A calibration of our model suggests that the potential for beneficial policy is very great. However, a final conclusion on this depends on a number of elasticities to do with mobility and spillovers for which we just do not have data, though what evidence we have presented suggests mobility is significant and growing.

References

Baldwin, R. A., and P. Krugman. 1988a. Industrial policy and international competition in wide-bodied jet aircraft. In *Trade policy issues and empirical analysis,* ed. R. E. Baldwin. Chicago: University of Chicago Press.

———. 1988b. Market access and international competition: A simulation study of 16K random access memories. In *Empirical methods for international trade,* ed. R. C. Feenstra. Cambridge: MIT Press.

Beath, J. A., Y. Katsoulacos, and D. Ulph. 1989. Strategic R&D policy. *Economic Journal* 99 (supplement): 579–583.

Bernstein, J. I. 1989. The structure of Canadian inter-industry R&D spillovers and the rates of return to R&D. *Journal of Industrial Economics* 37:315–28.

———. 1989. R&D and intra industry spillovers. *Review of Economic Studies* 56:249–67.

Bernstein, J. I., and M. I. Nadiri. 1988. Interindustry R&D spillovers, rate of return and production in high-tech industries. *American Economic Review* 78:429–34.

Bond, J. S. 1981. United States international transactions in royalties and fees—Trends and interpretation. Workshop on the Technological Balance of Payments, Organisation for Economic Cooperation and Development.

Brander, J., and B. Spencer. 1983. International R&D rivalry and industrial strategy. *Review of Economic Studies* 50:707–22.

Cantwell, J. 1989a. *Technological innovation and multinational corporations.* Oxford: Basil Blackwell.

Cantwell, J., 1989b. The international agglomeration of technological activity. University of Reading. Mimeo.

Caves, R. E. 1982. *Multinational enterprise and economic analysis.* Cambridge: Cambridge University Press.

Creamer, D., A. Apostolides, and S. Wang. 1976. *Overseas research and development by United States multinationals, 1966–1975: Estimates of expenditures and a statistical profile.* New York: Conference Board.

Cuneo, P., and J. Mairesse. 1984. Productivity and R&D at the firm level in French manufacturing. In *R&D, patents and productivity,* ed. Z. Griliches. Chicago: University of Chicago Press.

Dixit, A., and G. Grossman. 1986. Targeted export promotion with several oligopolistic industries. *Journal of International Economics* 21:233–49.

Evenson, R. E., and Y. Kislev. 1973. Research and productivity in wheat and maize. *Journal of Political Economy* 81:1309–29.

Federal Republic of Germany. 1988. *Report of the Federal Government on research, 1988.* Bonn: Federal Ministry of Research and Technology.

Griliches, Z. 1964. Research expenditure, education and the aggregate agricultural production function. *American Economic Review* 54:961–74.

———. 1980. Returns to R&D expenditures in the private sector. In *Developments in productivity measurement and analysis,* ed. J. W. Kendrick and B. N. Vaccara. Chicago: University of Chicago Press.

Griliches, Z., and J. Mairesse. 1984. Productivity and R&D at the firm level. In *R&D, patents and productivity,* ed. Z. Griliches. Chicago: University of Chicago Press.

Hirschey, R. C., and R. E. Caves. 1981. Research and transfer of technology by multinational enterprises. *Oxford Bulletin of Economics and Statistics* 43:115–30.

Hood, N., and S. Young. 1976. US investment in Scotland—Aspects of the branch factory syndrome. *Scottish Journal of Political Economy* 23:279–94.

Jaffe, A. 1986. Technological opportunity and spillovers of R&D: Evidence from firms' patents, profits and market value. *American Economic Review* 76:984–1001.

Lall, S. 1979. The international allocation of research activity by US multinationals. *Oxford Bulletin of Economics and Statistics* 42:313–31.

Ledic, M., and Z. A. Silberston. 1984. The technological balance of payments in perspective. *Greek Economic Review* 6:356–86.

Levin, R. C., and C. Reiss. 1984. Tests of a Schumpeterian model of R&D and market structure. In *R&D, patents and productivity,* ed. Z. Griliches. Chicago: University of Chicago Press.

Mansfield, E. 1968. *Industrial research and technical innovation.* New York: Norton.

Mansfield, E., J. Rapoport, A. Romeo, S. Wagner, and G. Beardsley. 1977. Social and private rates of return from industrial innovations. *Quarterly Journal of Economics* 91:221–40.

Mansfield, E., D. Teece, and A. Romeo. 1979. Overseas research and development by US-based firms. *Economica* 46:187–96.

Miniasian, J. 1969. R&D production functions and rates of return. *American Economic Review* 59(2): 80–85.

NSF (National Science Foundation). 1973. Immigrant scientists and engineers in the United States: A study of characteristics and attitudes. Document No. NSF 73-302. Washington, D.C.: National Science Foundation.

———. 1986. Immigrant scientists and engineers, 1982–84. Document no. NSF 85-326. Washington, D.C.: National Science Foundation.

———. 1988. Foreign citizens in US science and engineering: History, status and outlook. Document no. NSF 86-305. Washington, D.C.: National Science Foundation.

OSEP (Office of Science and Engineering Personnel). 1988. *Foreign and foreign-born engineering in the United States.* Office of Science and Engineering Personnel, Washington, D.C.

Pearce, R. D. 1986. The internationalisation of research and development by leading enterprises: An empirical study. Discussion Paper in International Investment and Business Studies, no. 99. University of Reading.

———. 1988. The determinants of overseas R&D by US MNEs: An analysis of industry level data. Discussion Paper in International Investment and Business Studies, no. 119. University of Reading.

Reddaway, W. B. 1968. *Effects of UK direct investment overseas: Final report.* Cambridge: Cambridge University Press.

SEPSU (Science Engineering Policy Studies Unit). 1987. *The migration of scientist and engineers to and from the UK.* London: The Royal Society.

Teece, D. J. 1976. *The multinational corporation and the resource cost of international technology transfer.* Cambridge, Mass.: Ballinger.

Terleckyj, N. E. 1974. *Effects of R&D on the productivity growth of industries: An exploratory study.* Washington, D.C.: National Planning Association.

8   Industrial Organization and Product Quality: Evidence from South Korean and Taiwanese Exports

Dani Rodrik

8.1   Introduction

For developing countries, probably the predominant question of strategic trade policy is, How can entry be facilitated into markets for sophisticated manufactured goods characterized by imperfect competition and well-entrenched oligopolists? Pessimism regarding the prospects for successful entry into such markets underlies the widespread unease with outward-oriented trade strategies. Yes, as the experiences of Japan and the East Asian tigers following on its heels have amply demonstrated, well-positioned entrants can always create room for themselves. These countries have diversified into manufactured products of increasing sophistication, demonstrating that even the tightest international oligopolies can be penetrated.

The broad reasons underlying the export success of the East Asian countries are well known. My focus in this paper is on a narrow but significant aspect of their performance: the transition from standardized, labor-intensive manufactures to sophisticated, skill-intensive products where quality plays an important role. While traditional factor-endowment considerations typically play the determinant role with the former group of products, the role of industrial organization comes into its own with the latter. Putting it somewhat crudely, the transition can be viewed as a shift from price to quality as the source of competitiveness. The higher-end products typically require not only a broader range of skills and technological sophistication, but also investment in product quality, customer loyalty, and reputation.

Dani Rodrik is professor of economics and international affairs at Columbia University, a research fellow of the Centre for Economic Policy Research, and a research associate of the National Bureau of Economic Research.

The author is grateful to conference participants and to Tyler Biggs, Brian Levy, Klaus Lorch, and Ray Vernon for helpful comments and owes special thanks to Brian Levy, who stimulated this research. Excellent research assistance was performed by Tina Poitevien.

The rate at which the transition takes place, if it takes place at all, is naturally influenced by a wide range of factors and country characteristics. Can industrial policy play a role here as well? As a first pass, I focus in this paper on broad patterns of industrial organization. We can identify two relevant models for policy here. In the first, policy would favor the formation of large firms and conglomerates and would direct resources toward them, discriminating against small firms and potential entrants. In the second, policy would be neutral, and a more fluid, diffuse industrial structure would result. Which pattern is more conducive to making the transition to high-end products? In the next section, I will discuss a simple theory which suggests that the transition can be achieved more easily when domestic industry is highly concentrated. The basic argument is that such industries are better able to cope with the inevitable reputational externalities involved in producing high-quality goods for foreign markets.

Is there any empirical evidence to support this proposition? Fortunately, South Korea and Taiwan provide as close to a controlled experiment for testing the hypothesis as can be hoped for in economics. Starting from a tiny base, both countries have been phenomenally successful in expanding and diversifying their manufactured exports. Their trade and macroeconomic policies have been broadly similar, as are their income levels. Yet, the two countries are radically different in their patterns of industrial organization. Korean industry is dominated by a handful of large conglomerates, and firm-concentration ratios are uniformly high. In Taiwan, large conglomerates are the exception rather than the rule, and individual industries are typically less concentrated than their Korean counterparts. It would be very surprising indeed if their respective trade patterns did not somehow reflect this difference. In light of the considerations discussed above, this paper looks for evidence of differential performance with respect to product quality. I find strong support for the hypothesis that industrial organization and product quality are related in the expected manner: the quality of Korean manufactured exports—with quality proxied by unit value—is systematically higher than that of Taiwanese exports.

The outline of the paper is as follows. The next section sketches out a simple theory which relates product quality to the number and size distribution of firms in an exporting industry. Section 8.3 compares briefly the industrial organization patterns in South Korea and Taiwan and discusses some of the reasons behind the differences. Analyzing the two countries' exports to the United States, section 8.4 presents evidence on their divergent performance with respect to product quality. The paper ends with concluding comments in section 8.5.

8.2   Product Quality and Industrial Organization: A Theoretical Sketch

New entrants into high-end product categories typically face an entry barrier altogether different from the usual obstacles. Perceived product quality is an important component of demand for such products; to be judged high-quality by consumers, entrants must invest in reputation or other means of communicating quality. The problem is even more serious for firms from developing countries, as they may have to surmount a reputation for shoddy quality frequently associated with developing-country goods.[1]

Such informational barriers to entry have been the subject of a number of theoretical papers. In the simplest framework, one could imagine that (foreign) consumers' familiarity with quality increases with cumulated exposure to the product in question. Provided the actual quality level of home exports exceeds the perceived level, there may then be a role for export subsidies in speeding up the process of product familiarization (Mayer 1984). When domestic firms are differentiated by quality, high-end firms can try to signal quality by selling at low prices initially (in anticipation of future profits); subsidies can facilitate such signaling strategies, at an overall welfare gain to the home economy (Bagwell and Staiger 1989). But the problem is that subsidies may also encourage additional domestic firms to enter at the low end of the quality spectrum, failing to improve the perceived quality of home exports and increasing the cost to high-quality producers of distinguishing themselves from their low-quality counterparts (Grossman and Horn 1988). In all these cases, the transition to higher-quality products is hampered by informational entry barriers.

These papers do not consider directly the importance of domestic market structure in determining the average level of product quality in exports. A recent article by Chiang and Masson (1988), motivated specifically by policy discussions in Taiwan, focuses on this issue in the context of a simple model of reputational externalities in product quality. Their basic point is that concentrated industries will do a better job of internalizing these and that they will therefore tend to produce at the higher end of the quality spectrum. In what follows, I will base my argument on the same point and sketch out a similar model with a few additional twists.

Consider an industry which is a price-taker in world markets and which exports all of its output. Since my objective is to trace the effects of industry structure on product quality, I will take as given the overall size of the industry and the size distribution of firms within it. This is tantamount to assuming fixed capacities and full capacity utilization. Let the price received by each firm be a linear function of perceived quality, $p_i = \tilde{q}_i$, where i indexes firms. Marginal costs of production are linear in output, but increasing and convex in *actual* quality, q_i. For ease of exposition, I let these costs be quadratic. What is the relationship between perceived and actual quality? I assume that $\tilde{q}_i$ will generally lie somewhere between the the firm's actual quality (q_i) and the *average* quality ($\bar{q}$) of home exports:

$$(1) \qquad \tilde{q}_i = \phi q_i + (1 - \phi)\bar{q},$$

---

1. On country stereotyping with respect to product quality, see for example, Khanna (1986).

where ø is (for now) taken to be fixed. As a firm's perceived quality level (and hence price) will be based partly on other exporters' quality choices, this formulation introduces the externality which drives this section's results. The average quality level is simply

(2) $$\bar{q} = \Sigma_j s_j q_j,$$

where s_j is firm j's (fixed) share in industry output.

Letting x_i denote firm i's (fixed) level of output, profits can be written as

(3) $$\pi_i = (\tilde{q}_i - \frac{1}{2} q_i^2) x_i$$

which yields the first-order condition for quality:

(4) $$q_i = \phi + (1 - \phi) s_i.$$

Note that the social optimum would require the reputational externality to be eliminated by setting $\tilde{q}_i$ equal to q_i, in which case the equilibrium level of q_i would be unity, irrespective of the firm's market share. As can be seen from (4), this case can be recovered in this framework when $\phi = 1$, i.e., when firms can costlessly and perfectly communicate their individual quality levels to foreign consumers. Note that ϕ denotes the weight attached to own-quality level in foreigners' perceptions. As long as $\phi < 1$, quality involves a positive externality, and firms' quality level will lie below unity. In the worst possible scenario, when firms are branded by the average quality level of the home industry ($\phi = 0$), q_i will equal the firm's share in the industry. In general, larger firms will choose higher levels of quality.

We can now investigate the effects of industry structure on average product quality. Suppose that ϕ is identical across firms. In the present framework, average quality then turns out to be a simple linear function of the Herfindahl index of concentration. Using (2) and (4) in conjunction with $\Sigma_j s_j = 1$, we get

(5) $$\bar{q} = \phi + (1 - \phi) H,$$

where $H \equiv \Sigma_j s_j^2$ is the Herfindahl index. As $\bar{q}$ is increasing in H, more concentrated industries will operate at higher quality levels than less concentrated ones. For a given scale of industry output, the Herfindahl index is influenced both by the number of firms and by the size distribution of firms, so both factors will come into play in determining $\bar{q}$. Note also that whether a firm operates below or above the industry-wide average will depend on the relationship between its market share and H:

(6) $$q_i - \bar{q} = (1 - \phi) (s_i - H).$$

Therefore, $q_i > \bar{q}$ whenever $s_i > H$.

As a tiny step toward added realism, consider now the case where firms can invest in advertising, marketing/distributional channels, brand names, and the like in order to differentiate their image from that of other firms in the home industry. Let the amount of such investment be denoted by f_i. I assume that investment of this type serves to close the gap between actual and perceived quality. In the present framework, this amounts to letting ϕ be an increasing function of f_i. So we can write $\phi = \phi(f_i)$, with $\phi(0) = 0$, $\phi(\infty) = 1$, $\phi' \equiv \partial\phi/\partial f_i > 0$, and $\phi'' \equiv \partial^2\phi/\partial f_i^2 < 0$. Firm profits now become

$$(7) \qquad \pi_i = \left(\tilde{q}_i - \frac{1}{2}q_i^2\right)x_i - f_i,$$

with $\tilde{q}_i$ defined as before in (1). Since it may not pay for a firm to invest in reputation building, we associate the Lagrange multiplier λ with f_i and write the Langrangian expression as

$$(8) \qquad \mathcal{L} = \left(\tilde{q}_i - \frac{1}{2}q_i^2\right)x_i - f_i + \lambda f_i.$$

The first-order condition for q_i remains unchanged from (4)—except that ϕ is no longer a constant. With respect to f_i,

$$(9) \qquad x_i\phi'(q_i - \bar{q}) - 1 + \lambda = 0.$$

Note that for firms that operate at or below average quality ($q_i - \bar{q} \leq 0$), this equality requires that $\lambda > 0$, implying $f_i = \phi = 0$. For low-end firms, it simply does not pay to communicate their true quality levels, as this hampers their free ride on higher-quality firms.

As (9) shows, firms that choose to invest in "reputation" will be those with sufficiently high quality relative to the average.[2] From our earlier discussion, these will be the firms with larger market shares. For such firms $\lambda = 0$, and we have

$$(9') \qquad x_i\phi'(q_i - \bar{q}) = 1.$$

Since ϕ'' is negative by assumption, high levels of q_i will be associated with high levels of f_i.

To determine the effect on the average level of quality in the industry, let us divide firms into two groups, one for which $f = 0$, and the other for which $f > 0$. Denote the second set by T (for top-quality firms). Since $\phi(0) = 0$, we have

$$(10) \qquad \bar{q} = \Sigma_{j\notin T}s_j^2 + \Sigma_{j\in T}(\phi_j s_j + (1 - \phi_j)s_j^2),$$

where ϕ_j denotes $\phi(f_j)$. This yields

$$(11) \qquad \bar{q} = H + \Sigma_{j\in T}\phi_j(s_j - s_j^2),$$

where H is once again the Herfindahl index. If firms were unable to distinguish themselves from their competitors, $\bar{q}$ would equal H (as $\phi(0) = 0$). As (11)

2. What "sufficiently" means in this context depends on the magnitude of $\phi'(0)$. The larger $\phi'(0)$, the smaller the threshold above $\bar{q}$ for investing in reputation.

shows, the ability of firms to communicate their true quality—as partial and costly it may be—raises the average quality level of exports.

The bottom line of this discussion is that, all else being equal, we would expect more concentrated industries to produce and export a higher-quality range of products. When firms have the ability to build reputation and brand loyalty, the expectation is that the quality differential between concentrated and unconcentrated industries will be even larger: this is because the incentive to undertake such investments depends on how skewed the size distribution of firms (and hence the quality distribution) is in the first place.

To be sure, the model presented here is no more than a parable. It focuses on only one possible link between industry structure and product-quality choice. We should certainly not expect it to provide great explanatory power regardless of context. But I suspect that for many developing countries the considerations raised here are likely to be important ones. Therefore, it would be useful to see if there is evidence which supports the basic hypothesis. Before I go on to discuss the evidence from Korean and Taiwanese exports, however, I provide a brief overview of industrial organization in the two countries.

8.3   Industrial Organization in South Korea and Taiwan

Probably nothing better illustrates the difference in the industrial organization of the two countries than the fact that South Korea has 11 firms in the Fortune International 500, compared to Taiwan's three.[3] Some of the major Korean conglomerates are now becoming household names in the industrialized countries (Hyundai, Samsung), while even sophisticated consumers would be hard pressed to come up with the name of a single Taiwanese firm—this despite the fact that Korean GNP per capita is a quarter lower than Taiwan's and the overall magnitude of the two countries' exports are similar.

The differences in the industrial structures of the two countries have received little attention to date, with a few notable exceptions. In his comparative account of economic development in the two countries, Tibor Scitovsky (1986) focused on these differences and stressed that the Taiwanese economy is organized much more along free-market lines than is the Korean one, with much greater competition among firms in Taiwan.[4] In a series of papers based on

3. The Korean firms in the top 500, with their ranks in parentheses, are: Samsung (21), Lucky-Goldstar (37), Daewoo (39), Sunkyong (82), Ssangyong (152), Korea Explosives (182), Hyundai Heavy Industries (187), Hyosung (195), Pohang Iron and Steel (216), Hyundai Motor Company (261), and Doosan (431). The three Taiwanese companies are Chinese Petroleum (104), Nan Ya Plastics (467), and China Steel (489).

4. Scitovsky takes it on faith that more-competitive industries will perform better. But he is forced to conclude, "Ironically, in Korea there is no evidence that the large profits and fast accumulation of great fortunes that Korea's economic policies made possible had any unfavorable effects on the drive, stamina, and efficiency of Korea's businesses." He ends, in a way that could easily give cultural explanations a bad name, by saying "perhaps this is due to the Chinese cultural background" (1986, 151).

case studies of Taiwanese and Korean firms, Brian Levy has investigated the implications of market structure on strategies and likely success of these firms in foreign markets (Levy 1987; Levy and Kuo 1987a, 1987b). He finds that firm strategies are predictably influenced by size but that small size has not adversely affected the ability of Taiwanese firms to break into high-technology markets, at least when investment requirements are not too large.

Direct, comparative evidence on industrial organization patterns in the two countries is hard to come by. Table 8.1 summarizes the broad size distribution of enterprises in the manufacturing industry. Because the size distribution is not sufficiently disaggregated, the data here are not particularly meaningful. They show that large enterprises (300 or more employees) account for 64 percent of total value added in Korea, compared with 59 percent in Taiwan. The share of small enterprises (5–19 employees) is 4 percent in Korea and 8 percent in Taiwan. These numbers do not point to a great discrepancy between the two economies, but this is highly misleading. For one thing, the table excludes the smallest firms (with fewer than five employees), as statistics are not compiled on such firms in Korea—which in itself is meaningful. These smallest firms account for almost half the total number of manufacturing firms in Taiwan. More important, the Korean industrial censuses collect data at the establishment (plant, factory, workshop, etc.) level rather than the firm or enterprise level, as in Taiwan. This naturally biases the Korean concentration figures downward. Moreover, the preponderance in the Korean economy of the *chaebul* (conglomerates) spanning diverse activities across subsectors introduces another important source of downward bias. In 1985, the top five *chaebul* accounted for 27.0 percent of Korean manufactured exports, and the top 30 for 41.3 percent (Lee 1988, table 20). There are few such giants in the Taiwanese economy. As a consequence, the figures in table 8.1 greatly underestimate the degree of concentration in Korea.

There are other indicators that suggest that the extent of competition in Taiwanese industries surpasses that of Korea. Scitovsky (1986, 146) draws the following interesting comparison: between 1966 and 1976 the number of manufacturing firms in Taiwan increased by 150 percent while the number of employees per firm increased by 29 percent; in Korea, the number of firms increased only by 10 percent, while average firm size (measured again by

Table 8.1   **Distribution of Value Added in the Manufacturing Industry (%)**

Size of Enterprise or Establishment (number of employees)	South Korea (1984)	Taiwan (1981)
5–19	4.3	7.8
20–299	32.0	33.2
300+	63.7	58.9

Sources: Biggs and Lorch (1988); Economic Planning Board (1986).
Note: We exclude enterprises/establishments with fewer than five employees.

employees) increased by 176 percent. The relative ease of entry into Taiwanese industries is also corroborated by the high rate of bankruptcy in that country (Scitovsky 1986, 151). In Korea, by contrast, bankruptcy is not even legally recognized, and business failure carries great moral stigma extending beyond the entrepreneur to his family (Michell 1983, 168–69).

The reasons behind these divergent patterns of industrial organization are due partly to historical circumstance and partly to policy. Among the former, possibly the key role in Taiwan was played by the immigration of overseas Chinese who brought substantial capital with them (30 percent of the total inflow of foreign capital) and used it to establish new enterprises (Scitovsky 1986, 146). With respect to policy, the Taiwanese government's attitude has been much more benign toward small enterprises, and there has been little overt support for large firms. In Korea, the situation has been quite different. "Since 1961," writes Michell (1983, 168), "it has been the continual mission of the Ministry of Commerce and Industry [of Korea] to prevent what is termed 'reckless overcompetition.'" Given the transactions cost of dealing with governmental bureaucracies, it is also likely that the more active role of the Korean government in industry (in credit allocation, for example) would have served to discriminate against small and medium-sized firms, even when policy had no such objective (see Levy 1987). Taking some license with terminology, it can be said that "industrial policy" favored industrial consolidation in Korea and was indifferent to firm size in Taiwan.

8.4   Evidence on Product Quality from U.S. Imports

I will now discuss the available evidence on product quality in Korean and Taiwanese exports. Note first that, by most relevant criteria, Taiwan is the more economically developed of the two countries (see table 8.2). Most important from our perspective, Taiwan is comparatively rich in human skills and education by virtue of having been an early starter compared to Korea. As table 8.2 shows, Korea now appears to have caught up with Taiwan in terms of *flow* additions to the educated work force, but Taiwan is still endowed with a proportionately larger stock of skilled and educated workers. On these grounds, then, we would expect Taiwan to be further along in the transition to high-end products than Korea. The industrial-organization effects discussed above go in the opposite direction.

To check for systematic differences in product quality, I examine the unit values for the two countries' exports to the United States, disaggregated at an appropriate level. A critical maintained hypothesis is that unit values are a good proxy for quality. For manufactured exports of the type that will be the focus of the analysis, this seems to be a sensible working hypothesis.[5] The

5. I have also computed unit values for Japanese expots to the United States (see app.). These are almost without exception higher than those for Korea and Taiwan. This is consistent with what we know about Japan's successful transition to products at the very high end of the quality spectrum.

Table 8.2   **Basic Indicators of Development**

Indicator	South Korea	Taiwan
GDP per capita (1983 $)	2,010	2,670
Electric power consumption per capita (kWh)	915	2,131
Life expectancy at birth (years)	65	72
Infant mortality (per 1,000 live births)	37	25
Daily calorie intake per capita	2,785	2,805
Daily protein intake per capita (grams)	70	78
Households with running water (%)	55	67
Households with TV sets (%)	79	100
School enrollment rates (% of age group):		
Primary	111	100
Secondary	76	80
College and universities	12	10

Sources: UNIDO (1986, table 1); Scitovsky (1986, tables 2 and 4).

analysis is restricted to the U.S. market in order to obtain closely comparable trade data for the two countries. The United States is by far the largest export market for both countries, accounting for roughly one-half of total sales. It is unlikely that substantial biases are introduced by restricting attention to the United States.

Selecting the level of disaggregation at which the comparison of unit values is carried out requires care. At too aggregated a level, there is always the danger of comparing apples to oranges. At too *dis*aggregated a level, on the other hand, the quality range of the product in question may be needlessly compressed, leaving out useful information about the upper and lower ends of the range.[6] I have chosen an intermediate level of disaggregation, using the four-digit Schedule A classification for U.S. import statistics (U.S. Department of Commerce 1986). These import data are recorded on a "customs value" basis, defined as "the price actually paid or payable for merchandise when sold for exportation in the United States, excluding U.S. import duties, freight, insurance and other charges incurred in bringing the merchandise to the United States."[7] In order to focus on products which are important exports for the two countries, I restrict the analysis to categories in which at least one of the countries had exports to the United States exceeding $100 million. In 1986, there were 49 such product groups. Exports included in these groups amount to $9.6 billion for Korea and $14.5 billion for Taiwan, substantial parts of each country's total exports to the United States.

Table 8.3 lists the respective unit values for each of these 49 categories for the two countries. The product groups are ranked in ascending order of (pro-

6. For example, the highly detailed seven-digit TSUSA classfication contains categories such as: "moccasins, soled, leather, for women, *not over $2.50* pair" (emphasis added).

7. The description further adds, helpfully, "In the case of transactions between related parties, the relationship between buyer and seller should not influence the Customs value" (U.S. Department of Commerce 1986).

Table 8.3   **Unit Values in Korean and Taiwanese Exports to the United States, 1986 ($ per 1,000 lbs.)**

Code	Description[a]	South Korea	Taiwan	Percent Differential
753.0	Automatic data processing (ADP) machines	6,347	6,214	2.1
891.0	Articles of rubber or plastics, nspf	940	913	3
658.9	Tapestries & made-up articles	3,080	3,212	−4.1
781.0	Passenger motor vehicles	2,410	2,529	−4.7
898.3	Sound, etc., recordings & blank media	3,430	3,603	−4.8
846.8	Under garments (including shirts) of textile nspf materials, knit	4,533	4,763	−4.8
845.5	Sweaters & other outerwear of textile materials, knit	5,587	6,029	−7.3
776.4	Integrated circuits	88,333	82,203	7.5
764.8	Audio and video tape players and records	7,038	6,514	8
764.9	Parts nspf of telecommunication & sound reproducing equip.	6,426	5,932	8.3
678.6	Pipes, tubes, & blanks, iron or steel	194	177	9.6
674.0	Plates & sheet, iron or steel	173	192	−9.9
699.1	Locks, safes, etc., of base metals	1,204	1,362	−11.6
635.9	Articles manufactured of wood, nspf	1,201	1,365	−12
749.2	Taps, cocks, valves, & parts	1,235	1,443	−14.4
762.0	Radio receivers (AM/FM) & combinations	4,309	3,759	14.6
844.1	Men's & boys' shirts cotton, wool, manmade fibers, not knit	4,860	5,752	−15.5
761.0	Television receivers & combinations	2,983	3,580	−16.7
699.8	Articles of cast iron,nspf	1,006	842	19.5
764.4	Electric telephone & telegraph equip. & parts	7,756	6,486	19.6
851.0	Footwear, new, excluding military or orthopedic	3,724	3,113	19.6
785.2	Adult cycles	1,151	1,463	−21.3
694.0	Nails, screws, & other fasteners of base metals	325	425	−23.5
588.8	Profile shapes, rubber & plastic	703	567	24
759.9	Parts of ADP & calculating office machines	2,009	2,703	−25.7
788.0	Parts nspf of motor vehicles & handling equip.	819	1,113	−26.4
879.2	Jewelry, etc., costume & semiprecious	7,530	5,911	27.4
763.8	Microphones, speakers, & audio amplifiers	2,297	1,758	30.7
634.7	Plywood, including wood veneer panels	220	326	−32.5
842.3	Slacks, etc., cotton, wool, manmade fibers	6,158	4,517	36.3
771.2	Nonrotating electric power equip.	6,840	4,999	36.8
775.8	Electro-thermic appliances nspf & parts	1,759	2,803	−37.2
812.4	Lighting fixtures and fittings	812	1,373	−40.9
773.1	Insulated electrical conductors (cables)	1,312	2,263	−42
821.8	Furniture & parts thereof, nspf	1,208	795	51.9
894.2	Toys, games, Christmas ornaments, etc.	2,705	1,780	52
697.2	Household & sanitary ware of iron or steel	1,247	807	54.5
848.1	Gloves, belts, other wearing apparel of leather, nspf	9,974	6,140	62.4

Table 8.3   (continued)

Code	Description[a]	South Korea	Taiwan	Percent Differential
843.7	Garments for rainwear; other outerwear, nspf	10,331	6,347	62.8
831.0	Luggage, handbags	2,926	1,763	66
635.4	Wood manufacturers, domestic & decorative use	1,946	1,157	68.2
884.2	Eyeglasses, eyeglass frames, & parts	10,823	6,250	73.2
775.7	Electro-mechanical household appliances nspf & parts	2,252	1,296	73.8
695.3	Hand tools, nspf of base metal	1,807	1,031	75.3
894.7	Sporting goods, etc., nspf	2,246	1,228	82.9
736.1	Metal-cutting machine tools	2,338	1,160	101.6
881.1	Still cameras & parts; flash apparatus	27,438	12,308	122.9
778.8	Ferrites nspf; elect machinery & equip. nspf	10,372	3,745	177
848.3	Fur clothing & other articles except headwear	38,801	10,474	270.5
	Unweighted average	6,431	4,826	26.7

Source: U.S. Department of Commerce (1986).

Note: nspf = not specially provided for.

[a]Commodity descriptions are abridged versions. Full descriptions can be found in U.S. Department of Commerce (1986).

portional) difference between Korean and Taiwanese unit values. A quick glance at the table reveals clearly that Korean exports tend to have higher unit values than Taiwanese exports. Of the 49 products, 30 exhibit higher unit values in Korean exports. Moreover, all of the larger discrepancies in unit values are in favor of Korea. The unweighted average differential between Korean and Taiwanese unit values is 27 percent. On the basis of weighted averages, Korean exports command a price premium of 19 percent (Korean export weights) to 22 percent (Taiwanese export weights) over Taiwanese exports.

Is the observed discrepancy in unit values statistically significant? An appropriate statistical test here is the Wilcoxon signed-ranks test, which takes into account both the frequency with which Korean unit values exceed Taiwanese ones *and* the relative magnitudes of the discrepancies (see DeGroot 1975, 483–86). Using this test, the null hypothesis that Taiwanese unit values are at least as high as Korean unit values is decisively rejected at the 5 percent confidence level, with a z-value of 2.75. Notice that this is a particularly stringent test of our hypothesis, as a priori we would expect Taiwanese products to be of higher quality than Korean ones on all grounds but industrial organization.

A related implication of the model is that Korean exporters would be more likely to specialize at the high-end of the quality spectrum *across* broad product categories, as they possess a comparative advantage there relative to Taiwan. Figure 8.1 shows that this is indeed the case. Ranking product groups by

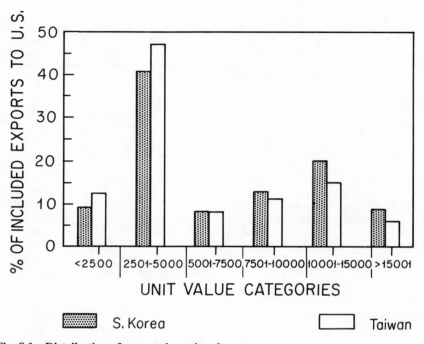

Fig. 8.1   Distribution of exports by unit value

Note: Product groups are ranked using Japanese unit values for each group. Unit values are in dollars per 1,000 lbs.

Japanese unit values to establish a rough quality hierarchy, we find that the distribution of Korean exports is relatively skewed toward the top end. Of Korea's (included) exports, 29 percent are in the "top" quality range (unit values greater than $10,000), compared to 21 percent for Taiwan. Korea has 50 percent of its exports at the low end (unit values $5,000 or lower) and Taiwan 60 percent.

A further test of a different nature would be to see whether the differences in unit values are proportionately more pronounced in products for which quality plays an important role. Remember that, in terms of our model, industrial organization becomes important only when quality is a predominant characteristic of the product group in question. Unfortunately, there is no clear-cut way of determining the products for which this is likely to be true. A shortcut is to assume that higher unit values are associated with "quality-intensive" products. Using Japanese unit values to rank industries by this criterion, the following regression results are obtained:

$$PREM = -1.03 + 0.15 \ln(JAP),$$
$$(0.06)$$
$$R^2 = 0.11, N = 49,$$

where PREM is the Korean unit-value premium over Taiwan (in percent) and JAP is the Japanese unit value for the corresponding product group. The standard error of the slope coefficient is in parentheses. This suggests that the Korean quality advantage over Taiwan increases as we move from low-end to high-end products. A doubling of the average level of product quality—as measured by unit values of Japanese exports—is associated with an increase of 15 percent in the Korean price premium over Taiwan. This finding is consistent with the discussion in section 8.2.

To sum up, these data reveal an interesting divergence in the export performance of the two countries.[8] It is of course entirely possible that these findings reflect some other unidentified statistical quirks. For example, Taiwanese exporters could be prone to underinvoicing. Or, the relatively greater downstream integration of the Korean exporters in the U.S. market may lead to high transfer prices being set on these exports, *provided* that it is viewed as preferable to hold income in South Korea rather than in the United States. In any case, the hypothesis that quality differentials between the exports of Korea and Taiwan are systematically related to their industrial organization patterns would appear to be worth a closer look.

8.5 Concluding Remarks

This paper has combined a simple—perhaps simplistic—theory with a simple test. The findings are twofold: (i) Korean exports tend to be systematically of higher quality than Taiwanese exports, at least when quality is proxied by unit value, and (ii) this is consistent with a model of quality choice in which reputational externalities are less damaging in heavily concentrated industries.

A crucial final point concerns the normative aspect of the analysis. Nothing that has been said here should be construed as advocacy of an industrial policy that actively pursues concentration. Before we can go from the positive analysis to policy prescription, we will need a more complete welfare analysis and a more complete model in which to carry it out. There are at least two sets of reasons, besides policymakers' obvious concern about quality upgrading, to suspect that the findings here have normative significance. First, higher-quality products may carry price premiums exceeding the additional cost of producing them, as excess profits serve as the carrot needed to sustain quality levels (Shapiro 1983). Public policies in pursuit of such excess profits can potentially improve welfare. Second, there may be significant skills generated as countries move up the quality spectrum, and these may in turn create substantial positive externalities for the rest of the economy. Once again, policy may have a role to play. If domestic industrial structure and export performance are indeed linked,

---

8. Based on a quick look at 1975, it would appear that earlier years show the same pattern as 1986. Among included categories, the Korean premium in 1975 ranges from 20.1 percent (Taiwanese export weights) to 30.9 percent (Korean export weights).

as the preliminary results presented here would indicate, these would be fruitful areas for further research.

References

Bagwell, Kyle, and Robert Staiger. 1989. A role for export subsidies when product quality is unknown. *Journal of International Economics* 27:69–89.

Biggs, Tyler, and Klaus Lorch. 1988. The evolution of Taiwan's industrial structure and the role of policy. Cambridge: Harvard Institute for International Development. Forthcoming.

Chiang, Shih-Chen, and Robert Masson. 1988. Domestic industrial structure and export quality. *International Economic Review* 29:261–70.

DeGroot, Morris H. 1975. *Probability and statistics.* Reading, Mass.: Addison-Wesley.

Economic Planning Board, Republic of Korea. 1986. *Report on mining and manufacturing survey 1984.* Seoul.

Grossman, Gene, and Henrik Horn. 1988. Infant-industry protection reconsidered: The case of informational barriers to entry. *Quarterly Journal of Economics* 103:767–87.

Khanna, Sri Ram. 1986. Asian companies and the country stereotype paradox: An empirical study. *Columbia Journal of Business* 21, no. 2 (Summer): 29–38.

Lee, Kyu-Uck. 1988. International trade and industrial organization: The Korean experience. Seoul: Korea Development Institute. Mimeograph.

Levy, Brian. 1987. Export intermediation and the structure of industry in Korea and Taiwan. EEPA Discussion Paper No. 13, Cambridge: Harvard Institute for International Development, October.

Levy, Brian, and Wen-jeng Kuo. 1987a. Investment requirements and the participation of Korean and Taiwanese firms in technology-intensive industries. EEPA Discussion Paper no. 11. Cambridge: Harvard Institute for International Development, October.

Levy, Brian, and Wen-jeng Kuo. 1987b. The strategic orientations of firms and the performance of Korea and Taiwan in frontier industries: Lessons from comparative case studies of keyboard and personal computer assembly. EEPA Discussion Paper no. 12. Cambridge: Harvard Institute for International Development, October.

Mayer, Wolfgang. 1984. The infant-export industry argument. *Canadian Journal of Economics* 17:249–69.

Michell, Tony. 1983. The Republic of Korea: Employment, industrialization and trade. World Employment Programme Research Paper. Geneva: International Labor Organization.

Scitovsky, Tibor. 1986. Economic development in Taiwan and Korea, 1965–81. In *Models of development: A comparative study of economic growth in South Korea and Taiwan,* ed. Lawrence J. Lau. San Francisco: ICS Press.

Shapiro, Carl. 1983. Premiums for high quality products as returns to reputation. *Quarterly Journal of Economics* 98 (November): 659–79.

UNIDO (United Nations Industrial Development Organization). 1986. Industrial policy in East Asia, 1950–1985. Document no. IS.636. Vienna: UNIDO, 29 May.

U.S. Department of Commerce, Bureau of the Census. 1986. *U.S. General Imports: Schedule A Commodity Groups by World Area.* Report FT150. Washington, D.C.: Government Printing Office.

Appendix

Table 8A.1   **Unit Values and Exports of Korea, Taiwan, and Japan, 1986**

Category Description[a]	Unit Value ($ per 1,000 lbs.)			Total Value (million $)		
	South Korea	Taiwan	Japan	South Korea	Taiwan	Japan
588.8 Profile shapes, rubber and plastic	703	567	1,349	28.8	100.6	165.5
634.7 Plywood, including wood veneer panels	220	326	422	6.4	122.4	25.6
635.4 Wood manufactures, domestic & decorative use	1,946	1,157	2,517	2.2	164.5	5.9
635.9 Articles manufactured of wood, nspf	1,201	1,365	1,616	5.8	102.4	4.9
658.9 Tapestries & made-up articles	3,080	3,212	6,226	40.5	156.8	14.9
674.0 Plates & sheet, iron or steel	173	192	233	258.95	23.35	1,096.7
678.6 Pipes, tubes, & blanks, iron or steel	194	177	280	169.7	52.97	397.1
694.0 Nails, screws, & other fasteners of base metals	325	425	748	111.3	207.2	384.4
695.3 Hand tools, nspf of base metal	1,807	1,031	2,262	17.4	193	113.1
697.4 Household & sanitary ware of iron or steel	1,247	807	1,803	68.7	111.7	42.6
699.1 Locks, safes, etc., of base metals	1,204	1,362	2,364	18.97	175.9	127.1
699.8 Arts nspf of cast iron	1,006	842	1,286	50.5	122.1	102.3
736.1 Metal-cutting machine tools	2,338	1,160	4,161	10.8	106.9	745.6
749.2 Taps, cocks, valves, & parts	1,235	1,443	3,493	28.5	100.8	235.4
753.0 Automatic data processing (ADP) machines & auxiliaries	6,347	6,214	10,223	362.9	713.96	2,781.1
759.9 Parts of ADP & calculating office machines	2,009	2,703	2,461	94.1	399.97	1,957.2
761.0 Television receivers & combinations	2,983	3,580	6,335	442.3	445.2	869
762.0 Radio receivers (AM/FM) & combinations	4,309	3,759	12,344	214	263.7	1,785.4
763.8 Audio & video tape players and records	7,038	6,514	12,009	352.2	187.6	5,364.8
764.2 Microphones, speakers, & audio amplifiers	2,297	1,758	4,204	45.2	133.2	500.4
764.4 Electric telephone & telegraph equip. & parts	7,756	6,486	21,586	153.3	287.2	1,095.4
764.4 Integrated circuits	88,333	82,203	132,704	442.3	240.4	929.5
764.9 Parts nspf of telecommunication & sound reproducing equip.	6,426	5,932	12,109	313.1	491.6	1,734.5
771.2 Nonrotating electrical power equip.	6,840	4,999	9,815	19.2	125.3	237.7
773.1 Insulated electric conductors (cable)	1,312	2,263	5,359	32.6	304.6	177.3
775.7 Electro-mechanical household applicances nspf	2,252	1,296	3,888	38.9	117.1	71.8

(*continued*)

Table 8A.1   (continued)

Category Description[a]	Unit Value ($ per 1,000 lbs.)			Total Value (million $)		
	South Korea	Taiwan	Japan	South Korea	Taiwan	Japan
775.8 Electro-thermic applicances nspf & parts	1,759	2,803	2,654	300.1	94.97	592.6
778.8 Ferrites nspf; electrical machinery & equip. nspf	10,372	3,745	5,743	96.5	236.1	750
781.0 Passenger motor vehicles (except buses)	2,410	2,529	3,321	798.7	2.4	2.2
785.2 Adult cycles	1,151	1,463	4,057	13.7	199.5	68.4
788.0 Parts nspf of motor vehicles & handling equip.	819	1,113	2,486	56.3	204.7	2,972.3
812.4 Lighting fixtures & fittings	812	1,373	3,863	19	288.6	20.1
821.8 Furniture & parts thereof, nspf	1,208	795	3,184	53.5	968	177.4
831.0 Luggage, handbags	2,926	1,763	4,317	331.1	522.8	33.6
842.3 Slacks, etc., wool, mmf	6,158	4,517	12,532	65.6	157.8	16.2
843.7 Garments for rainwr; other outerwear nspf	10,331	6,347	8,517	328.4	401.1	174.1
844.1 Men's & boys' shirts, cotton, wool, manmade fibers, not knit	4,860	5,752	14,582	270.3	199.7	2.8
845.5 Sweaters & other outerwear of textile materials, knit KT	5,587	6,029	8,203	647.4	765.4	40
846.8 Undergarments (including shirts) of textile materials, nspf, knit	4,533	4,763	9,146	237.9	336.6	28.7
848.1 Gloves, belts, other wearing apparel of leather, nspf	9,974	6,140	11,115	347.3	141.8	9.9
848.3 Fur clothing & other articles except headwear	38,801	10,474	33,778	120.4	5.6	0.3
851.0 Footwear, new, excluding military or orthopedic	3,724	3,113	4,304	1489	2,101.1	13.1
879.2 Jewelry, etc., costume & semiprecious	7,530	5,911	32,946	79.4	106.6	63.5
881.1 Still cameras & parts; flash apparatus	27,438	12,308	47,152	17.5	105.1	792.4
884.2 Eyeglasses, eyeglass frames, & parts	10,823	6,250	39,687	31.4	114	86
891.0 Articles of rubber or plastics nspf	940	913	3,148	100	699	374.9
894.2 Toys, games, Christmas ornaments, etc.	2,705	1,780	3,789	519.5	787.1	346.2
894.7 Sporting goods, etc., nspf	2,246	1,228	4,004	163	534.8	143.3
898.3 Sound, etc., recordings & blank media	3,430	3,603	5,669	173.8	35.7	961.1

Source: U.S. Department of Commerce (1986).

Note: nspf = not specially provided for.

[a]Commodity descriptions are abridged versions. Full descriptions can be found in U.S. Department of Commerce (1986).

9 Import Surveillance as a Strategic Trade Policy

L. Alan Winters

The European Community (EC) policy of import surveillance entails the public announcement that henceforth the commission will collect detailed statistics on particular imports either prior to or immediately after their importation. This paper considers two aspects of surveillance. First, it studies—for the first time, to my knowledge—the effects of import surveillance on the volumes, prices, and origins of EC imports. Second, it argues that through such a study it is possible to cast light on the existence of strategic behavior among firms and policymakers. Prima facie surveillance appears unlikely to have a material impact on imports, for it seems to amount merely to the collection of detailed trade statistics. But, if the imposition of surveillance affects exporters' subjective probabilities about further trade measures, then it is easy to imagine it affecting trade flows. This would transform it from the category of innocuous statistical procedures to that of subtle nontariff barriers to trade, an issue of immediate and direct interest to trade economists and policymakers. My results suggest that, at least sometimes, surveillance curtails imports.

On the second objective, if import surveillance does indeed affect import flows, it is evidence of strategic behavior—that is, "actions . . . taken to induce favourable responses by rivals" (Grossman 1987, 49). Surveillance has a negligible direct impact on the costs and revenues of undertaking trade; hence any observed reduction in imports due to surveillance must stem from indirect, or strategic, pressures, whereby exporters feel that by altering their behavior they can influence the subsequent actions by the importing country government.

L. Alan Winters is professor of economics at the University of Birmingham and codirector of the international trade program at the Centre for Economic Policy Research.

The author is grateful to Jim Anderson, Paul Brenton, Mike Finger, Peter Goate, David Greenaway, Carl Hamilton, Brian Hindley, John Marshall, Patrick Messerlin, Anne Stoddard, and conference participants for comments on an earlier draft, to Paul Brenton and John Sheehy for research assistance, and to Elena Ellis and Sue James for typing.

That is, by responding "cooperatively" to surveillance they can avoid something worse. The identification of strategic behavior among exporters is of interest in itself, but it is more important in the context of the present conference because of the light it sheds on the empirical relevance of "strategic trade policy."

Strategic trade policy has been around for about ten years. Its first five years produced a series of theoretical models which showed how, under certain circumstances, trade policies could manipulate foreign firms' reactions to the advantage of the home country. Its second five years has been oriented more toward the empirical implementation of these models; however, given their complexity and the difficulties of measuring some of the crucial variables, studies have entailed calibration and simulation rather than estimation and hypothesis testing.

Calibration studies are useful for illustrating the mechanisms of the models they treat and for assessing the relative sizes of the effects they postulate, and with sufficient sensitivity analysis they can produce robust results of direct relevance to policymakers. They are, however, only the first step toward the full empirical investigation of strategic trade policy. Baldwin (1989) suggests a second step—namely a more thorough attempt to estimate the relevant parameters from many (or at least several) data points. In this paper I explore a third level of empiricism—an attempt to test directly for the presence of strategic effects. At one level, empirical testing could involve estimating the parameters of a fully specified econometric model and then asking whether at a suitable level of significance they fall within the ranges necessary to produce strategic behavior. There are at least two disadvantages to such an indirect approach. First, it requires the precise specification of a model in terms of parameters and observables, a task of immense complexity and, given our present ignorance, arbitrariness. Second, the circumstances necessary for strategic behavior cannot usually be boiled down to a single parameter, but rather entail the interaction of many parameters and data. The resulting multivariate statistical tests are not only difficult to formulate and interpret, but are also, when confronted with poor data such as trade economists have, prone to be very weak.[1]

In this paper, therefore, I adopt a different, nonparametric, approach. On the basis of verbal reasoning I identify the qualitative changes in trade behavior that would be consistent with strategic responses to import surveillance. I then move immediately to the data to see if they can reject the hypothesis of no change in favor of that of "strategic" changes. The results are almost universally more consistent with the latter hypothesis than the former but do not often achieve the degree of definition necessary to reject the former at conventional

1. In fact, it is actually quite difficult to devise models in which the existence (as opposed to the magnitude) of strategic behavior may be represented parametrically. Certainly the well-known examples of strategic trade models, such as Baldwin and Krugman (1988), presume strategic behavior if markets are not perfectly competitive.

significance levels. Moreover, I must also admit that, although the tests conducted here are grounded in real data, what they gain in terms of contact with the real world they lose in terms of theoretical sophistication. Indeed, while I shall argue that import surveillance has genuinely strategic dimensions, the test proposed deals only indirectly with one of the principal features of the current theory—namely imperfect competition. Nonetheless, the attempt is justified, for identifying strategic behavior in very simple cases is a reasonable first step toward finding it elsewhere.

9.1 Import Surveillance

The empirical work of sections 9.3 and 9.4 below considers the effects of the European Community's policy of import surveillance on its import flows. Two forms of surveillance exist. The first, which concerns trade between EC member countries, is designed to identify the "need" for, and then support the application of, an Article 115 ruling which imposes quantitative limits on the circulation of foreign goods within the EC.[2] Such rulings are the means to market segmentation among member states and a necessary prop for members' own national trade restrictions. They are applied most frequently to textile trade in order to enforce the "burden sharing" provisions of the Multifiber Arrangement (MFA) but also occur for other sectors.[3] While the existence of a surveillance stage prior to, rather than simultaneous with, the imposition of an Article 115 ruling suggests that the Commission may believe that surveillance affects behavior, I have not examined the effects of such surveillance because it is so obviously and so readily supplemented by directly trade-restricting measures.

The second form of surveillance is of imports into the Community from nonmember countries. Surveillance and other trade policies toward third-country imports are governed by Article 113 of the Treaty of Rome as implemented in the Council Regulations "Common Rules for Imports." For the analysis of this paper, Regulation No. 288/82 of 1982 (*Official Journal, [OJ]*, no. L35/1, 1982) will be taken as representative of the legal position. This regulation strictly covered only imports from Western countries over the period 1982–86, but previous and subsequent regulations (e.g., nos. 926/79 and 1243/86) were virtually identical in the nature of their surveillance provisions.

Article 1 of Regulation No. 288/82 states that the importation of goods into the EC shall be free except under certain listed circumstances, of which surveillance is *not* one. That is, surveillance is not recognized de jure as curtailing imports at all. Moreover, the mechanics of surveillance, as set out in Article 11 of the regulation, are not particularly arduous, so it would be difficult to main-

2. I refer to Article 115 of the Treaty of Rome. Some details of the article and its application are given in Volker (1987).

3. The MFA is negotiated with exporters by the European Community, but quotas are then distributed among member states to spread the "burden" of cheap imports.

tain that surveillance represented a direct barrier to imports. Thus if the imposition of surveillance has detectable effects on imports, it must be for strategic reasons. That is, because exporters, realizing that their environment has changed, believe it advantageous to change their behavior. Moving one stage back, surveillance will have been used strategically, as well as having acted strategically, if the European Commission, realizing this possibility, has adopted or manipulated surveillance to induce the changes in exporter behavior that it wishes to see.

The likelihood of such strategic use of surveillance becomes apparent as soon as one goes into the details of Regulation No. 288/82. Either the Commission or a member-state government may initiate consultations on an import flow, and if the prima facie evidence suggests the need for action (surveillance or protection) a full investigation into the case may be instituted. At both stages "the trend of imports . . . and substantial injury or threat of substantial injury to Community producers resulting from such imports" are examined, paying particular attention, *inter alia,* to the rate of increase of imports, significant price undercutting relative to Community producers, and trends in local output, employment, profits, and the like.

"Where developments . . . threaten to cause injury to Community producers and where the interests of the Community so require, importation . . . may be made subject to either retrospective or prior surveillance" (Article 10). By contrast, "where a product is imported . . . in such greatly increased quantities . . . as to cause, or threaten to cause, substantial injury to Community producers," and where there is great urgency, the Community may "alter the import rules," that is, impose licensing and quantitative restrictions (Article 15). Thus the difference between the circumstances in which surveillance and quantitative restrictions may be imposed is one of degree rather than of nature. Surveillance is not primarily an information-gathering tool—that comes at the investigation stage—but rather an explicitly forward-looking policy addressing threatened injury. Article 15 on protective measures admits the possibility that surveillance may be superseded by protection by discussing the transitional arrangements from one to the other (par. 1 [a]), but there is no presumption that surveillance leads to protection nor that protection should be preceded by surveillance. Surveillance does, however, expedite the statistical analysis of affected imports and, with prior surveillance, put in place some of the machinery for controlling imports. Thus it does imply an increased threat of future import restrictions.

Prior surveillance is clearly the more threatening form of the policy. Not only does it institute a system of documentation which might readily be transformed into an authorization system, but it also requires national authorities to report monthly in arrears both actual trade statistics and the value and volume of trade for which documents have been issued. Because these documents must be obtained prior to importation the monthly reports act at least partly as an early warning system. An import document is required to state, inter alia, the nature and origin of the product, the quantity and price of the transaction, and the place and date of importation. It *must* be authorized free of charge by an EC national authority within five days of presentation, and importation must await authorization. Interestingly, the prices and quantities quoted on the document are treated respectively as lower limits on the actual prices and upper limits on the actual quantities that may be traded. This alone suggests something of the intentions of the policy. Import licenses are issued to the importer on the basis of invoices for firm orders. These are the documents that firms will require for their own accounts, so that the extra work entailed in satisfying prior surveillance is very slight. Certainly, it could not account for significant trade diversion to nonsurveyed suppliers.

The previous paragraph notwithstanding, however, it would be easy to exaggerate the distinction between prior and retrospective surveillance. The procedures of consultation and investigation described above may all be bypassed by the Commission or member states in cases of perceived urgency.[4] and the administrative machinery required to stop imports while licensing procedures are introduced is not great. Thus even though retrospective surveillance entails only the prompt transmission to Brussels of ex post trade statistics in the affected product groups and is quite invisible to private traders, I will treat it as equivalent to prior surveillance.

Two further features of surveillance should be noted briefly. First, it is imposed for a finite period only—usually for the remainder of the year of imposition and the next year in the first instance. However, it may simply be extended by a new Commission regulation and so de facto can be indefinite. That said, however, we do observe instances in which it is removed. Second, surveillance is usually applied discriminatorily—only certain exporters are named in the regulations of application. Moreover, GATT notwithstanding, the European Community's recent import restrictions have also usually been discriminatory, so we may interpret discriminatory surveillance as having a quite country-specific message. Countries facing surveillance will thus generally interpret it as a potential precursor to selective import controls, so that the effects of responses to surveillance can generally be held to be internal to the group of surveyed countries.[5]

Over time the use of surveillance appears to have increased and its application to have become less constrained by the regulation. It is now applied in broader circumstances and makes less of its nonrestrictive nature than previously. Thus Regulation No. 646/75 (*OJ*, no. L67/21, 1975) imposing surveillance on zip fasteners noted that surveillance was "purely documentary" and

4. That is, they may be done retrospectively after surveillance has been introduced.

5. Regulation No. 288/82 is implicitly based on GATT's Article XIX, which allows only nondiscriminatory emergency actions, but since the European Community uses other means for import restrictions this fact does not disturb the interpretation in the text. Indeed in 1982, Regulation No. 288/82 was the basis of no EC-wide import restrictions but did support many national restrictions, a high proportion of which were discriminatory.

did "not affect in any way freedom of importation"; such disclaimers are not encountered in recent legislation. Moreover, while during the late 1970s other countries' import restrictions were quoted as reasons for increased imports, they have more recently been noted in justification of surveillance because they *threaten* increased imports: thus Regulation No. 418/87 (*OJ*, no. L42/25, 1987) on imports of urea from Eastern Europe notes "the addition of trade measures concerning urea by certain third countries, including the United States of America, *may* lead to a considerable increase in exports from producer countries to the Community" (emphasis added). A similar case was Regulation No. 1245/87 which established prior surveillance on imports of personal computers, electrical hand tools, and color televisions expressly because of the punitive duties imposed on these goods by the United States. Finally, surveillance has recently been introduced independently of the Common Rules, as in Council Regulation No. 1909/86 (*OJ*, no. L165/1, 1986). This notes that because "the United States of America has imposed restrictions on imports of certain products from the Community," and because "these measures threaten to cause injury to the Community producers concerned . . . it is necessary for the Community to introduce surveillance for imports of certain products originating in the United States." This is strategic use writ large.

9.2   Responses to Surveillance

Exporters' responses to surveillance must be considered on at least two levels—the individual firm and the exporting country government.[6] A third, intermediate, level might be a trade association which institutes collective action but without the force of law. The crucial factor determining an exporter's response to surveillance is the extent to which *any* action it takes could influence the types or probabilities of more formal protective measures being imposed at a later date; this in turn relates to the likely responses of the surveying government to changes in total exports and the extent to which the individual firm can influence total exports.

The simplest and most direct form of strategic behavior occurs if an exporting firm believes that surveillance is the precursor to an effective antidumping action. It would then have an immediate and direct incentive to raise prices and reduce trade. The incentive would be immediate because in the European Community, unlike the United States, once an antidumping action is started it refers to historical prices and there is no obligation on the commission to accept an undertaking to charge higher prices instead of imposing duties. It is direct because any antidumping duty imposed will be perfectly negatively correlated with the import price and will be calculated and levied on the

---

6. In preparing this section I have benefited from seeing some unpublished notes by Carl Hamilton.

specific firm concerned: all the incentives to modify behavior are internalized and point the same way. It is virtually impossible to assess whether firms do see surveillance as the precursor to antidumping actions, but several factors suggest that it may not be a very plausible view: the frequency with which antidumping actions are introduced without previous surveillance, which suggests no constraint on the European Community to introduce the policies in sequence, the separate legislative bases of the two approaches, and the fact that antidumping actions entail more detailed information collection than surveillance. Finally, and most significantly, in only one of our cases below have antidumping actions followed the imposition of surveillance, in three cases antidumping actions have preceded surveillance (by several years), and in a number of cases antidumping actions have been taken against closely related but not identical products to those suffering surveillance.[7] All this seems to indicate a substantial degree of independence between the two forms of trade policy.

If surveillance is seen as the harbinger of inevitable quantitative restrictions, no firm will have an incentive to reduce its exports and most will wish to expand them immediately. Expansion may merely reflect an intertemporal shift in sales—an attempt to get the goods in before the door is shut or before tariffs are imposed. It may also, however, have a strategic dimension. The rents which quantitative restrictions (QRs)—especially voluntary export restraints (VERs)—create are proportional to sales, and sales quotas for individual firms are more often than not related to past sales. Thus a firm expecting to face a QR will believe itself likely to do better the higher its base-year exports. Moreover, this is likely to be so regardless of whether the quota allocation is made by the importing or the exporting countries. Given that the majority of new protectionism has taken the form of discriminatory QRs, this jockeying for position seems a strong possibility. Yoffie (1983), for example, reports such behavior on the part of Taiwanese and Korean exporters of footwear to the United States in 1976: protection seemed inevitable, but a principal policy objective was to postpone it long enough to build up base levels from which to negotiate. Yoffie tells the story more from the point of view of the trade associations and governments than from that of individual firms, but the principle is the same. Under these circumstances surveillance is likely to be greeted by booming import volumes and stable or decreasing import unit value from the surveyed sources.[8]

---

7. I am grateful to Patrick Messerlin for providing the information concerning EC antidumping actions.

8. Since nearly completing this work, I have seen Hoekman and Leidy (1989) and Anderson (1989) which formalize some of the ideas of this paragraph. The latter, which my discussant is too modest to mention below, shows that if the probability of a VER is exogenous any industry will seek to increase its exports while it has the chance. If, on the other hand, the probability is endogenous and the industry is imperfectly competitive, self-restraint may be optimal.

If, contrary to the previous case, exporters are strongly convinced that surveillance will not be followed by protection—perhaps because of broader political considerations—we should expect no change in export behavior.

The notion that future protection is quite independent of import behavior under surveillance is not convincing. The European Community has the means to impose import restrictions immediately if it is determined to do so, and so is presumably using surveillance to probe exporters' reactions. Moreover the information collected during surveillance can be a potent weapon in any debate about an import restriction. Thus overall it seems more likely that the probability of future restrictions will be positively related to the current import level, and that there will be some incentive to curtail exports in the face of surveillance. There may, however, be difficulties in doing so.

Ignoring dynamic considerations, the individual exporter faces a prisoner's dilemma. Even if he accepts the need for restraint overall, his own incentives are toward unrestrained exporting. Moreover, if he believes that everyone else is exercising restraint, he may even find it profitable to increase his own exports to take advantage of their restraint.[9] The outcome of this situation depends partly on the number of exporters involved: the fewer the firms, the more likely that effective cooperation (restraint) will occur. Thus *ceteris paribus* we should expect surveillance to have a stronger restraining effect on imports the less competitive the supplying industry. Competitiveness is difficult to assess, but, given the scope for market segmentation and the greater likelihood of technical differences between firms, it seems likely to be lower in sophisticated goods (e.g., hi-fi equipment) than in simple ones (e.g., footwear).

Another condition making for cooperation is the role of government or collective trade associations. Industries and countries with strong traditions of government involvement in exporting are more likely to be able to restrain exports than others.[10] Indeed, the imposition of surveillance may be the signal to create an export control system which had previously been suppressed for fear of infringing antitrust law. Previously competitive exporters may indeed appeal to governments to police export restraint agreements in order to avoid free-rider problems. This is particularly likely if any resulting restraint drives up export prices, for then incumbent firms will be anxious to ensure that their efforts are not undermined by new entrants.

Even if exporting governments do not wish to create or police an export management scheme, they may be forced into closer association with the industry than previously. If surveillance contains even a hint of future protection,

9. A suggestion of this kind of behavior is evident in Taiwanese exports of footwear to the United Kingdom in the mid-1980s. These were ostensibly governed by an industry-to-industry restraint agreement; the Taiwanese claimed to be trying to enforce it, but by 1984 it was being overshipped by 150 percent. After the U. K. industry refused to sign it in 1985, exports fell.

10. Even cooperation developed for quite different purposes—e.g., over the enforcement of standards—probably makes export control easier. This may further strengthen the tendency for imports of sophisticated goods to respond more directly to surveillance than do those of simpler goods.

the government will probably wish to prepare its negotiating strategy. At a minimum this is likely to entail collecting information.

It is difficult to identify a priori countries which are more likely to be able to impose constraint, but anecdote suggests that perhaps Korea and Japan fall into the category. Both have strong traditions of "administrative guidance," and Wakasugi (1989) suggests that in Japan the Ministry of International Trade and Industry (MITI) has a well-established tradition of watching for and responding to trade threats of this kind. Less speculatively, however, we might expect that where more than one country falls under surveillance, export restraint is less likely to result because the prisoner's dilemma will be more difficult to solve between countries than between firms. Even here, however, if there is a possibility that subsequent protection could discriminate between exporters, individual countries may still wish to restrain.

In this section, I have argued that surveillance may affect imports either positively or negatively. Tentatively, the probability of a negative effect seems greater (i) the fewer the countries whose imports are surveyed, (ii) the less competitive the exporting industry, (iii) the more sophisticated the goods concerned, and (iv) the greater the role in exporting assumed by government or trade associations. The probability of a positive effect is most closely related to (i) the strength of the threat of future protection, and its sensitivity to changes in the level of imports, and (ii) the extent to which existing trade will influence quota distribution under any future restrictions. Several of these observations are testable, and thus in principle we are able to test for the existence of strategic behavior. There are, however, a number of practical difficulties to overcome first.

9.3 The Tests

An ideal test of surveillance would construct a model of import behavior with which to predict imports in the absence of surveillance (an *anti-monde*), and then ask whether actual imports differed significantly from predicted levels. This is what I do here, in principle, but my anti-mondes are far from ideal. Taking each of several instances of surveillance I seek to identify material changes in the levels or growth rates of imports, their geographical composition, and their prices (unit values) at the times of the imposition and removal of surveillance. So far as possible the data cover the period from five years before the imposition to five years after its removal, bounded by 1972 and 1987. They are drawn from Eurostat Commodity Trade Statistics; the external trade data refer to the European Community as a whole, although separate data are collected on intra-EC trade in the surveyed commodities.

The sample of instances of EC surveillance considered excludes all occurrences in agricultural products, textiles, and steel. These are the sectors most prone to surveillance, but they are also subject to such widespread and vigorous directly trade-restricting policies that it is impossible to disentangle the effects of surveillance from the other effects. Similarly, among the remaining commodities I excluded any years for which there was strong evidence of other community trade policy (apart from tariffs) such as unofficial VERs.[11] Finally, a number of instances of surveillance could not be studied because of data difficulties—especially the subdivision and recombination of the relevant headings in the trade statistics. Table 9.1 describes the final sample of cases investigated.

The engineering products in which Japan was subject to surveillance in the early 1980s are particularly difficult to interpret. In all, 10 commodities were subject to discussions between the European Community and Japan as "sensitive products." In February 1983 Japan agreed to "moderate" its exports, while at the same time, the European Community continued or introduced retrospective import surveillance. The terms of the export moderation agreement remain secret, but the broad outline was published in the *EC Bulletin* (no. 2, 1983). It recognizes five categories of goods

(i)   general export moderation: in the case of five products in particular— light utility vehicles (vans), fork-lift trucks, motor cycles, quartz watches and hi-fi equipment—consultations could be held in the event of failure to observe this principle;

(ii)   continuation of the moderation introduced in 1982 for exports of cars and numerically controlled machine-tools;

(iii)   for colour television cathode tubes, a specific level of moderation for three years (1983, 1984 and 1985);

(iv)   moderation of exports of colour television sets for two years (1983 and 1984); renewable for a third year;

(v)   an *ad hoc* solution for video recorders (assurances as to prices and quantities).

On the basis of this report I assume in the main analysis that surveillance was overridden by effective QRs for color-TV cathode ray tubes, color televisions, and videocassette recorders during the period 1983–85. Data definition difficulties prevent us from considering cathode ray tubes, and videocassette recorders experienced domestic tax increases and a tariff increase from 8 to 14 percent in 1986; we therefore include only color TVs in this exercise, and assume that from 1986 onward surveillance was the principal policy extant.[12] The five commodities in category (i) appear to have had little more than surveillance in operation over 1983–85, and I therefore proceed as if the "general

11. Surveillance is sometimes thought to represent the official dimension of industry-to-industry arrangements, and it is possible that such private deals lie behind some of our examples. If so, any strategic component of any observed changes in trade behavior is reduced, but the fact of the changes themselves is not altered. Moreover, if hidden VERs cause the changes reported below, surveillance is still affecting trade to the extent that the private arrangements cannot be made effective without it.

12. I include imports of Korean video tape recorders below because trade increased despite the tariff increase and surveillance. Thus there is no danger of confusing the effects of the two policies.

Table 9.1   **Sample of Instances of EC Surveillance**

Product and NIMEXE Heading[a]	Type of Surveillance:[b] Initial Regulation	Cited Exporters	Period[c]	Analytical Group[d]
Slide fasteners:		All[e]	1975–79	I
98.02-10	P: 646/75			
98.02-90				
Phosphate fertilizers:				
31.05-12	P: 440/77	All	1977–83	I
Titanium:		All	1987	I
81.04-59				
81.04-61				
81.04-63				
Footwear:				
64.02-40	P: 716/78 (5/78–10/78)	DCs[f]	1978–87	II
64.02-61	R: 78/560 (after 10/78)			
64.02-69				
64.01-65				
64.03-00				
64.05-31				
Certain machine tools:[g]				
84.45-12	R: 536/81	Japan	1981–87	III
84.45-14			[1981–82, 1986–87]	
84.45-16				
84.45-36				
84.45-37				
84.45-51				
84.45-94				
84.45-48	R: 653/83	Japan	1983–87	IV
			[1986–87]	
Color TVs:[g]				
85.15-25	R: 537/81	Japan	1981–87	III
	P: 1245/87 (after 3/87)		[1981–82, 1986–87]	
Quartz watches:[g]				
85.15-21	R: 653/83	Japan	1983–87	IV
85.15-25				
Hi-fi equipment:[g]				
85.14-40	R: 653/83	Japan	1983–87	IV
85.14-60			[1986–87]	
92.11-10				
92.11-32				
92.11-34				
92.11-37				
Light commercial vehicles:[g]				
87.02-86	R: 3544/82	Japan	1983–87	IV
			[1986–87]	

(*continued*)

Table 9.1   (continued)

Product and NIMEXE Heading[a]	Type of Surveillance:[b] Initial Regulation	Cited Exporters	Period[c]	Analytical Group[d]
Motorcycles:[g]				
87.09-59	R: 3543/82	Japan	1983–87 [1986–87]	IV
Videocassette recorders:[h]				
92.11-80	R: 235/86	Korea	1986–87	V

[a]Heading in initial year of imposition.
[b]R = retrospective; P = prior.
[c]Years of imposition. Dates in brackets are years in which surveillance was the principal policy.
[d]Group in which the heading is put for subsequent analysis.
[e]Japan is named in text of the regulation, but not singled out for surveillance.
[f]Effectively all major footwear-exporting developing countries—Brazil, Hong Kong, Korea, Malaysia, Pakistan, Spain, Taiwan, China, Czechoslosvakia, Poland, and Rumania.
[g]See section 9.3 of text for details.
[h]Tariff increase from 8 to 14 percent in 1985.

moderation" had no effect. Similar arguments may be made about motor vehicles and machine tools. However, although there is no official record of the moderation agreements from 1982, the national restrictions on imports of motor vehicles in France, Italy, the United Kingdom, and, according to Bronkers (1987), Belgium and Germany from 1981 were sufficiently strong that I felt obliged to ignore this commodity in this analysis. For machine tools the situation is more complex. Press comment during 1983–85 suggested that an effective VER existed over that period, and so I treat machine tools analogously to the goods in EC category (iii). I omit one surveyed category (NIMEXE category 84.45–64), however, because its trade was exceedingly small prior to surveillance, which distorts the growth rates I consider below.

I measure the effects of import surveillance on the affected suppliers in four obvious ways: the volume of imports, the import share, the unit value of imports, and the unit value of imports relative to that of intra-EC imports.

It is clearly important to consider the absolute effects of surveillance on imports and their prices, but the two relative statistics are likely to be the more informative ones. Not only do they allow crudely for the inherent trends of the markets involved, but they are also among the indicator variables named in the trade regulations, and so may be imbued with a direct strategic relevance.[13]

A potential problem of using the intra-EC unit value as the norm for the

13. The share measure essentially incorporates market demand into the anti-monde, along with time, which enters when we consider growth rates. It is difficult to think of a more sophisticated anti-monde for modeling price/quantity outcomes without detailed commodity-level investigation, which is plainly inappropriate for a study of this kind.

import unit value is that international trade policy is designed at least partly to support EC prices; thus the relative unit value measure may understate the extent of the surveillance-induced increase in import prices (if any). The sign of the relativity should be robust, however, for it is extremely unlikely that an x percent increase in import prices will generate a larger than x percent increase in intra-EC trade prices. In the absence of explicit models of import demand from which to derive the anti-mondes, I use two simple statistical constructs—the extrapolation of past trends and no change from the last nonsurveillance year.

In nearly every instance, surveillance has been imposed in response to rapidly increasing imports from the surveyed sources. When comparisons are made between imports under surveillance and extrapolations of these growth rates, the results indicate strong negative responses to surveillance. Extrapolating at the average growth rate of the previous four years (fewer in certain cases where data deficiencies required it) I calculated the ratio of actual to predicted import volumes for the first year of surveillance. Out of the 35 ratios, 27 were below unity, as shown in figure 9.1. The effects on the volume share are even stronger, as are those for later years of surveillance. On this basis, therefore, there is very strong evidence that import surveillance curtails imports, and, although there are differences between commodity groups, they are dominated by the general tendency.

Perhaps more informative is an analysis based on the conservative antimonde of no change from the last presurveillance year. Table 9.2 reports two

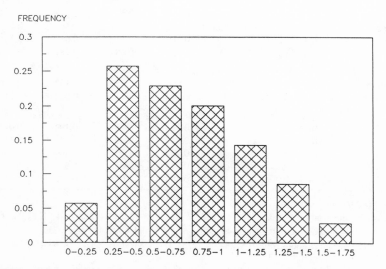

Fig. 9.1   Ratio of actual to predicted imports: First year of surveillance

Table 9.2   **Effects of Surveillance relative to "No-change" Anti-Monde**

| | Number of Positive Deviations | | | | | Mean Proportionate Deviation | | | |
	A	B	C	D	N	A	B	C	D
Group I									
Year 1	5	3	3	4	6	0.208	−0.034	−0.045	0.108
Year 2	3	1	3	3	3	0.474	−0.010	0.208	0.241
Year 3	3	1	3	3	3	0.601	−0.029	0.346	0.304
Year 4	3	1	3	3	3	0.302	−0.021	0.594	0.348
Year 5	3	1	3	2	3	0.389	−0.023	0.577	0.331
Group II									
Year 1	2	2	3	0	6	−0.179	−0.019	−0.001	−0.076
Year 2	3	4	5	3	6	0.091	0.000	0.093	−0.023
Year 3	5	5	5	3	6	0.485	0.048	0.239	−0.059
Year 4	4	3	6	3	6	0.452	0.056	0.444	0.064
Year 5	5	3	6	4	6	0.477	0.047	0.564	0.074
Year 6	6	4	6	2	6	0.517	0.069	0.584	−0.016
Year 7	5	4	6	3	6	0.609	0.069	0.826	0.095
Group III									
Year 1	3	3	8	6	8	−0.123	−0.019	0.236	0.131
Year 2	2	3	8	4	8	−0.297	−0.066	0.242	0.049
Year 3									
Year 4									
Year 5									
Year 6	2	1	8	6	8	0.019	−0.075	0.493	0.129
Year 7	1	1	8	6	8	−0.151	−0.102	0.469	0.088
Group IV									
Year 1	6	7	14	12	15	−0.097	−0.019	0.371	0.183
Year 2	9	9	15	13	15	0.054	−0.015	0.318	0.184
Year 3	6	7	13	14	15	0.036	−0.024	0.473	0.203
Year 4	5	2	10	9	10	0.260	−0.045	0.617	0.161
Year 5	6	3	8	8	8	0.459	−0.054	0.781	0.148
Group V									
Year 1	1	1	0	0	1	4.500	0.050	−0.152	−0.234
Year 2	1	1	0	0	1	16.193	0.142	−0.215	−0.217
Total									
Year 1	17	16	28	22	36	0.198	−0.009	0.194	0.071
Year 2	18	18	31	23	33	0.647	−0.005	0.240	0.117
Year 3	14	13	21	20	24	0.238	−0.007	0.400	0.137
Year 4	10	3	23	17	19	0.277	−0.017	0.526	0.111
Year 5	11	4	21	16	17	0.466	−0.013	0.638	0.117

Notes: Definition of Groups:

Group I: Universal surveillance (98.02-10,98.02-90, 31.05-12, 81.04-59, 81.04-61, 81.04 - 63)

Group II: Footwear (64.01-65, 64.02-40, 64.02-61, 64.02-69, 64.03-00, 64.05-31)

Group III: Japanese goods from 1981 (84.45-12, 84.45-14, 84.45-16, 84.45-36, 84.45-37, 84.45-51, 84.45-94, 85.15-25)

Table 9.2   (continued)

Group IV: Japanese goods from 1983 (84.45-48, 91.01-21, 91.01-25, 87.07-21, 87.07-24, 87.07-25, 87.07-27, 92.11-10, 92.11-32, 92.11-34, 92.11-37, 85.14-40, 85.14-60, 87.02-86, 87.09-59)

Group V: Korea (92.11-80)

Definition of Columns:

A: Proportionate change in volume of imports to the European Community from surveyed country(ies)

B: Change in share of surveyed countries in EC imports including intra-EC trade

C: Proportionate change in unit value of imports from surveyed countries

D: Proportionate change in the unit value of imports from the surveyed countries relative to the unit value intra-EC trade.

sets of results for five groups of commodities. The first four columns of the table report the number of instances in which actual imports (share, unit value, or relative unit value) exceeded the presurveillance value, and the last four columns the unweighted means of the proportionate deviations of actual imports from presurveillance values. Unweighted sums and means are appropriate because I am investigating the existence of trade effects rather than trying to quantify their overall impact. The table reports data for up to seven years of surveillance, although given the usual amounts of change in trading conditions the later years should not be taken too seriously. The number of cases varies from year to year because not all surveillance lasted or could be observed for seven years. Group III refers to goods from Japan first surveyed in 1981 but for which the years 1983–85 were covered by "moderation" agreements—hence the three missing years. Group I includes goods with different starting dates for surveillance, but the remaining groups are homogeneous in that regard: group II, starting in 1978; group III, 1981; group IV, 1983; and group V, 1986.[14]

The no-change anti-monde almost certainly biases the results toward finding too many positive trade effects associated with surveillance, for, over the years concerned, trade in most headings of NIMEXE grew significantly. On the other hand, this anti-monde poses fewer problems when looking at the effects of surveillance after several years, and any negative effects it uncovers seem likely to be genuine cases of trade curtailment. Prima facie the totals at the foot of table 9.2 suggest virtually no systematic effects of surveillance at all. The loss of import share (column B) is consistently negative, but the mean effect is small and at least for the first three years only half or fewer of the individual instances record declines in share.

14. Such homogeneity is a disadvantage for this analysis, because it makes it more difficult to disentangle the effects of *n* years' surveillance from those of general shifts in import behavior over real time, for example, in response to exchange rate changes or the business cycle. On the other hand, the consistency of our results over groups and their consistency with our predictions offer at least some comfort. See Anderson's comment, which follows this paper, for more on this difficulty.

The results for the individual groups are more informative than the totals, however. Three groups display a consistent tendency for surveillance to be accompanied by rising relative unit values and declining market shares—cases of universal surveillance (group I) and the two Japanese groups (III and IV). The latter two are consistent with several of our hypotheses: the goods are sophisticated, only one country was surveyed, and Japan is sometimes held to have well-developed mechanisms for cooperation. The only concern about this result is the possibility that there were covert moderation agreements behind these groups for more years than we have allowed. However, since the only legal teeth to such agreements was surveillance, even in this case one may still argue that surveillance is having its predicted effects. Besides, in section 9.4 I consider a much more restrictive selection of years and commodities for seeking surveillance effects and find the results largely unaffected.

Groups II and V generally record negative responses in relative unit values (column D) and positive import share responses (column B). These also appear explicable in terms of the arguments above. For footwear (group II), 11 developing country sources were surveyed; these countries have no traditions of mutual cooperation, and footwear is a highly fragmented industry in most of them. Thus it is not surprising that effective restraint was hard to organize.[15] Moreover, it is not clear that it was ever required, for the European Community has steadfastly resisted calls for community-wide protection in footwear; in these cases the implicit threat may have been rather weak.[16]

Group V contains only one case, but it provides no refutation of our hypotheses. Korea had a small share of the EC videocassette recorder (VCR) market in 1986. Despite earlier restrictions on Japan, the sector was still sensitive in the European Community in 1986, and Korea had experienced many previous instances of restrictions. Thus an aggressive attempt to establish a market position while the opportunity lasted looks like a rational response to surveillance. In 1987, the European Community instituted antidumping actions against Korean VCRs; however even if this was in retaliation for Korea's "aggressive selling" during 1986 and 1987, the "aggression" may well have been optimal, for Japanese exporters were also faced by antidumping investigations at the same time. Thus Korea had arguably managed to attain a reasonable share of the market before the undertakings extracted by the EC antidumping authorities cartelized it.

Group I—the cases of universal surveillance—appears to refute the arguments of section 9.2 above. Because surveillance refers to all countries, one might expect severe difficulties of coordination to produce the same outcome

15. The initial fall in volume may be explicable in terms of the U. K. and French restrictions on Taiwan introduced in 1977.
16. EC footwear protectionism has been national—although in the recent instances of Italian and French restrictions on Korean and Taiwanese footwear the measures have been formally introduced and validated by the European Community.

as observed for footwear (group II), but in fact this case is consistently one of rising relative unit values and falling market shares. This could reflect the early dates of two of the three cases; surveillance of industrial products was unusual in 1975 and 1977, and European *dirigisme* was strong at least in terms of articulated views of economic management if not in terms of implemented trade policies. More likely, however, it reflects the structure of imports. Although ostensibly universal, surveillance was effectively focused on only one or two countries because of their high shares of EC imports. For our two types of slide fasteners Japan accounted for 73 and 88 percent of the last presurveillance year's extra-EC imports, while for phosphate fertilizers the U.S. share was 92 percent, and for titanium the United States and Japan jointly accounted for 99 percent of each heading. Thus overall the negative effect of surveillance on imports seems quite explicable.

The consistency of the results in table 9.2 is striking. However, one must be cautious in interpreting them, because the changes observed are only rarely statistically significantly different from zero. Under a null hypothesis of no surveillance effect the five declines in market share recorded for group III (column B, years 1 and 2) could have occurred by chance with probability 15 percent, and the seven declines (in years 6 and 7) only with probability 3.5 percent. Otherwise the sign counts on market shares are wholly insignificant. Those on the relative unit values are stronger, but even then not overwhelmingly so. Similarly I calculated standard deviations for year-on-year changes in the four indicators from historical data (i.e., changes in the four years before surveillance) in order to check the statistical significance (difference from zero) of the first year's results for each group in table 9.2.[17] The absolute and relative increases in unit values for groups III and IV and the relative increase for group I are the only significant ones. The market share changes generally have ratios to their standard errors of just over unity. Even the changes described in figure 9.1 are only occasionally significant. Using historical data to calculate the expected change in volume and its standard error, only for six trade headings can we reject the hypothesis that the change in the first year of surveillance comes from the same population as prior changes. On the other hand, 27 out of 35 negative changes does significantly reject the hypothesis that surveillance has no systematic effect.

The lack of statistical significance in the results is disappointing, but it is not surprising given the small sample of cases available for investigation and the extreme noisiness of finely disaggregated trade data. Moreover, although the data cannot generally reject the hypothesis of no surveillance effects at say 95 percent significance, they nonetheless suggest that the alternative hypothesis of some effect provides a better explanation of observed phenomena than the null hypothesis of no effect.

17. This could not be done for group V because only one year's prior data are available.

9.4   Further Analysis

The consequences of removing surveillance are not the opposite of those of imposing it. As we have seen, there is a marked tendency for the import share of the surveyed country to fall during the period of surveillance, but it shows no sign of recovering subsequent to its removal. This suggests that surveillance is removed only after the "danger" has passed, which is a perfectly plausible conclusion in light of what we know of the way that governments set trade policy. Although not particularly damaging to my hypotheses, neither does this observation lend them much prima facie support, however, unless one interprets it as evidence that surveillance eventually causes exporters to move out of the surveyed markets permanently. The observation does, however, reinforce the view that surveillance has adverse effects on the volume of imports.

The second extension of the analysis asks which countries gain market share as a result of the losses inflicted on surveyed countries. For group I—the cases of universal surveillance—the answer is obvious—intra-EC trade, for that is all that escapes surveillance. Thus from table 9.2 it is plain that following surveillance EC supplies of the surveyed goods became on average more competitive (column D) and increased their market shares. It is also true, however, that the dominant suppliers lost some market share to their smaller rivals, despite the fact that the latter were also under surveillance.

For the Japanese cases, groups III and IV, the results on trade diversion are displayed in table 9.3. Here I am able to distinguish between nonsurveyed extra-EC sources of imports and intra-EC sources. No general tendency is evident. For group III, extra-EC imports fall initially along with those from the surveyed countries, which may indicate a spillover of strategic behavior to nonsurveyed countries. The corresponding increase in the intra-EC share is strong. By years 6 and 7, however, some of the trade destruction is undone as nonsurveyed extra-EC suppliers show the greatest increase in trade above base levels.

Turning to group IV, the effects are rather different, with surveyed suppliers generally being replaced by nonsurveyed extra-EC suppliers—that is, trade diversion. These results suggest that intra-EC trade gains virtually nothing from third-country import surveillance, whose principal effect is simple trade diversion. One cause of this outcome is apparent from columns C and D. With the Japanese constrained, European suppliers raise their prices by 10–20 percent over the first three years of surveillance (compare columns C and D of table 9.2), but the nonsurveyed extra-EC suppliers do so hardly at all (column C of table 9.3). By years 4 and 5, however, these effects are also starting to reverse.

The evidence of table 9.3 is ambiguous and, of course, says nothing about the levels of domestic sales in EC member states. It does suggest, however, that it is far from certain that surveillance diverts sales significantly from the surveyed sources to local firms. This is in line with analyses of other nontariff barriers, which also frequently appear to result primarily in trade diversion.

Table 9.3   **Trade Diversion and Trade Destruction Due to Import Surveillance**

	Number of Positive Deviations				Mean Proportionate Deviation			
	A	B	C	D	N	A	B	C	D
					Group III				
Extra-EC trade									
Year 1	2	3	8	6	8	−0.201	−0.043	0.260	0.156
Year 2	3	3	7	5	8	−0.110	−0.004	0.416	0.163
Year 6	7	6	7	4	8	0.755	0.071	0.380	0.031
Year 7	5	6	7	3	8	0.611	0.031	0.389	−0.006
Intra-EC trade									
Year 1	5	7	6		8	0.065	0.062	0.102	
Year 2	2	5	7		8	−0.063	0.070	0.204	
Year 6	7	4	8		8	0.318	0.005	0.333	
Year 7	7	7	8		8	0.519	0.071	0.376	
					Group IV				
Extra-EC trade									
Year 2	8	10	8	8	15	0.301	0.047	0.028	−0.038
Year 3	10	11	10	6	15	0.407	0.064	0.084	−0.021
Year 4	7	7	8	5	10	0.405	0.001	0.174	−0.001
Year 5	5	4	7	4	8	0.803	−0.016	0.179	−0.033
Intra-EC trade									
Year 1	3	7	12		15	−0.033	−0.001	0.073	
Year 2	6	7	13		15	0.008	−0.032	0.087	
Year 3	8	6	13		15	0.051	−0.040	0.142	
Year 4	9	8	10		10	0.662	0.038	0.182	
Year 5	8	6	8		8	1.024	0.050	0.230	

Definitions: See definitions for table 9.2.

As the discussion in section 9.3 suggests, there is considerable uncertainty outside the relevant bits of MITI and the European Commission as what were the exact terms of the EC-Japan trade agreement of 1983. Above I interpreted it rather liberally, arguing that, for several of the goods mentioned, "general moderation" amounted to no more than surveillance. I also faced uncertainty as to when (and if) known export restraint agreements expired. It is useful, therefore, to rework parts of the analysis under more rigid interpretations. This is done in table 9.4, which presents results for the surveillance of Japanese goods in two new classes. The new classification uses information from Jones (1987) on British VERs and assumes that if any of the categories mentioned in surveillance regulations were identified by Jones as facing British VERs, they were also covered by EC-wide VERs. Thus if it errs, table 9.4 errs on the side of caution. This adjustment excludes all Japanese products over the period 1983–85 and several others either previously or subsequently. Group III' now refers only to the years 1981 and 1982, while group IV' refers to 1986 and

Table 9.4   Effects of Surveillance, Alternative Classifications

	Number of Positive Deviations					Mean Proportionate Deviation			
	A	B	C	D	N	A	B	C	D
Group III'									
1981	2	2	7	5	7	−0.162	−0.024	0.245	0.130
1982	1	2	7	3	7	−0.363	−0.077	0.243	0.039
Group IV'									
1986	3	2	9	6	9	0.208	−0.058	0.645	0.116
1987	3	2	7	5	7	0.134	−0.065	0.612	0.043

Notes: Definition of Groups:
   Group III': 84.45-12, 84.45-14, 84.45-16, 84.45-36, 84.45-37, 84.45-51, 84.45-94
   Group IV': 84.45-36, 84.45-37, 84.45-48, 84.45-51, 84.45-94, 85.14-40, 85.14-60; 87.09-59, 92.11-80

Definition of Columns:
See definitions for table 9.2.

1987 regardless of whether surveillance was instituted in 1981 (group III) or 1983 (group IV). Given the smallness of the sample this seemed a more useful classification than that used in tables 9.2 and 9.3. The revision of the classification makes no difference to the conclusions above.

Fundamental to the whole of this analysis is that exporters believe that surveillance increases the probability of future QRs but that if they restrain themselves the probability is offsettingly reduced. It would be of interest to know whether such a view has any foundation. Unfortunately, our data shed little light on the matter, for we do not know the levels at which the European Community's triggers for further protection, if any, were set. Given that the pressures for, and politics of, protection differ so much between industries and time periods these triggers are bound to differ from case to case.

Among our categories only groups III and III' moved from surveillance to QRs. They, in fact, showed the strongest reduction in the surveyed countries' market shares that we observed, which might suggest that strategic responses to the threat implied by surveillance was misplaced. There are, however, a number of special factors that encouraged the imposition of the VER in 1983 and which could plausibly outweigh any strategic considerations. The European Community and Japan were negotiating VERs on other goods, and the European Community was anxious to obtain a comprehensive package to bolster its trade-policy-making role in the face of challenges from national governments. Surveillance had stimulated intra-EC shares; thus there was more incentive to defend its results by formalizing them than if trade diversion had occurred. Machine tools—the only commodity in group III—were held to be a highly strategic sector at the time. It is also possible that the factor that permits a cooperative response to surveillance—namely, a concentrated or well-organized industry—also facilitates creating a VER, for it is clear with whom the European Community should negotiate (even if indirectly via Japanese officials), and on the export side it is easier to prevent dissenting or newly entering firms from disrupting the process.

The fact that surveillance is removed only when the "danger" has passed lends some credence to the endogeneity of trade policy, but overall it is clear that a firm ruling on this possibility must await a different exercise. All I can conclude here is that my results are not inconsistent with the maintained hypothesis that the probability of surveillance transforming into something worse depends on the level of imports under surveillance.

9.5 Conclusions

The conclusions of this analysis come on two levels. In terms of description we have shown that more often than not imposing import surveillance, which ostensibly entails only collecting detailed trade information, curtails imports. In some cases it induces an absolute fall in imports, in a majority it causes the surveyed countries' market shares to fall, and in nearly all it reduces the rate of growth of imports. It raises the prices of the surveyed imports and probably also those of the European Community's local production. In some cases it diverts trade toward extra-EC nonsurveyed suppliers and in others toward intra-EC trade. In short, import surveillance has detectable and lasting protective effects, and this is so whether the reasons are strategic or otherwise.

Analytically I have provided a model which distinguishes the circumstances in which surveillance is likely to reduce imports from those where it might increase them. The former was predicted to occur when exporters plausibly believed that they could influence the probability of future QRs. In part this depended on perceptions of the European Community's propensity to protect certain sectors, but it was also argued to be more likely if surveillance was discriminatory and concerned goods from relatively concentrated industries. These factors allowed me to predict which groups of instances of surveillance were most likely to cause trade reductions. Although the empirical results were imprecise and frequently did not attain usual standards of statistical significance, they showed a strong general tendency to support the predictions. Certainly, given the underlying amount of noise, they did not contradict the hypotheses advanced.

The significance of the results is that the model's predictions rely heavily on strategic behavior. Since surveillance barely affects the actual costs of or returns to trading, its effects, if any, must stem from its influence on exporters' perceptions of their environment. Specifically, if exporters believe that the imposition of surveillance increases the probability that the European Community will protect a sector, but that they can reduce that probability by exercising voluntary restraint, then the model predicts that restraint will be more likely to occur. This is strategic behavior, albeit of a very simple kind. The results above indicate the existence of such strategic behavior.

Substantial effort has gone into building models of strategic behavior over the last decade, but virtually none has been devoted to testing their implications on real data. Thus while such models might provide persuasive parables, we have virtually no handle on their ability to explain the world as we observe it. This paper, on the other hand, does explore the positive implications of strategic behavior and, in a very simple context, finds them vindicated. I stress that my results do not prove the existence of strategic behavior of the types postulated by strategic trade policy models, but at least they suggest that it is worth looking for them. Moreover, I would argue that until we have tested the positive predictions of these models we should not recommend, even implicitly, their use in the real world.

References

Anderson, J. E. 1989. Domino dumping, I: Competitive exporters. Working Paper no. 186, Department of Economics, Boston College.

Baldwin, R. E. 1989. Taking the calibration out of calibration studies. Columbia University Business School. Mimeograph.

Baldwin, R. E., and P. R. Krugman. 1988. Market access and international competition: A simulation study of 16K random access memories. In *Empirical methods for international trade,* ed. R. C. Feenstra. Cambridge: MIT Press.

Bronkers, M. C. E. J. 1987. A legal analysis of protectionist measures affecting Japanese imports into the European Community—Revisited. In *Protectionism and the European Community,* ed. E. L. M. Volker, 57–120. Dewenter: Kluwer.

Grossman, G. M. 1987. Strategic export promotion: A critique. In *Strategic trade policy and the new international economics,* ed. P. R. Kurgman. Cambridge: MIT Press.

Hoekman, B. M., and M. P. Leidy. 1989. Dealing with "market disruption": Designing a system of emergency protection. Geneva: General Agreement on Tariffs and Trade. Mimeograph.

Jones, C. D. 1987. *Tariff and non-tariff barriers to trade.* Government Economic Service Working Paper no. 97. London: Department of Trade and Industry.

Volker, E. L. M., ed. 1987. *Protectionism and the European Community,* 2d ed. Deventer: Kluwer.

Wakasugi, R. 1989. Export restraints in Japan—A reconsideration. Paper presented at a conference on the Political Economy of Export Restraint Arrangements, Trade Policy Research Center, Washington, D.C., June.

Yoffie, D. 1983. *Power and protectionism.* New York: Columbia University Press.

Comment   James E. Anderson

This paper is a pioneering empirical effort to see whether the prospect of future trade intervention influences current trade volumes. Surveillance is a way of raising the subjective probability all agents place on the event of a VER. Competitive firms should export more in the hope of claiming more export licenses in the future. Cournot duopolists (or firms in countries which cartelize exports) should export less in the hope of reducing the probability of a VER, since profits will be lower in the event of a VER. The investigation shows that they do, more or less. I have reservations about the methods used but have no doubt that the topic is worthwhile. I also suspect that the findings may hold up after a deeper investigation. I have two sorts of objections, to the theory, and to the econometrics.

Theory

There is no formal theory, but a discussion. Moreover, this structure is not adequate to bear the weight assigned to it.

1. A reduction in trade following surveillance is taken to be evidence of strategic behavior, but there is a simpler explanation. Any type of firm will dump less if surveillance is the signal that antidumping action is contemplated. Winters attempts to rule this out by noting that antidumping action is always available to a government and quicker than surveillance. Therefore, agents believe that if antidumping were intended, it would be done directly. The argument is ingenious, but not convincing. It is plausible that the enforcement of antidumping is welfare-decreasing for the importing country (a model is needed to sort this out), and if so the threat of enforcement is a useful added tool. It would be nice to find a way to disentangle the antidumping aspect from the strategic, but I concur with the author that it is hard to see how.

2. Some instances of strategic behavior are associated with increased trade. If the VER system will reduce competition among exporting rivals, depending on the level of trade, it could increase profits; hence strategic exporting will be greater in the hope of raising the probability of the VER.

Econometrics

It is always difficult to pick out one clear refrain from the clamor of many, but the usual approach is to set out a tolerably complete model which can be used to subdue the dogs in the pound of *ceteris paribus*. Rather than that, Winters compares trade growth before and after the surveillance episode. Nonparametric methods have some attraction here, especially in light of the difficulty of modeling such fine micro behavior, but is surveillance the only important shift parameter in the demand, cost, or institutional structure?

James E. Anderson is professor of economics at Boston College

1. One major confounding factor is the European recession of the 1980s. I was unable to determine from the presentation of table 9.1 and figure 9.1 the extent to which this might account for the low import growth after surveillance.

2. Another major confounding factor is the eclipse of the Japanese by new Asian competitors. Again, I could not determine whether this might account for slow import growth after surveillance in a number of cases.

3. A major cause of changes in absolute advantage in the 1980s was large relative movements in exchange rates. Does this account for a number of cases of slow import growth?

4. Winters attempts to control for other political-economic factors which might have shifted the subjective probability of a VER by excluding some industries and years on the basis of explicit actions taken. This is no doubt a proper step so far as it goes, but a full model of the probability of a VER is needed to control for many other possible important influences in the importing country, such as electoral or opinion poll results, domestic increases or decreases in unemployment, and so forth.

Contributors

James E. Anderson
Department of Economics
Boston College
Chestnut Hill, MA 02167

Richard G. Harris
Department of Economics
Simon Fraser University
Burnaby, B.C. V5A 1S6
Canada

Heather A. Hazard
Institute of International Economics and
    Management
Copenhagen School of Business
Nansensgade 19, 7
1366 Copenhagen K
Denmark

Kathleen Hogan
Oracle Corporation
500 Oracle Parkway
Redwood Shores, CA 94065

Gernot Klepper
Institut für Weltwirtschaft
Kiel Universität
P. O. Box 4309
D-2300 Kiel 1
Germany

Kala Krishna
Kern Graduate Building, Rm 403
Department of Economics
Pennsylvania State University
University Park, PA 16802

Paul Krugman
Department of Economics
Room E52–383
Massachusetts Institute of Technology
50 Memorial Drive
Cambridge, MA 02139

James Levinsohn
Department of Economics
University of Michigan
Ann Arbor, MI 48109

Victor D. Norman
Norwegian School of Economics and
    Business Administration
N-5035 Bergen-Sandviken
Norway

Dani Rodrik
Department of Economics, 1312
Columbia University
420 W. 118th Street
New York, NY 10027

Garth Saloner
Graduate School of Business
Stanford University
Stanford, CA 94305

Alasdair Smith
School of European Studies
University of Sussex
Brighton GN1 9QN
United Kingdom

Siri P. Strandenes
Norwegian School of Economics and
    Business Administration
N-5035 Bergen-Sandviken
Norway

Phillip Swagel
Federal Reserve System
20th Street and Constitution
    Avenue, NW
Washington, DC 20551

David G. Tarr
Room H9079
The World Bank
1818 H St., NW
Washington, DC 20433

David Ulph
Department of Economics
University College London
Gower Street
London WC1E 6BT
United Kingdom

Anthony J. Venables
Department of Economics
London School of Economics and
    Political Science
Houghton Street
London WC2A 2AE
United Kingdom

L. Alan Winters
Department of Economics
School of Social Sciences
University of Birmingham
Edgbaston
Birmington B15 2TT
United Kingdom

Author Index

Abreu, D., 39
Adams, W., 39
Airbus Industrie, 110, 116
Anderson, J. E., 217n8
Anderson, S., 14n7, 68

Bagwell, Kyle, 197
Baldwin, Richard E., 5, 12n3, 46, 86, 102, 112, 127, 131–32, 181, 212
Barnett, D., 140, 141n7
Baumol, William J., 109, 127
Beath, J. A., 171
Berg, Hartmut, 104, 106
Bernstein, J. I., 192
Biggs, Tyler, 201t
Boeing Company, 110
Bond, J. S., 188
Brainard, Lael, 112, 127
Brander, James A., 2, 106, 107, 118, 119, 121, 158
Brock, J. W., 39
Bronkers, M. C. E. J., 222

Cantwell, J., 158, 191
Caves, R. E., 188, 189, 190
Chiang, Shih-Chen, 197
Coopers & Lybrand, 107
Cox, D., 4, 5
Crandall, R. W., 133, 134n3, 140, 141n7
Creamer, D. A., 189
Cuneo, P., 181

Deaton, A. S., 45
Degroot, Morris H., 205

De Melo, Jaime, 18n9
De Palma, A., 14n7, 68
DeVaney, A. S., 86
Dixit, A., 1n1, 3, 4, 5, 11, 12, 13, 14, 42, 46, 68, 77, 127, 132, 158, 188
Douglas, G. W., 86
Driskill, R., 35

Eaton, J., 3, 11, 13n5, 28, 35, 55
Economic Planning Board, South Korea, 201t
Economist, 111
Emerson, M., 5
Ethier, W., 1n1
Evenson, R. E., 191

Federal Republic of Germany, 190
Feenstra, R., 35
Flam, Harry, 5, 86, 102
Froot, Kenneth, 39

Griliches, Zvi, 181, 191
Grossman, G. M., 3, 11, 13n5, 28, 55, 158, 188, 197, 211

Halberstam, D., 23n15
Harris, R. G., 4, 5, 133n2, 150n10
Helpman, E., 1n1, 12, 86
Heston, Alan, 112
Hirschey, R. C., 188, 189
Hoekman, B. M., 217n8
Hofton, Andy, 105f
Hogan, Kathleen, 16n8, 19n11
Hood, N., 189
Horn, Henrik, 197

Subject Index

Air transportation demand model: simulation, 86–88
Available seat miles (ASM), 92, 93

Barriers to entry. *See* Trade barriers
Bertrand behavior: in airline deregulation model, 86; in air transportation demand model, 89–90, 95–96; in auto firm calibration model, 23–25, 34; firms as price setters, 4–5; in steel minimill pricing, 152–53; in trade policy effect model, 44, 47, 62
Brander-Spencer model: in R&D analysis, 158, 161–62, 166; tournament model of R&D, 172–73; of trade policy under imperfect competition, 2–3

Calibration: of air transportation demand model, 91–94; of European car market model, 70–73, 80; parameters and data in steel market model, 139–42; in policy experiments, 58, 60–61; in trade policy effect model, 45–49; of trade policy effect model, 58–62; of transport aircraft industry model, 110–14. *See also* Equilibrium concept
Calibration models: alternative to Dixit's, 12, 14–20; market behavior in, 21–25; for optimal trade policy, 11–12; parameter value results, 20–25; with product differentiation, 14; quality effects, 35; use of conjectural variations in, 11–12
Calibration technique: defined, 4–5; refining, 5–6; in trade policy under imperfect competition, 46

Car market model. *See* European car market model
Cecchini Report, 5
Competition: in air transportation demand model, 95–99; analysis in auto firm calibration model, 21–28; calibration procedure for different forms, 46–47; comparison of Korean and Taiwanese industries, 200–201; conditions for strategic behavior with, 3; conjectural variations to capture firms' behavior in, 11–12; in European car market model, 68; in international steel industry, 131, 133–34; knowing degree of product differentiation, 46; for labor rents, 158; learning-effects model, 102; modeling intertemporal, 132; in steel minimill sector, 137, 140–41; in trade policy effect model, 43–44, 47, 53, 55, 62; in transport aircraft industry, 104–6; in transport aircraft market, 117. *See also* Bertrand behavior; Cournot behavior; Firm behavior
Conjectural variations (CVs): in auto firm calibration model, 24, 30–31; in calibration models, 11–12, 14–19; in calibration of steel industry model, 152; solving for parameter, 46
Consumer preferences: in air transportation demand model, 86–88, 89–90; in markets with product differentiation, 68; in trade policy effect model, 64–66
Contestable-markets theory, 137–38
Cost function: in aircraft industry output, 108–9, 114–15; calibration in transport air-